Inventing New Orleans

Inventing
New Orleans

Writings of Lafcadio Hearn

EDITED, WITH AN INTRODUCTION BY

S . F R E D E R I C K S T A R R

For Melba Judy
With Regards to
a New Orleans - Brooklyn
original
Fred S
2001

University Press of Mississippi • *Jackson*

www.upress.state.ms.us

Reproduction and restoration of woodcuts by Lafcadio Hearn included
in this volume were funded by a grant from Louisiana Endowment for the Humanities,
the state affiliate of the National Endowment for the Humanities.

09 08 07 06 05 04 03 02 01   4 3 2 1

∞

Library of Congress Cataloging-in-Publication Data

Hearn, Lafcadio, 1850–1904.
Inventing New Orleans : writings of Lafcadio Hearn / edited, with introduction by
S. Frederick Starr.
p.   cm.
Includes bibliographical references.
ISBN 1-57806-352-3 (alk. paper) — ISBN 1-57806-353-1 (pbk. : alk. paper)
1. New Orleans (La.)—Literary collections.   2. New Orleans (La.)—Description
and travel.   I. Starr, S. Frederick.   II. Title.
PS1916.S83 2001
813'.4—dc21
00-065461

British Library Cataloging-in-Publication Data available

CONTENTS

Contents

Contents

ACKNOWLEDGMENTS

The idea of issuing this selection of Lafcadio Hearn's writings on Louisiana arose from my friend, Professor Maurice DuQuesnay of the University of Louisiana, Lafayette. A New Orleans native and ardent champion of Louisiana letters, DuQuensnay brings to his study a deep knowledge of American literary and intellectual currents as a whole that frees him (and his students) from all provincialism, at the same time making him all the more sensitive to what is distinctive to the region's culture. This volume is an outgrowth of the lecture on Hearn that I delivered in Lafayette for the Flora S. Levy Series in the Humanities, which Professor DuQuesnay has long directed.

The task of locating, identifying, verifying, and preparing the texts was an important one that required both ingenuity and literary judgment. It was capably handled by Delia LaBarre, of New Orleans and Baton Rouge, who served as assistant editor. Initially I had expected to include only works previously identified as Hearn's and reissued elsewhere. But when Ms. LaBarre succeeded in identifying many heretofore anonymous works as Hearn's, the scope of this volume expanded significantly.

Outside of Japan, the best collections of Hearn materials are in Louisiana and from these holdings the selections offered here were drawn. Thanks, therefore, to the staffs of the Williams Research Center, Historic New Orleans Collection; Special Collections, Loyola University Library; the Louisiana Collection of the New Orleans Public Library; and the Howard-Tilton Library of Tulane University, especially to Special Collections, which houses the Lafcadio Hearn Room, for preserving what are perhaps the only two surviving volumes of the New Orleans *Daily City Item* of those years Hearn wrote for that paper. Thanks also to the courteous and helpful staffs of the Louisiana Collection, Louisiana State Library, under the direction of Judy Smith, and of Hill Memorial Library Special Collections, Louisiana State University, directed by Faye Phillips, especially to Mark Martin, imaging specialist, for special attention to the reproduction of the engraved portrait of Lafcadio Hearn appearing on the cover of this volume. The assistance of Alex Landry, Louisiana State Library, in Baton Rouge, by making volumes of Hearn's works accessible, eased some of the tasks of research and preparation of texts. Invaluable to the preparation of the texts from archives to manuscript were computer and internet services, including electronic transference of manuscripts and correspondence, provided by the Goodwood and Bluebonnet locations of the East Baton Rouge Parish Libraries. The guidance of Professor Louis Day of the Manship School of Mass Communication, Louisiana State University, was helpful in identifying Hearn's anonymous works.

The woodcuts included herein have been rescued from near extinction thanks to support received through a grant from the Louisiana Endowment for the Humanities, whose offices are located in New Orleans. Thanks to Maria Biondo for artistic consultation in restorations. And special thanks to Grant Dupré of Dupré's Printing and Copying, Baton Rouge, who generously offered his photographic and printing expertise in directing the process of restoration and digitization of the woodcuts.

SFS

INTRODUCTION

The Man Who Invented New Orleans

What is a "Louisiana Writer"? To many, the answer is obvious: a Louisiana writer is a writer from Louisiana. As the Louisiana State Library proudly reminds us, in the Bayou State growing writers is a cash crop, albeit mainly for export. Some of the earliest, like the romantic novelists Father Adrien Emanuel LaRoquette or Alfred Mercier, playwright Placide Canonge, or the poet Arnold Lanusse, wrote in French. Others, like the ambivalent chronicler of Creole New Orleans, George Washington Cable, the worldly Truman Capote, or the mordent bard of the 1960s, John Kennedy Toole, wrote in English.

But not all authors from Louisiana write about Louisiana, while some of the best writers about Louisiana have come from elsewhere. If the criterion of a "Louisiana writer" is extended to include all those who wrote about the state and its peoples, then the cast expands to include such luminaries as William Faulkner, Tennessee Williams, Walker Percy, or Kate Chopin, not to mention such lesser-known figures as Henry Clay Lewis, who anticipated both Twain and Hearn in his uproariously funny *Odd Leaves from the Life of a Louisiana Swamp Doctor* (1850). Tens of countries in the UN cannot claim ever to have attracted the attention of half so much literary talent.

This is no accident. Write about Colorado or New Hampshire, Malaysia or Chile, and you write about, well, Colorado or New Hampshire, Malaysia or Chile. Nothing less, nothing more. Set your novel in Louisiana, especially South Louisiana, and your themes start to multiply like the outlets of the Mississippi Delta. Involuntarily you will find yourself holding forth on ethics, pleasure, mortality, and what Monty Python called "The Meaning of Life."

For in the realm of the written word, Louisiana is less a place than an idea, less a physical reality than a symbol.[1] A symbol of what? Of everything that the New England tradition in American literature and culture and thought is not. Louisiana represents the heart over the intellect, spontaneity over calculation, instinct over reason, music over the word, forgiveness over judgment, impermanence over permanence, and community over the isolated and alienated individual. Any writer who uses a Louisiana setting to address these themes is *ipso facto* a Louisiana writer.

Arguably the first writer to employ Louisiana settings to explore the entirety of this rich and provocative mélange of topics, and to do so with an artistry that set the tone for most who followed, was Lafcadio Hearn (1850–1904). Whether one speaks of genre, content, or literary form, this Anglo-Greek who spent only a decade in New Orleans before moving on to a new life and global fame in Japan, "wrote the book" on literary Louisiana. As we shall see, he virtually invented the notion of Louisiana, more specifically New Orleans, as idea and symbol.

It would be hard to conceive a more enigmatic person than Hearn.[2] He stood barely five foot three and had a colorless, bulbous left eye and poor vision in the right. He was born in 1850 on the Greek island of Lefkas, where his father, a stern British military doctor, was briefly stationed. His mother was a bewitchingly beautiful Greek woman of humble background. The couple named the boy after his place of birth. This union of seeming opposites was doomed from the start. Doubly orphaned, Hearn was abandoned first by his father, who took up a station in the Caribbean, and then by his mother, who could not endure the rigors of life with her in-laws in cold and brooding Ireland.

From earliest childhood Lafcadio believed himself to be beset by ghosts. Neither his upbringing by a straight-laced Irish great-aunt nor his rigorous but incomplete education at Catholic school in England and France dispelled his natural predilections for the morbid, the melancholy, and the macabre.

Even his warmest admirers admit that Hearn was a notoriously difficult human being. When he was only thirteen, a schoolmate declared that he was "slightly off his mental balance." A female friend in Louisiana felt "he was not happy, or calculated to make others happy." His closest male friend, the later renowned doctor Rudolph Matas, recalled that "both in taste and temperament he was morbid and in many respects abnormal." His editor at the New Orleans *Times-Democrat* considered him a rare genius but concluded that "taken altogether he was quite impossible."[3]

It is no surprise that Hearn fit in nowhere and spent his entire life searching for a place he could call home. But if Thomas Wolfe could not go home again, Hearn could neither find nor build himself an enduring nest. Young Lafcadio's formal education ended when his family's resources ran out. He was then placed in the care of a guardian in London, where his life went from bad to worse. When his guardian disinherited him, Hearn abandoned England and sought his fortune in the booming Ohio River city of Cincinnati, where he arrived at the age of nineteen in 1869. He found work as a cub reporter for the Cincinnati *Enquirer,* where he gained notoriety for his sensationalized pieces on the sordid underworld of that brawling meat-packing center, known as "Porkopolis." He also took time to absorb the latest works of French literature in the original and to begin his lifelong quest for self-education. As a result of his marriage to a half Irish ex-slave named Alethea "Mattie" Foley, however, the *Enquirer* fired him. Lafcadio and Mattie proved quite incompatible and within months Hearn initiated a separation that closely paralleled his own father's actions towards his Greek wife. After a stint with the Cincinnati *Commercial* Hearn set out once more to find the place where he could fit in. In 1878 he found his place of respite in New Orleans, where he remained until 1888.

Lafcadio Hearn was neither the first nor the last writer to arrive in New Orleans nearly broke and nursing the wounds of rejection or difficulties elsewhere. This had been Walt Whitman's fate and it was to be William Faulkner's as well. After his reverses in Cincinnati, the New Orleans of 1877 seemed to the young Hearn to be nothing less than "a land of perfume and dreams." Fortunately, the Cincinnati *Commercial* had commissioned a series on Louisiana and the fees for these sustained Hearn until he found a post with the New Orleans *City Item.*

The newly founded *City Item* was still on the margins of New Orleans journalism when Hearn arrived. Working at a feverish tempo, he poured out such a stream of colorful articles on local life (most of which were unsigned) that the paper quickly soared in popularity. Until his eyes began to weary from the strain of close work, Hearn illustrated his articles with often charmingly naive wood block prints based on drawings that he himself produced in an effort to boost circulation. These were the first illustrations to appear in the southern press.

This torrent of activity soon attracted the attention of the editor of the solid establishment paper, the *Times-Democrat,* with which Hearn was to be associated from 1882 until his departure from Louisiana. As his fame spread, he also secured assignments from *Scribner's Magazine, Harper's Weekly, Cosmopolitan, The Century Magazine,* and *Harper's Bazar.* Besides writing his articles on New Orleans, he also traveled to Lake Borgne and the Bayou Teche and Atchafalaya country in 1883, Grand Isle in 1884 and 1886, and to Florida the following year.

Few of Hearn's friends of these years failed to record his fascination with New Orleans' demimonde. He frequented brothels of every race and nationality and explored the world of *voudou.* He tried unsuccessfully to learn Chinese from an immigrant who ran the city's first Chinese eatery, and examined Greek-born New Orleanians in an effort to discern even an iota of Homeric nobility in their grubby lives. He used his knowledge of Creole French to draw out draymen and washerwomen and frequented dives of every description during the hours when the rest of his fellow journalists were asleep. This nocturnal life, combined with his marginal existence in an endless series of shabby boarding houses, made him notorious among the men with "great shoulders and preponderant deportment" who comprised the local business elite.

During his decade in New Orleans Hearn worked like a dynamo, pouring out several thousand pages in a variety of genres. His prowling through the seamier *foubourgs* may have raised eyebrows, but it also constituted the field research on which he drew for both fiction and non-fiction works. The songs he collected for the well-known New York music critic Henry Edward Krehbiel remain an important contribution to ethnomusicology, just as his studies of Creole French made their mark in linguistics.

In his effort to fit in, Hearn "went native" during his New Orleans days, just as he was later to do in the very different world of Japan. But his self-education also proceeded apace, causing him to turn outward to the bigger world, even as he was focusing on the local. He learned Spanish, studied the world's main religions, read the epics of every culture, translated volumes of French literature, and sought out virtually everyone in New Orleans who shared his omnivorous interest in what we would now call comparative anthropology. All this study, combined with his "field research" in those parts of town least affected by modernity, assured that Lafcadio Hearn's writing in every genre combined almost tactile specificity with a keen sense of how the New Orleans microcosm fit into the global macrocosm.

Lafcadio Hearn lived in New Orleans barely a decade, between 1877 and 1888. When he departed, he was only thirty-eight years old. Viewed in the context of his life as a whole, Louisiana was only a preparatory phase of his development. When he achieved world renown as a writer, his great passion and invariable subject matter was not New Orleans but Japan. Even today, every Japanese child reads Hearn in school. His home in the Japanese city of Matsue is a museum, and Japanese publishing houses regularly reissue his works, which are rightly considered classics. Abroad, such works as his *Glimpses of Unfamiliar Japan, Kokoro,* or *Out of the East* are translated into a dozen languages and widely admired for their enduring insights on Japanese life, as well as for their engaging style.

The fame of Hearn's Japanese works has utterly eclipsed his writings from Louisiana. This is as regrettable as it is unjust. On the one hand, the sheer quantity of his published output during his New Orleans decade is staggering. As was the custom of newspapers at the time, the thousands of pieces Hearn wrote for the New Orleans press were unsigned. Only a fraction of his total *oeuvre* from Louisiana has even been identified up to now, let alone reissued. On the other hand, Hearn's literary interests blossomed profusely while he was in New Orleans. Whether measured by quantity, range, or the high level of quality he achieved in several genres, both fiction and nonfiction, Hearn deserves a place at or near the top of the pantheon of Louisiana writers.

Enormously diverse in both form and content, the writings of Lafcadio Hearn from his Louisiana period fall into eight categories.[4]

First, there are nearly two thousand news articles. Hearn's practice was to rewrite national and international stories coming in on the telegraph, often adding his own flourishes. Beyond this, he highlighted many otherwise obscure national and local developments, using his colorful style to give them a visibility they would otherwise never have achieved. Happily for Hearn, the concept of "news" in the 1880s was still capacious, allowing the journalist a far greater freedom to elaborate and ornament than would be acceptable today. Whether at the *City Item* or the *Times-Democrat,* "news" was whatever Hearn decided was newsworthy, which included just about everything that happened to interest him personally at the time. Occasionally he used news stories as a form of civic boosterism, skewing his coverage in the process. Thus, he published laudatory reports on the 1885 Cotton Centennial Exposition in New Orleans, while confessing privately that it was all "a big fraud."

Second, Hearn penned scores of editorials. In spite of his having been an ardent Republican since his Cincinnati days, he avoided most of the hottest national issues, focusing his reforming zeal instead on such targets as police brutality in New Orleans, the local penal system, and the board of health. He also regaled his readers with intriguing editorial ruminations on everything from the possibility of eye transplants in humans, the advantages of cremation over burial, the advance of Russian colonial power in Central Asia, to the politics of insects.[5] Thanks to his picturesque style, even topics as seemingly obscure as "Icelandic Prospects" or "A Defense of Pessimism" elicited an interested readership.

Third, Hearn turned out hundreds of reviews, covering books on philosophy, literature, religion, music, and travel. Any topic that piqued his curiosity was fair game. In practice, this meant that Hearn passed over most bestsellers of the day in favor of collections of Sanskrit literature, anthologies of Japanese folklore, or ponderous editions of Chinese philosophy. It is doubtful that any American newspaper ever fed its readers a more exotic diet of reviews. The extraordinary bluntness of some of his judgments doubtless attracted many readers who would otherwise have had no interest in the book being reviewed. Who else would title a review simply "Translation or Mutilation?" Together, Hearn's book reviews offer a comprehensive guide to his thought on everything from politics to religion to aesthetics.

Fourth, Hearn was a passionate and gifted translator of French. Thanks to his seemingly boundless energy, New Orleanians could read works by Théophile Gautier, Anatole France, Hearn's old schoolmate Guy de Maupassant, and the immensely popular Pierre Loti (*nom de plume* of the French naval officer Louis-Marie Julien Viaud) long before they were available to American readers elsewhere. Hearn grew steadily as a translator and gravitated increasingly towards the most economical and expressive stylists of the *fin de siècle*. In the process of translating these contemporary classics he also burnished his own prose style both for nonfiction and fiction.

Fifth, Hearn even ventured into poetry. Such doggerel verses as "The Amateur Musician" or "The Fatal Plunge" were so concise and pungent that they could be memorized by anyone and spouted over a beer at The Crescent Hall or Le Pelerin.

Sixth, Hearn produced volume after volume of his own *belles lettres*. Some, like his *Stray Leaves from Strange Literatures* (1884) and *Some Chinese Ghosts* (1885), were his personal renderings of tales and stories culled from his readings in ancient European and Asian texts. As he once explained to a correspondent, these should rightly be considered original creations, just as we accept fairy tales by the Brothers Grimm or Krylov's fables as independent works of literature.

Hearn also wrote a sizable group of short stories, most of which consisted of barely a page or two. Many were fictional pieces written in the style of his nonfiction sketches on New Orleans. While none has entered the ranks of major American short stories of the era, all reveal Hearn's deep appreciation both of French romanticism and especially of the new wave of realism launched by Baudelaire, and his effort to prod English letters in that direction.

His one Louisiana novel, *Chita: A Memory of Last Island* (1889), is a minor classic that combines a romantic tale, involving Spanish and French Creoles in the aftermath of a tragedy on a doomed island with wild nature painting worthy of Chateaubriand. Unfairly classified as a "regional" work, *Chita* awaits the critical acclaim that it amply deserves.

Seventh, even while he was pouring out this fountain of fiction and nonfiction, Hearn found time to research and write two landmark contributions to the study of Creole culture. A Creole, in the original sense of the word, was anyone of European parentage who was born and raised in the New World colonies of France or Spain, as opposed to new immigrants. In popular usage this was extended to African Americans of mixed blood who shared the amalgam of Catholic Latin and African cultural traits that distinguished them to greater or lesser degree from the rest of the population and, in New Orleans, especially from the "Americans," whether white or black. Hearn respected the ability of members of the old white Creole elite to protect their world by walls of privacy, as described in "A Creole Courtyard." He was fascinated with so-called "Creoles of color" because he detected in their daily life evidence of ancient folkways extending deep into the Caribbean past to France and to Africa.

Hearn drew on both groups for his *La Cuisine Créole* (1885), the first of the now endless stream of books devoted to the culinary arts in New Orleans. Along with the *Times-Picayune's* classic *Creole Cookbook* of 1901, which it inspired, it is still among the best. A related study is his pioneering work of comparative linguistics entitled *Gombo Zhèbes: A Little Dictionary of Creole Proverbs* (1885). Based on extensive research, this slim volume presented scores of proverbs as they appear in no fewer than six Creole dialects of Louisiana and the Caribbean. Appearing just a few years after George Washington Cable's horrifying portrayal of French Creole life in *Old Creole Days* (1879) and *The Grandissimes* (1880), these studies present the

Creole world in all its skin tones as a separate culture guided by its own principles and values. With none of the tendentiousness that marred Grace King's later "defense" of the Creoles, Hearn suggests that Creole life should be appreciated for its own sake, much the way an anthropologist might suspend judgment as he seeks to discern the underlying patterns of another culture.

Overshadowing all of the other categories of Hearn's Louisiana writings was his vast corpus of descriptive essays, impressionistic writings, whimsical pieces, portraits, poems in prose, historical sketches, and occasional pieces describing the variegated life of New Orleans and South Louisiana. A capriciously selected sampling of these appeared in a 1924 volume (subsequently reissued) entitled *Creole Sketches*. Most remain unknown and even undiscovered, since Hearn's name appeared on them only in those rare cases when they found their way into national journals. In the present volume these pieces are divided into two subgroups, "Descriptions and Impressions" and "Sketches."

These sketches erase the line between nonfiction and fiction. Most begin with some actual person, place, or situation that Hearn encountered in his daily rounds through the neighborhoods of New Orleans. In most cases he then takes off, spinning a web of reflections and speculations that leave the reader far from the homely real-world starting point. His palette is extremely varied. In back-to-back sketches he might offer a glimpse of timeless beauty and one his "grotesques," mordant humor and a flight of romantic fancy. Many are in the form of the French *feuilleton,* the infinitely flexible essay that was the glory of nineteenth-century Parisian journalism. The best, which would fill an entire volume, are among the most evocative and enduring writings ever devoted to the Crescent City.

Hearn, still in his thirties during his New Orleans days, used these shorter pieces like a painter's sketchbook, recording fleeting events, experimenting with new techniques, and toying with fresh ideas. Few, if any, had any didactic purpose. Taken as a group, however, they exhibit a number of recurring themes and preoccupations that, together, reveal the author's world view at the time.

Few writers have judged the United States more severely than Lafcadio Hearn. An outsider's outsider, he despised technological progress as he had observed it in North America and Europe, the tub-thumping Babbitry that sustained it, and the solid, cold men who were benefitting from it. All this reminded him of the world of his father and guardian, both of whom had turned their back on him and whom he rejected in return. In New Orleans it took Hearn no time to plug the triumphant business class into this template and to develop an Oedipal loathing of its materialistic members.

By contrast, the French and Creole world of South Louisiana went straight to Hearn's heart. He reveled in what he was sure was its authenticity, and contrasted it to what he was equally convinced was the artificial world of business, politics, and male striving. This better world of Creole culture he conceived as feminine and its chief glories—language, music, and cuisine—as the essence of civilization at any time or place.

The fact that this better reality was all but invisible to casual observers made it all the more delicious to Hearn. He cast himself as the Columbus of Creole Louisiana, its discoverer and the sole propagator of its inner truths.

The late nineteenth century was the age *par excellence* of archaeology and anthropology. It was the time when Heinrich Schliemann could stun the world with his exotic discoveries at Troy, and a painter like Gauguin could introduce his public to remote and primitive peoples. Hearn was fully part of this pan-European movement in the social sciences and arts. To label his writings simply as the Gulf South variant of a southern literary current that celebrated "local color" is to diminish his intentions and achievement.

All such explorers carried the same message: that ancient and simpler cultures are more vital and authentic than the culture of modern Europe and North America but are ultimately doomed by the march of so-called progress. Hearn saw the Creole *patois* of Louisiana as "a plant that has almost ceased to flower"; New Orleans itself he termed a world of "beauty and decay." Indeed, his very first impression of nature in Louisiana, set down in a letter to his Cincinnati friend and mentor, Henry Watkins, was of infinite beauty, of impermanence and immanent death.

There were two further essential ingredients in the recipe for Hearn's literary Louisiana: race and eros. His involvement with both topics flowed directly from the idiosyncrasies of his background and inner life. For Hearn, Creole Louisiana in general emanated an enticing cultural bouquet. Because of the reclusiveness of many members of the white Creole elite, Hearn's contact with that group was limited mainly to its intellectual leaders who banded together in the "Athenée Louisiannais" and published the respected *Les Comtes Rendue*. For Hearn, the entirety of Creole culture had a sensuous texture that was absent in what he dismissed as the sterile Anglo-Saxon world. Here, too, he was obviously favoring the Mediterranean world of his mother over the more northern world of his British father. It is no wonder that his writings all but ignore the large and booming north European and "American" segment of New Orleans society, in spite of the fact that virtually all his readers belonged to this group.

While Hearn was drawn back again and again to the fascinating world of the old Creole elite, he identified more fully with "Creoles of color," and especially the underclass of that group, whom he judged more "authentic" and hence more vital than their more solidly bourgeois fellows. Nonetheless, he piled up evidence to show that both their language and culture were ultimately doomed, a judgment that both reflected and reinforced the cultural pessimism that lay at the center of his own consciousness and of his art.

In his interest in the Crescent City's black population, Hearn recalls his New Orleans contemporary and sometimes friend, writer George Washington Cable. But where Cable's concern was mainly social and political, Hearn's was cultural and aesthetic. Cable crusaded for what he believed to be social justice and civic betterment. Hearn, a bleak pessimist, was content to plunge into what he was convinced was the dying hybrid culture of the Creoles of color, to feel at one with it, and to extol its fading beauty.

To identify with this milieu was the easier for Hearn because he viewed himself as a racial and cultural hybrid and hence a kindred spirit to the Creoles of color. Further, he saw himself as a cultural victim whose world had been diminished by the advances of modern Anglo-American civilization in much the way he believed the Creoles' world was being threatened. In all this Hearn was an early practitioner of a kind of "victimology" that was to gain popularity in America a century later.

Beyond this, Hearn saw himself as a son of eros, the product of an erotic but ill-fated union between an English officer and a simple, passionate Mediterranean beauty from the island of Lefkos. His very name "Lafcadio" memorialized the female and elemental side of his family tree and somehow validated his own commitment to the world of eros. Back in Cincinnati Hearn had been fascinated by the writings of John Humphrey Noyes, founder of the Oneida Community in New York State and proponent of the idea of "serial marriage" or free love. Once in New Orleans Hearn not only applied this to his own life but he enshrined it as a central element of his conception of South Louisiana culture as a whole. Thus, years before Gauguin set out for the South Seas, Hearn presented himself as both the analyst and poet of primitivism. He was at once the artist of the sensual and the elemental and, in part, his own subject matter.

Except for the fact that he had amassed a good library, Hearn left New Orleans as he had arrived: broke. In the end, Louisiana disappointed him, not because it was backward but because it was not backward enough. With his one not very good eye he saw it rapidly modernizing and abandoning its solid old ways in order to wallow in crass and soulless materialism.

He spent the first two years after his departure in Martinique, where he had gone in search of Creole civilization in its most undiluted form. He found it in the town of Saint-Pierre, which he idealized as a smaller version of New Orleans but without ambition, commerce, materialism, or accursed progress. The enchantment gradually wore off. Worse, Hearn was soon broke again and had no choice but to accept an assignment from *Harper's* to travel to Japan and send back an account of that country. This marked the end of his infatuation with Creole culture.

There had always been something morbid about Hearn's involvement with New Orleans and Saint-Pierre, and he judged both to be doomed. Twelve years after Hearn departed for Japan, nature echoed his judgment when a volcanic eruption all but obliterated Saint-Pierre. New Orleans struggled on, its French and Creole values slowly fading.

From the first moment he arrived in Japan, Hearn felt he had discovered the one place that he could truly call home. Repeating the pattern he set in New Orleans, he "went native" with a vengeance. He turned his back on his editor in New York, took a Japanese wife, shed western attire in favor of traditional Japanese dress, and assumed Japanese citizenship and even a Japanese name, Yakumo Koizumi.

When Hearn arrived in Japan in 1890, that country was already *à la mode* throughout Europe and America. Its woodblock prints (*ukioye*) had inspired French painters, and soon western architects like Charles Rennie Macintosh in Glasgow and Frank Lloyd Wright in Chicago were to be studying its traditional buildings for inspiration. Hearn may not have known it, but a small army of western travel writers was hastily crisscrossing Japan gathering materials for books that would "explain" that country to western readers.

How did it happen, then, that a writer-journalist who arrived not speaking a word of Japanese could, within a few years, establish himself as the premier interpreter of Japanese culture to the English-speaking and European world?[6] More to the point, how could an outsider, even an outsider who had adopted Japanese ways, create a literary picture of Japan that Japanese themselves would come to admire as an image of their better selves?

Literary critics of the postmodern school would pose the question differently: how did Lafcadio "construct" his verbal Japan? What materials did he use to create this edifice and how did he put them together? The answer must be sought partly in his earlier writings on Louisiana.

Back in Louisiana Hearn had mastered the art of precise observation. He had learned how to convey the telling detail succinctly and to relate it to larger traits of culture. Equally important, he had developed a Manichean world view that pitted Good against Evil in an unequal struggle. His notion of a gentle, aesthetically rich, feminine, sensual, and fragile Creole culture gradually losing out to the Anglo-Saxon world of Mammon could be transferred wholesale to Meiji-era Japan. He had only to change the names for his idealization of the victims of modernization in Louisiana to fit the conditions he encountered in Japan.

In short, Hearn constructed a Creolized version of Meiji Japan using ideas and techniques he first developed while working at the New Orleans *City Item* and *Times-Democrat*. There were differences, of course, especially the absence of a strong erotic element in Japanese culture (which an older Hearn now applauded) and the racial homogeneity that prevailed there. But those aspects of Hearn's portrait of Japan that most appealed to the Japanese themselves were already stowed in his intellectual and artistic baggage when he arrived, the fruits of his years in Louisiana and of his own tortured inner life.

Considering how deeply Hearn affected how western readers and Japanese themselves conceived Japan, is it possible that his earlier writings on Louisiana similarly shaped the way American readers and New Orleanians themselves view the old city on the Mississippi? Recall that Louisiana and New Orleans have become as much ideas and symbols as physical or social realities. The question, then, touches on the origins of literary images that have become part of our everyday consciousness.

Before delving into their genealogy, it is worth pausing to review the vivid set of images that now cling to New Orleans and South Louisiana.

Who has not heard of New Orleans as "The Big Easy" or "The City That Care Forgot"? Tourist agencies and even New Orleans's official tourism commission have touted both slogans in order to lure travelers and conventions. Then there is the image of New Orleans as a wicked (or at least naughty) place where normal constraints are relaxed and where sensuality reigns, especially during Mardi Gras.

At a slightly deeper level is the notion that New Orleans is not quite American, and that its "otherness" derives from the continuing if subterranean influence of Creole culture by its bearers of all nationalities and races. The diligent traveler does not simply *visit* New Orleans; he or she explores it, seeking out the invisible but authentic reality that is more real than whatever can be discerned on the surface.

To succeed at this quest, one must discover an obscure but indisputably authentic Creole restaurant maintained by some anonymous culinary genius; one must plunge into the world beyond Bourbon Street to *ferret out* a remote bar or dance hall where *real jazz* is played, preferably by self-taught elderly musicians who purportedly cannot read music but play with unchallenged *authenticity*. Better still, visit a back street church filled with *ecstatic* singing, or find some little-visited cemetery where *voudou* rites are said still to be practiced. If there is perceived to be an element of danger in such peregrinations, so much the better. The invisible world of South Louisiana will not yield up its secrets without a struggle.

The glue holding together the various elements of this composite image is the imminent threat of destruction that hangs over it all. Creole folkways are dying, quaint buildings are being destroyed, authenticity in music is not being passed on to the rising generation, fine old neighborhood eateries are closing their doors, and so forth. The visitor must rush to experience the remaining morsels before they are gone, preserving his or her impressions with notebook, camera, and tape recorder, so as to be able later to savor them in a mood of sweet lyrical melancholy—and, with luck, some day to guide a fiancé or friend through the same itinerary.

And what is the force that is obliterating this fragile flower of authentic New Orleans and Louisiana culture? Why, it is modern capitalism with its bloodless efficiency, franchised restaurants, canned music, and spiritual emptiness. It is modernity itself, or globalization, as we now say. Never mind that one uses the latest technologies to book a ticket, fly to Louisiana, stay cool in one's hotel, and send e-mails back home. Never mind, also, that Hearn himself came to long for a solid modern home with all its conveniences, rather than the idyllic Creole courtyard he had extolled in print. To experience *authentic* New Orleans is, for the moment, to reject the modern world of which one is a part and to revel in an innocent world of beauty and eros in the moments before its demise.

These, then, are a few of the elements that make up the image of New Orleans that prevails among millions of Americans, Europeans, and Asians. Others could be added, just as some of these might be muted for a few years, before emerging again. It is curious that they are all essentially literary in character, rather than sociological, economic, or even historical. Yet these literary images have conquered all, confirming the thesis of Daniel Boorstin's seminal 1962 study, *The Image,* namely, that in the modern world images are more "real" than reality.

Evidence of this truth is the way in which many residents of New Orleans and South Louisiana have themselves accepted this set of images. Who cares that the region can boast of its major port, thriving businesses, a serious scientific tradition, major accomplishments in engineering and technology, and more than a few achievements in medicine? When locals are called on to describe their world, they are more likely to trot out the above set of literary and cultural images and to ignore these impressive if more mundane realities.

The composite vision of fading grandeur, cultural hybridization, noble simplicity, eroticism, authenticity of expression (and a hint of danger) provides the underpinnings for scores of books and films on New Orleans and for the programs of more than a few local cultural and educational institutions. The City of New Orleans has long since accepted this image as a true representation of itself and—for better or worse—has made tourism the center of its strategy for economic development. The booming tourist industry rests squarely on the foundation of these same images and supposed verities. In short, the literary image of New Orleans has been successfully commodified, to the point that it has taken on an economic life of its own.

This, then, is the notion of New Orleans and South Louisiana that took root and prevailed throughout the world in the twentieth century and which many residents of the region themselves have come to accept. Because it is less an analytic description than a literary construct, it is worth enquiring once more into its origins and genealogy.

Some might argue that it just grew up. Even though a literary construct, it is rooted in a reality that many writers over the past two centuries have tried to describe. In support of that claim they might cite travelers' accounts from the early nineteenth century and even from the eras of French and Spanish rule.[7]

But while this argument has a degree of validity, it is flawed on two counts. First, it cannot account for the fact that very few writers until the late nineteenth century presented this colorful set of literary images that acknowledged the region's workaday political, economic, and social circumstances. Second, and more compelling, until Lafcadio Hearn appeared at the *City Item,* not one writer had consistently developed every one of the elements of this literary gumbo, to the exclusion of all others, and done so in so lively and evocative a style that it commanded the attention of a wide readership not only in New Orleans but, increasingly, across the United States.

The titles of Hearn's countless writings on New Orleans and Louisiana read like an index to the main themes of literally hundreds of novels, movie scripts, travel guides, tourist brochures, monographs, and dissertations devoted to the region. Local and national writers and musicians who make a profession of explaining the Crescent City to the uninitiated tirelessly march through Hearn's table of contents without even realizing they are doing so. But it was Hearn who, more than anyone else, identified the elements of what became the prevailing image of New Orleans and commanded the literary skills needed to communicate that composite to a large general readership.

Was Hearn a writer of the very first rank? Probably not. But he belongs firmly in the upper ranks of those secondary writers who nonetheless succeed in influencing how millions of people view a given subject. It is pointless to compare him to Faulkner, Percy, or Williams, whose aspirations had little in common with Hearn's. Better to think of the French writer Eugene Sue, whose *Les mysteres de Paris* (1843) created a literary image of the French capital that was so compelling and enticing that it shaped how nineteenth-century painters, poets, and Bohemians thought about that city, influenced, directly or indirectly, the work of novelists as far away as Dostoevsky in Russia, and later became the basis for the tourist industry's own portrayal of Paris. Or one might compare Hearn to America's great western painters like Bierstadt, who may not have been artists of the first rank but changed forever how millions perceived the Rockies.

It is in this sense that we might conclude that Lafcadio Hearn, the one-eyed gnome from a remote island in the Greek Aegean, the morbidly sensitive social misfit and self-described "wandering ghost," *invented* New Orleans. Anyone who delights in that world, whether as literary image or concrete reality, is in his debt.

The goal of the present volume is to present a sampling of Lafcadio's writings on Louisiana and New Orleans. The selections are drawn from a mass of works in many genres which, together, would fill several volumes. Of necessity, whole categories of Hearn's writings have been passed over. His fictional works, notably his intriguing novel, *Chita,* are here excluded. Hearn was also an addictive and engaging correspondent, often signing his letters "Your Creolized friend." Even though many of these revealing letters have never appeared in print, they will have to await another publication.

And the principle of selection? Whatever pieces seem to represent most fully this complex and contradictory writer, whatever works reflect best his multi-faceted and nuanced vision of New Orleans, and whatever writings most appeal to this particular reader and admirer of Hearn have found their way into these pages. Even after scores of pieces that might have claimed the reader's attention were excluded, the collection was still far too big to fit into one volume, let alone one that might comfortably be read on a bench along the Riverwalk, on a grassy levee in the Ninth Ward, or in Audubon Park. And so I have made various excisions, which, following Hearn's own practice, are indicated with ellipses.

S. Frederick Starr
Washington and New Orleans
August, 2000

1. Symbol and myth, of course, are different, but Violet Harrington Bryan's *The Myth of New Orleans in Literature* (Knoxville, 1993) is nonetheless relevant to this discussion, especially chapter 1.

2. The biography that captures this quality best is Jonathan Cott, *Wandering Ghost: The Odyssey of Lafcadio Hearn* (Tokyo, New York, London, 1990).

3. Cott, chapter 5.

4. The largest collection of Hearn's writings is the sixteen-volume *The Writings of Lafcadio Hearn* (Boston, 1922), but a comprehensive edition would be much larger.

5. *Editorials by Lafcadio Hearn,* Charles Woodward Hutson, ed., Boston, 1926.

6. S. Frederick Starr, "The Creole Japan of Lafcadio Hearn," International House, Tokyo, 2000, *Louisiana Cultural Vistas,* vol. 12, no. 2, Louisiana Endowment for the Humanities, New Orleans, summer 2001.

7. *Louisiana Sojourns: Travelers' Tales and Literary Journeys,* Frank de Caro, ed., Rosan Augusta Jordan, assoc. ed., Baton Rouge, 1998.

Inventing New Orleans

PART I

The Outsider as Insider

IMPRESSIONS

Hearn was by profession a journalist, but most "news" simply bored him. During a decade in Cincinnati he specialized in covering the most brutal and squalid sides of local life, passing stern judgments on what the locals had come to accept as normal. In the process he developed a style as lurid as his subject matter.

In Louisiana he underwent a change of heart. Deeply drawn to this unfamiliar world, he strove to present it with sympathy and love. To readers around the country he was now an insider, describing and explaining what they could barely imagine. In the process, he defined many of the themes that dominate subsequent writings on New Orleans. Later, he made good use of this reportorial style, which might be called "affectionate impressionism," in his landmark writings on Japan.

Memphis to New Orleans

NOVEMBER 14, 1877.

...One leaves Memphis with little regret, despite those lovely sunsets, for rain and storms are more frequent than fine days. The day of my departure I watched the cottonboats being loaded, being myself upon a cottonboat; and the sight, at first novel, became actually painful as the afternoon waned and the shadows of the steamboat chimneys lengthened on the levee. Cotton, cotton, cotton,—thump, thump, thump,—bump,

bump, bump; until everything seemed a mass of bagging and iron bands, blotched with white, and one felt as if under the influence of a cotton nightmare. Just when the boat was leaving the levee, it suddenly occurred to me that the color of the face of the bluffs and the color of the new cotton bales piled along the slope were almost precisely the same; and the irregularly broken brownness of the bluffs themselves helped out the fancy that Memphis was actually built upon bales of cotton. Allegorically speaking, this is strictly true.

—I once thought when sailing up the Ohio one bright Northern summer that the world held nothing more beautiful than the scenery of the Beautiful River,—those voluptuous hills with their sweet feminine curves, the elfin gold of that summer haze, and the pale emerald of the river's verdure-reflecting breast. But even the loveliness of the Ohio seemed faded, and the Northern sky-blue palely cold, like the tint of iceberg pinnacles, when I beheld for the first time the splendor of the Mississippi.

"You must come on deck early to-morrow," said the kind Captain of the *Thompson Dean;* "we are entering the Sugar Country."

So I saw the sun rise over the cane fields of Louisiana.

It rose with a splendor that recalled the manner of its setting at Memphis, but of another color;—an auroral flush of pale gold and pale green bloomed over the long fringe of cottonwood and cypress trees, and broadened and lengthened half way round the brightening world. The glow seemed tropical, with the deep green of the trees sharply cutting against it; and one naturally looked for the feathery crests of cocoa-nut palms. Then the day broke gently and slowly,—a day too vast for a rapid dawn,—a day that seemed deep as Space. I thought our Northern sky narrow and cramped as a vaulted church-roof beside that sky,—a sky so softly beautiful, so purely clear in its immensity, that it made one dream of the tenderness of a woman's eyes made infinite.

And the giant river broadened to a mile,—smooth as a mirror, still and profound as a mountain lake. Between the vastness of the sky and the vastness of the stream, we seemed moving suspended in the midst of day, with only a long, narrow tongue of land on either side breaking the brightness. Yet the horizon never became wholly blue. The green-golden glow lived there all through the day; and it was brightest in the south. It was so tropical, that glow;—it seemed of the Pacific, a glow that forms a background to the sight of lagoons and coral reefs and "lands where it is always afternoon."

Below this glow gleamed another golden green, the glory of the waving cane fields beyond the trees. Huge sugar mills were breathing white and black clouds into the sky, as they masticated their mighty meal; and the smell of saccharine sweetness floated to us from either shore. Then we glided by miles of cotton-fields with their fluttering white bolls; and by the mouths of bayous;—past swamps dark with cypress gloom, where the gray alligator dwells, and the gray Spanish moss hangs in elfish festoons from ancient trees;—past orange-trees and live-oaks, pecans and cotton-woods and broad-leaved bananas; while the green of the landscape ever varied, from a green so dark that it seemed tinged with blue to an emerald so bright that it seemed shot through with gold. The magnificent old mansions of the Southern planters, built after a generous fashion unknown in the North, with broad verandas and deliciously cool porches, and all painted white or perhaps a pale yellow, looked out grandly across the water from the hearts of shadowy groves; and, like villages of a hundred cottages, the negro quarters dotted the verdant face of the plantation with far-gleaming points of snowy whiteness.

And still that wondrous glow brightened in the south, like a far-off reflection of sunlight on the Spanish Main.

—"But it does not look now as it used to in the old slave days," said the pilot as he turned the great wheel. "The swamps were drained, and the plantations were not overgrown with cottonwood; and somehow or other the banks usen't to cave in then as they do now."

I saw, indeed, signs of sad ruin on the face of the great plantations; there were splendid houses crumbling to decay, and whole towns of tenantless cabins; estates of immense extent were lying almost untilled, or with only a few acres under cultivation; and the vigorous cottonwood trees had shot up in whole forests over fields once made fertile by the labor of ten thousand slaves. The scene was not without its melancholy; it seemed tinged by the reflection of a glory passed away—the glory of wealth, and the magnificence of wealth; of riches, and the luxury of riches.

O, fair paradise of the South, if still so lovely in thy ruin, what must thou have been in the great day of thy greatest glory!

White steamboats, heavily panting under their loads of cotton, came toiling by, and calling out to us wild greeting long and shrill, until the pilot opened the lips of our giant boat, and her mighty challenge awoke a thousand phantom voices along the winding shore. Red sank the sun in a sea of fire, and bronze-hued clouds piled up against the light like fairy islands in a sea of glory, such as were seen, perhaps, by the Adelantado of the Seven Cities.

"Those are not real clouds," said the pilot, turning to the west, his face aglow with the yellow light. "Those are only smoke clouds rising from the sugar-mills of Louisiana, and drifting with the evening wind."

The daylight died away, and the stars came out, but that warm glow in the southern horizon only paled, so that it seemed a little further off. The river broadened till it looked with the tropical verdure of its banks like the Ganges, until at last there loomed up a vast line of shadows, dotted with points of light, and through a forest of masts and a host of phantom-white river boats and a wilderness of chimneys the *Thompson Dean*, singing her cheery challenge, steamed up to the mighty levee of New Orleans.

At the Gate of the Tropics

NEW ORLEANS, NOVEMBER 19, 1877.

Eighteen miles of levee! London, with all the gloomy vastness of her docks, and her "river of the ten thousand masts," can offer no spectacle of traffic so picturesquely attractive and so varied in its attraction.

In the center of this enormous crescent line of wharves and piers lie the great Sugar and Cotton Landings, with their millions of tons of freight newly unshipped, their swarms of swarthy stevedores, their innumerable wagons and beasts of burden. Above the line of depot and storehouse roofs, stretching southward, rises the rolling smoke of the cotton-press furnaces. Facing the Sugar Landing, stretching northward, extend a line of immense sugar sheds, with roofs picturesquely-peaked, Sierra-wise. Below, along the wooden levee, a hundred river boats have landed without jostling, and the smoky breath of innumerable chimneys floats, upward-eddying, into the overarching blue. Here one sees a comely steamer from the Ohio lying at the landing, still panting, after its long run of a thousand miles; there a vast Mississippi boat lies groaning, with her cargo of seven thousand bales, awaiting relief by a legion of longshoremen. At intervals other vessels arrive, some, like mountains of floating cotton, their white sides hidden by brown ramparts of bales built up to the smokestacks; some deeply freighted with the sweet produce of the cane fields. Black tugs rush noisily hither and thither, like ugly water-goblins seeking strong work to do; and brightly-painted luggers, from the lower coasts,— from the oyster beds and the fruit tree groves—skim over the wrinkled water, some bearing fragrant freight of golden oranges, and pomegranates, and bananas richly ripe; some bringing fishy dainties from the sea. Ocean steamers are resting their levitation sides at the Southern piers, and either way, along the far-curving lines of wharves, deep-sea ships lie silently marshaled, their pale wings folded in motionless rest. There are barks and brigs, schooners and brigantines, frigates and merchantmen, of all tonnages—ships of light and graceful build, from the Spanish Main; deep-bellied steamers, with East Indian names, that have been to Calcutta and Bombay; strong-bodied vessels from Norway and all the Scandinavian ports; tight-looking packets from English ports; traders under German, Dutch, Italian, French, and Spanish flags; barks from the Mediterranean; shapely craft from West Indian harbors....

—It is not an easy thing to describe one's first impression of New Orleans; for while it actually resembles no other city upon the face of the earth, yet it recalls vague memories of a hundred cities. It owns suggestions of towns in Italy, and in Spain, of cities in England and in Germany, of seaports in the Mediterranean, and of seaports in the tropics. Canal street, with its grand breadth and imposing façades, gives one recollections of London and Oxford street and Regent street; there are memories of Havre and Marseilles to be obtained from the Old French Quarter; there are buildings in Jackson Square which remind one of Spanish-American travel. I fancy that the power of fascination which New Orleans exercises upon foreigners is due no less to this peculiar characteristic than to the tropical beauty of the city itself. Whencesoever the traveler may have come, he may find in the Crescent City some memory of his home—some recollection of his Fatherland—some remembrance of something he loves....

I find much to gratify an artist's eye in this quaint, curious, crooked French Quarter, with its narrow streets and its houses painted in light tints of yellow, green, and sometimes even blue. Neutral tints are common; but there are a great many buildings that can not have been painted for years, and which look neglected and dilapidated as well as antiquated. Solid wooden shutters, painted a bright grass-green, and relieved by walls painted chocolate color, or tinted yellow, have a pretty effect, and suggest many memories of old France. Few houses in the quarter are without them. . . .

Most of the finer public buildings must have been erected at a time when expense was the least consideration in the construction of an edifice. They are generously and beautifully built; yet it is sad to see that many of them are falling into decay. Especially is this the case in regard to the old St. Louis Hotel—now the State House—with its splendid dome, frescoed by Canova, and its grand halls. To repair it would now require an outlay of hundreds of thousands. It has been outraged in a manner worthy of Vandals; soldiers have been barracked in it; mould and damp have written prophecies of ruin within it. Hither it was that the great planters of the South dwelt in the old days when they visited New Orleans, and under their rich patronage the hotel prospered well, till the war swept away their wealth, and, for a time at least, ruined New Orleans. I doubt if any of the great hotels here are now doing well.

The St. Charles, with its noble Greek façade, is the handsomest of these. From the entrance of the rotunda looking outward and upward at the vast Corinthian columns, with their snowy fluted shafts and rich capitals, their antique lines of beauty, their harmonious relation to each other, the sight is magnificent. I find a number of noble Greek façades in the city, the City Hall, the Methodist Church, on Carondelet street, and other structures I might name, are beautiful, and seem to illumine the streets with their white splendor. This elegant, gracious architecture appears adapted to this sky and this sunny clime; and, indeed, it was under almost such a sky and such a sun that the Greek architecture was born.

But, after all, the glory of the city is in her Southern homes and gardens. One can not do justice to their beauty. The streets broaden there; the side-paths are bordered with verdant sod as soft and thick as velvet and overshadowed with magnolias; the houses, mostly built in Renaissance style, are embowered in fruit-bearing trees and evergreen gardens, where statues and fountains gleam through thick shrubbery, cunningly trimmed into fantastic forms. Orange and fig trees; bananas and palms; magnolias and myrtles; cypresses and cedars; broad-leaved, monstrous-flowering plants in antique urns; herbs with leaves shaped like ancient Greek sword-blades, and edged with yellow. . . And you can walk through this paradise hour after hour, mile after mile; and the air only becomes yet more fragrant and the orange trees more heavily freighted with golden fruit, and the gardens more and more beautiful, as you proceed southwardly. . . .

NOVEMBER 20.

I have just witnessed a terrible exhibition of the power of the machinery. Friends had advised me to visit the huge cotton press at the Cotton Landing, and I spent several hours in watching its operation. Excepting, perhaps, some of the monster cotton presses of India, it is said to be the most powerful in the world; but the East Indian presses box the cotton instead of baling it, with enormous loss of time. This "Champion" press at the New Orleans Levee weighs, with all its attachments, upwards of three thousand tons, and exerts the enormous pressure of four million pounds upon the bales placed in it. When I first arrived at the gate of the building where the machinery is placed, they were loading the newly pressed bales upon drays—bales much smaller than the ordinary plantation bales. I was considerably surprised to see three or four negroes straining with all their might to roll one of these bales; but I was not then aware that each of the packages of cotton before me weighed upward of *one thousand pounds.* . . .

The spectacle of this colossal press in motion is really terrific. It is like a nightmare of iron and brass. It does not press downward, but upward. It is not a press as we understand the term generally, but an enormous mouth of metal which seizes the bale and crushes it in its teeth. The machine did not give me the idea of a machine, it seemed rather some vast, black genie, buried up to his neck in the earth by the will of Soliman, the pre-Adamite Sultan.

Fancy a monstrous head of living iron and brass, fifty feet high from its junction with the ground, having pointed gaps in its face like gothic eyes, a mouth five feet wide, opening six feet from the mastodon teeth in the lower jaw to the mastodon teeth in the upper jaw. The lower jaw alone moves, as in living beings, and it is worked by two vast iron tendons, long and thick and solid as church pillars. The surface of this lower jaw is equivalent to six square feet.

The more I looked at the thing, the more I felt as though its prodigious anatomy had been studied after the anatomy of some extinct animal,— the way those jaws worked, the manner in which those muscles moved.

Men rolled a cotton bale to the mouth of the monster. The jaws opened with a low roar, and so remained. The lower jaw had descended to a level with the platform on which the bale was lying. It was an immense plantation bale. Two black men rolled it into the yawning mouth. The titan muscles contracted, and the jaw closed, silently, steadily, swiftly. The bale flattened, flattened, flattened—down to sixteen inches, twelve inches, eight inches, five inches. Positively less than five inches! I thought it was going to disappear altogether. But after crushing it beyond five inches the jaws remained stationary and the monster growled like rumbling thunder. I thought the machine began to look as hideous as one of those horrible, yawning heads which formed the gates of the *teocallis* at Palenque, and through whose awful jaws the sacrificial victims passed. . . .

—Do you remember that charming little story, "Père Antoine's Date-Palm," written by Thomas Bailey Aldrich, and published in the same volume with "Marjorie Daw" and other tales?

Père Antoine was a good old French priest, who lived and died in New Orleans. As a boy he had conceived a strong friendship for a fellow student of about his own age, who, in after years, sailed to some tropical island in the Southern Seas, and wedded some darkly beautiful woman, graceful and shapely and tall as a feathery palm. Père Antoine wrote often to his friend, and their friendship strengthened with the years, until death dissolved it. The young colonist died, and his beautiful wife also passed from the world; but they left a little daughter for some one to take care of.

The good priest, of course, took care of her, and brought her up at New Orleans. And she grew up graceful and comely as her mother, with all the wild beauty of the South. But the child could not forget the glory of the tropics, the bright lagoon, the white-crested sea roaring over the coral reef, the royal green of the waving palms, and the beauty of the golden-feathered birds that chattered among them.

So she pined for the tall palms and the bright sea and the wild reef, until there came upon her that strange homesickness which is death; and still dreaming of the beautiful palms, she gradually passed into that great sleep which is dreamless. And she was buried by Père Antoine near his own home.

By and by, above the little mound there suddenly came a gleam of green; and mysteriously, slowly, beautifully, there grew up towering in tropical grace above the grave, a princely palm. And the old priest knew that it had grown from the heart of the dead child.

So the years passed by, and the roaring city grew up about the priest's home and the palm tree, trying to push Père Antoine off his land. But he would not be moved. They piled up gold upon his door-steps and he laughed at them; they went to law with him and he beat them all; and, at last, dying, he passed away true to his trust; for the man who cuts down that palm tree loses the land that it grows upon.

"And there it stands," says the Poet, "in the narrow, dingy street, a beautiful dreamy stranger, an exquisite foreign lady, whose grace is a joy to the eye, the incense of whose breath makes the air enamored. May the hand wither that touches her ungently!"

Now I was desirous above all things to visit the palm made famous by this charming legend, and I spent several days in seeking it. I visited the neighborhood of the old *Place d'Armes*—now Jackson Square—and could find no trace of it; then I visited the southern quarter of the city, with its numberless gardens, and I sought for the palm among groves of orange-trees overloaded with their golden fruit, amid broad-leaved bananas, and dark cypresses, and fragrant magnolias and tropical trees of which I did not know the names. Then I found many date-palms. Some were quite young, with their splendid crest of leafy plumes scarcely two feet above the ground; others stood up to a height of thirty or forty feet. Whenever I saw a tall palm, I rang the doorbell and asked if that was Père Antoine's date-palm. Alas! Nobody had ever heard of the Père Antoine.

Then I visited the ancient cathedral, founded by the pious Don André Almonaster, Regidor of New Orleans, one hundred and fifty years ago; and I asked the old French priest whether they had ever heard of the Père Antoine. And he answered me that they knew him not, after having searched the ancient archives of the ancient Spanish cathedral.

Once I found a magnificent palm, loaded with dates, in a garden on St. Charles street, so graceful that I felt the full beauty of Solomon's simile as I had never felt it before:

"Thy stature is like to a palm tree."

I rang the bell and made inquiry concerning the age of the tree. It was but twenty years old; and I went forth discouraged.

At last, to my exceeding joy, I found an informant in the person of a good-natured old gentleman, who keeps a quaint bookstore in Commercial Place. The tree was indeed growing, he said, in New Orleans street, near the French Cathedral, and not far from Congo Square; but there were many legends concerning it. Some said it had been planted over the grave of some Turk or Moor,—perhaps a fierce corsair from Algiers or Tunis,—who died while sailing up the Mississippi, and was buried on its moist shores. But it was not at all like the other palm trees in the city, nor did it seem to him to be a date-palm. It was a real Oriental palm: yea, in sooth, such a palm as Solomon spake of in his Love-song of Love-songs.

"I said, I will go up to the palm tree; I will take hold of the boughs thereof."

. . . I found it standing in beautiful loneliness in the center of a dingy wood-shed, on the north side of Orleans street, towering about forty feet above the rickety plank fence of the yard. The gateway was open, and a sign swung above it bearing the name "M. Michel." I walked in and went up to the palm tree. A laborer was sawing wood in the back shed, and I saw through the windows of the little cottage by the gate a family at dinner. I knocked at the cottage door, and a beautiful Creole woman opened it.

"May I ask, Madame, whether this palm tree was truly planted by the Père Antoine?"

"Ah, Monsieur, there are many droll stories which they relate of that tree. There are folks who say that a young girl was interred there, and it is also said that a Sultan was buried under that tree—or the son of a Sultan. And there are also some who say that a priest planted it."

"Was it the Père Antoine, Madame?"

"I do not know, Monsieur. There are people also who say that it was planted here by Indians from Florida. But I do not know whether such trees grow from Florida, I have never seen any other palm tree like it. It is not a date-palm. It flowers every year, with beautiful yellow blossoms the color of straw, and the blossoms hang down in pretty curves. Oh, it is very graceful! Sometimes it bears fruit,—a kind of oily fruit, but not dates. I am told they make oil from the fruit of such palms."

I thought it looked so sad, that beautiful tree, in the dusty wood-yard, with no living green thing near it. As its bright verdant leaves waved against the blue above, one could not but pity it as one would pity some being, fair and feminine and friendless in a strange land. *"Oh, c'est bien gracieux,"* murmured the handsome Creole lady.

"It is true, Madame, that the owner of the land loses it if he cuts down the tree?"

"Mais oui! But the proprietors of the ground have always respected the tree, because it is so old, so very old!"

Then I found the proprietor of the land, and he told me that when the French troops first arrived in this part of the country they noticed that tree. "Why," I exclaimed, "that must have been in the reign of Louis XIV!" "It was in 1679, I believe," he answered. As for the Père Antoine, he had never heard of him. Neither had he heard of Thomas Bailey Aldrich. So that I departed, mourning for my dead faith in a romance which was beautiful.

The City of the South

NEW ORLEANS, NOVEMBER 29, 1877.

I paid a good deal of attention to the old Spanish Cathedral here, founded by Don André Almonaster, Regidor and Álferez-Real of his Most Catholic Majesty. It is called the oldest church in the country, excepting one, I believe, in St. Augustine, Florida; and it is now always spoken of as the French Cathedral. But I was terribly disappointed about it. It is not now the same Cathedral that the Spanish Regidor built. Don André did not build for the centuries; and one day his church-towers crumbled down into the Plaza, and the whole Cathedral had to be pulled down and reconstructed. It was reconstructed Frenchily, and has lost its Spanish features.

You may still find those features preserved in certain old prints that hang, yellow with age and spotted with fly-specks, in the offices of certain ancient Notaries of the French Quarter; and you will find that Don André built the cathedral after that curiously mixed, but not unimposing style that characterizes the old cathedrals of Spanish-America. It had towers with Roman-arched windows, and cupolas of brick; and it looked very picturesque and quaint. Now it looks quaint enough, but less picturesque. I observed that the clock-face was broken to pieces, and that several of the pieces had been lost; and I supposed they do not wish to mend it, lest they should impair the venerable look of the façade—the yellow façade, the triple-pointed façade. And the beauty of the thing is enhanced by the fact that on either side stands one of the oldest-looking structures one could wish to see—buildings nearly two hundred years old, formerly called the "Mairie" and the "Palais-de-Justice." This Palais-de-Justice, or, in Spanish, *casa curial,* was also built, they say, by Don Almonaster, and is still the Courthouse of New Orleans. Both buildings have ponderous piazzas under the second story, supported by thickset Roman arches.

But the French Cathedral still contains two venerable objects of inter-est—two ancient tombs. One is the tomb of Don Almonaster; the other is the family tomb of the noble French family De Marigny de Mandeville, ante-revolutionary, aristocrats all, who may have strutted in those pic-turesque costumes we are familiar with in the paintings of the period; who belonged in the age in which gentlemen bowed and took snuff with an ineffable grace which this uncultivated generation are powerless to conceive of.

Ancient, in good sooth, is the tomb of Don André Almonaster. It is marked by a great marble slab, flush with the church pavement, and situ-ated opposite the side altar of the southern aisle. Benches are placed over it. The feet of more than four generations of worshipers have oblit-erated the carven helmet with its knightly plumes, and blotted out the noble armorial bearings of the carven shield. Only their outline is dimly visible; but the inscription, deeply cut, remains.

...I was talking the other day with an old gentleman who has long been a resident of New Orleans.... I asked him why it was that the early French colonists had chosen the pelican for the arms of Louisiana. "It was probably suggested to them," he replied, "by the fact that pelicans were so common in the country; and the pretty fallacy about the bird's devotion to its young made it seem a still more appropriate emblem for so fertile and bountiful a land as this. I suppose you know the arms were changed."

"No, sir," I replied, "I did not hear of it. Who could have had the bad taste to change them?"

"Why, the Radical carpet-baggers and scallawags, of course. Nobody else would have done such a thing. Do you know why they did it? Because, sir, those arms were a perpetual sarcasm upon their scoundrelism—a stand-ing rebuke to their thievery. The pelican had ceased to feed its young with its own blood; its blood was drained by the vultures who came down here to prey upon Louisiana. The mother State was no longer able to feed her own young, because the thieves and carpet-baggers had robbed her of her very life-blood. So the thieves had a new seal made. The peli-can was no longer represented as feeding her young with her blood; but the young were represented alone in the nest, and the mother pelican *coming from a distance* with something in her mouth. If you see some of the bonds issued in Warmoth's time, you will see how the arms were changed."

"But now they have been restored, have they not?" I asked.

"Yes, sir; now we have some reform and honesty in the State and Municipal Governments; and the Pelican, thank God, is again able to feed her young."

New Orleans has long been celebrated for the beauty of her women, and most deservedly so, I think. It is not, however, their comeliness of feature that especially impresses the stranger; it is their grace; it is that supple shapeliness which the French term *sveltess,* and for which the English tongue has no word. The opaline skin, the sun-golden hair of Northern beauty are seldom visible here; it is the rich, dark beauty of the Spanish and French types that one finds in New Orleans. A comely Creole woman's figure will often impress one as a startling realization of the Greek ideal of grace,—a statue by Lysippus animated and garbed—a living Venus of flushed bronze. This elegant, close-embracing costume now in fashion— the only modern dress, surely, that Cytherea would acknowledge well becoming a graceful woman—is admirably adapted to such figures. I have never seen the long dresses—made to be held up while walking, so as to show a gleam of snowy linen—so perfectly worn and perfectly managed as by the ladies who promenade Canal street of a sunny afternoon. And their robes make the air odorous as they pass, by the exquisite perfume of the South, the breath of orange flowers. I can not say I think beauty of feature a common gift of the women of New Orleans; indeed, I think it a rare one, comparatively speaking; but when one does find it, he straightway dreams of Titian and Veronese and Tintoretto.

I find that a large proportion of the lodging houses here are kept by colored women. Especially is this the case in the French Quarter; and all these colored concierges speak both French and English. Their English, however, is often deficient, and is invested with the oddest French accent imaginable. Somehow or other the French language sounds to me far more natural than our own in a black mouth; and it seems to be spoken by the blacks much better than English. It has been often observed that the negro acquires Spanish with facility. Southern tongues flow melodiously from his lips, being musically akin to the many-voweled languages of Africa. The *th*'s and *thr*'s, the difficult diphthongs and guttural *rr*'s of English and German pronunciation have a certain rude Northern strength beyond the power of Ethiopian lips to master. French is barren of rugged sounds; and it is common to hear these Southern negroes, with all the "politenesses" and "tendernesses" of which the sweet, smooth language is capable. The day after my arrival in the city I must have examined twenty-five or thirty furnished rooms offered for rent by colored housekeepers, and it was very pleasant to hear them speaking the speech of their old masters. . . .

Yesterday evening, the first time for ten years, I heard again that sweetest of all dialects, the Creole of the Antilles. I had first heard it spoken in England by the children of an English family from Trinidad, who were visiting relatives in the mother country, and I could never forget its melody. In Martinique and elsewhere it has almost become a written dialect; the school children used to study the "Creole Catechism," and priests used to preach to their congregations in Creole. You can not help falling in love with it after having once heard it spoken by young lips, unless indeed you have no poetry in your composition, no music in your soul. It is the most liquid, mellow, languid language in the world. It is especially a language for love-making. It sounds like pretty baby-talk; it woos like the cooing of a dove. It seems to be a mixture of French, a little Spanish, and West African dialects—those negro tongues that are voluminous with vowels. You can imagine how smooth it is from the fact that in West Indian Creole the letter "r" is never pronounced; and the Europeans of the Indies complain that once their children have learned to speak Creole, it is hard to teach them to pronounce any other language correctly. They *will* say "b'ed" for bread, and "t'ed" for thread. So that it is a sort of wopsy-popsy ootsy-tootsy language.

The patois of Louisiana is not nearly so soft. It is simply corrupted French, and when written, a Frenchman can understand a good deal of it, though he could hardly understand it when spoken. . . .

—If this be not the cosmopolitan city of the world, it is certainly the cosmopolitan city of the Americas. While standing in the bar-room of the St. Charles Hotel recently, where the auction sales of real estate are held, a friend pointed out to me foreigners from almost all parts of the world. I saw Herzegovinians, Cubans, Spanish-Americans, Italians, Englishmen, old-country French and Creole French, Portuguese, Greeks from the Levant, Russians, Canadians, Brazilians. We were a little party of four at the time, and within the space of twenty minutes I heard my three Southern friends converse with business acquaintances in the following languages: French, Portuguese, Spanish, and Modern Greek. I thought it a good example of the cosmopolitan character of New Orleans. . . .

There are many Greeks, sailors and laborers, in New Orleans, but I can not say that they inspire one with dreams of Athens or of Corinth, of Panathenaic processions or Panhellenic games. Their faces are not numismatic; their forms are not athletic. Sometimes you can discern a something National about a Greek steamboatman—a something characteristic which distinguishes him from the equally swarthy Italian, Spaniard, "Dago." But that something is not of antiquity; it is not inspirational. *It is Byzantine!* And one is apt to dislike it. It reminds me of Taine's merciless criticism of the faces of Byzantine art. But I have seen a few rare Hellenic types here, and among these some beautiful Romaic girls,—maidens with faces to remind you of the gracious vase-paintings of antiquity.

—I must tell you a New Orleans ghost-story which I have just heard. In these days ghosts have almost lost the power to interest us, for we have become too familiar with their cloudy faces, and familiarity begetteth contempt. An original ghost is a luxury, and a rare luxury at that. Now I think this one is unique enough to excuse me for presuming to relate it.

There was an old house on Melpomene street which nobody could live in. Many good folk had attempted to take up their residence in it, but none ever dwelt there more than one night. Sometimes people would send their furniture there in the morning and have the place fitted up, only to find everything outraged and violently upset in the afternoon. Carpets had been torn from the floor and stuffed up the chimney, or flung into the center of the room in an elfish shape, mockingly suggestive of a corpse with its hands crossed. Invisible footsteps shook the house with thundering tread, and bolted doors opened mysteriously at the touch of viewless hands. As the years flitted by the Goblin of Decay added himself to the number of the Haunters; the walls crumbled, and the floors yielded, and grass, livid and ghastly-looking grass, forced its pale way between the chinks of the planks in the parlor. The windows fell into ruin, and the wind entered freely to play with the ghosts, and cried weirdly in the vacant rooms. At last the police authorities resolved to solve the mystery of the house.

Stephen Leary was then Chief of Police. He visited the house one evening, accompanied by a picked detachment of six men, all armed with double-barreled shot-guns double-shotted. When the seven entered the crumbling building it was twilight. The chief ordered the detachment to form a hollow square in the middle of the old parlor, facing outward, and he himself filled the center of the square, lest the ghost might arise in the midst and seize every man by the back of the neck at the same time.

"Now," quoth he, "whencesoever it may approach we can blow it back to h— without hurting each other." And the hollow square remained stationary in the position of "ready."

Then the clocks commenced to strike the hours. There seemed to be at least a hundred clocks within hearing,— each one a little faster or a little slower than the rest. They told the time regularly in a hundred different keys, till it became "the dead waste and middle of the night." One after another, all the hundred clocks struck the hour of twelve. Then a vast and awful silence fell. The seven men brought up their muskets to "Present," and stared wildly in seven different directions.

Suddenly a gust of wind blew the light out; and they heard It coming;— an invisible and irresistible force seemed to burst up the flooring under the feet of the policemen;—*and each one simultaneously felt himself seized from below and violently flung against the ceiling. . . .*

And yet the city would not pay the bills of the seven doctors who attended the faithful men thus grievously injured "while in the discharge of their duty."

The Streets

. . . New Orleans, alone of American cities, has preserved all the romance of its earlier days in the titles of its streets, and with a simple directory one can recall the entire history of the French and Spanish dominion. Having changed its ownership no less than five times, having passed under so many masters, having witnessed such vicissitudes of fortune, New Orleans has a history full of incident and romance, and this it tells in its street nomenclature.

The old *carré* or parallelogram of the original city still preserves the names given by Le Blond de la Tour, who laid it out. There have been few changes here. The rue de l'Arsenal, Arsenal street, has given way to the rue des Ursulines, named in honor of the Ursuline nuns, who erected their convent here a century and a half ago. The rue des Quartiers, Barracks street, and the rue de l'Hôpital, Hospital street, are titles given to unnamed streets, because the government barracks and hospital were erected on them. Similarly the rue de la Douane, or Customhouse street, received its title, not from the massive granite customhouse that now stands there, but from the old wooden building, devoted to the same purpose, erected by the Spaniards a century and a quarter before. The boundary streets of the city, which marked the line of the old wall, all bear military titles referring to the old fortifications. Esplanade street was where the troops drilled; Rampart, rue des Remparts, marks, like the boulevards of Paris, the destroyed walls; while Canal street was the old fosse or canal which surrounded the city and which was continued as a drainage canal to the lake, and filled up only a few years ago.

Of the old streets only two have disappeared, rue de l'Arsenal into Ursulines, and rue de Condé into Chartres.

There have been some few corruptions in the old names. The rue de Dauphiné, named after the province of Dauphiny, in France, has dropped the accent on the *e*, and become simply Dauphine (pronounced Daupheen) street, as if it were named after the Dauphin's wife. The street named in honor of the Duc du Maine has got the preposition for ever mixed with the noun, and is, and will be ever, Dumaine, instead of Maine street.

In naming the streets of the city as it grew beyond its original boundaries, a dozen different systems were pursued. The gallantry of the French Creoles is commemorated upon old city maps by a number of streets christened with the sweetest and prettiest feminine names imaginable. Some of these were christened after the favorite children of rich parents, but again not a few were named after favorite concubines. The old maps of New Orleans were covered with such names as Suzette, Celeste, Estelle, Anelie, Annette, and others; many of these have died away into later titles, but not a few still survive. The religious tendency of the population showed itself in giving religious names to many of the streets. There are several hundred saints so honored, and scarcely one in the calendar has escaped a namesake in the Crescent City. There are besides these, such streets as Conception, Religious, Nuns, Assumption, Ascension, etc.

At the time of the French revolution there was an outbreak in France of Roman and Greek fashions. The modern French tried to imitate the ancient classics by assuming the Roman dress and Roman names. The Creoles who, although dominated by the Spaniards, were red republicans in these days, followed that fashion and all the names of antiquity were introduced into Louisiana and survive there to this day. Achille (Achilles), Alcibiade (Alcibiades), Numa, Demosthène (Demosthenes), came into fashion. The streets found a similar fate and the new faubourg Ste. Marie was liberally christened from pagan mythology. The nine muses, three graces, the twelve greater gods and the twelve lesser ones, and the demi-gods, all stood godparents for streets. The city fathers went beyond this, and there was a Nayades and a Dryades street, a Water Work, a Euphrosinè street, and so on without end.

Then came the Napoleonic wars, and with them, intense enthusiasm over the victories of the Corsican. A General of Napoleon's army who settled in Louisiana after the St. Helena captivity named the whole upper portion of the city in honor of the little Emperor. Napoleon Avenue, Jena and Austerlitz streets are samples which survive to this day.

In addition to these came the names and titles of the early Louisiana planters, such as Montegut, Clouet, Marigny, Delord, the early Governors of Louisiana, Mayors of New Orleans, and distinguished citizens.

These, however, failed to supply the 500 miles of streets that New Orleans boasts of, with a sufficiency of names.

In the naming of streets the French are not quite so matter of fact as the Anglo-Saxons, and they have shown this in some titles they have left behind. In New Orleans no Anglo-Saxon, for instance, would ever think of naming a street Goodchildren street, *rue des Bons Enfants,* or Love street, *rue de l'Amour,* Madman's street, Mystery street, Piety street, etc. Old Bernard Marigny christened two thoroughfares in the faubourg Marigny which he laid out, "Craps" and "Bagatelle" in honor of the two games of chance at which he lost a fortune. A curious mistake was that of the first American directory-maker who insisted upon translating Bagatelle into English and described it as Trifle street.

But even when a person is acquainted with the names of the New Orleans streets, the next thing is to know how to pronounce and spell them. This is very important, for they are seldom pronounced as they would seem to be. Tchoupitoulas—pronounced Chopitoulas—and Carondelet are the shibboleth by which foreigners are detected. No man is ever recognized as a true Orleanais until he can spell and pronounce these names correctly; and the serious charge made against an Auditor of the State, that he spelled Carondelet, Kerionderlet, aroused the utmost indignation of the population, who could never forgive this mistake.

The classical scholar who visits New Orleans and hears the names of the muses so frightfully distorted may regard it as unfortunate that Greek mythology had been chosen. The explanation of the mispronunciation, however, will relieve the people of New Orleans of any charge of ignorance. The Greek names are simply pronounced in the French style. Thus the street that the scholar would call Melpomene, of four syllables and with the last "e" sounded, would be in French Melpomène, and is translated by the people of New Orleans into Melpomeen. So Calliope is Callioap; Terpsichore, Terpsikor; Euterpe, Euterp; and others in the same way. Coliseum is accented like the French Colisée, on the second instead of the third syllable; and even Felicity street—it is named, by the by, after a woman (Felicité), not happiness—is actually called by many intelligent persons Filly-city. The influence of the old French days is seen in the spelling of Dryades, instead of Dryads, as the word is pronounced, and in a number of other apparent violations of orthoëpy or orthography, the truth being that the old French pronunciation and spelling are preserved and have become current among the English-speaking portion of the population.

The constant annexation to New Orleans of suburban villages and towns, with streets of the same name produces considerable inconvenience to strangers and even to natives of the city. There is a duplicate to nearly every name, and sometimes four or five streets bearing the same title.

Thus there is a North Peter's and a South Peter's miles apart, one in the First, the other in the Second district; then there is a simple Peter's in the Sixth district, and a Peter's avenue in the same division, while in the Fifth district there is a Peter street, and in the Third a Petre, pronounced Peter. A fine chance this to get confused.

There are Chestnut streets in the First, Fourth, Fifth and two in the Sixth district. And much more confusion of the same sort.

Another circumstance that is likely to deceive and mislead strangers is the preservation of the ancient names of the streets. These have been changed time and time again with the names, until even the residents on the streets get confused. Suppose you start down Rampart street, some will call it Love (the old name), and some Rampart. Beyond Canal you will see a building called the Circus street infirmary—this was, of old, Circus street. A little further on and you will hear that it is Hercules street, and when you get well up town, exactly half the population will swear it is St. Denis, and the other half stick to Rampart.

You want to go to the Moreau street Methodist Church and inquire for Moreau street. There is none; it is now Chartres; while the Craps street Church is not on Craps, but on Burgundy, its successor. When, in addition to this, it is remembered that few of the streets in New Orleans have any signs on the corners, that these signs one encounters are often in French, and that the numbering of the houses is very imperfect and defective, it will be seen that without a map or a good street-guide, giving not only the names of the streets to-day, but those they used to hear some years ago, a stranger can very easily lose himself in New Orleans.

The French Market

...As you near Jackson square a stream of busy-looking people appears, laden with baskets and bundles. Following this current of life, you are whirled forward to the corner, opposite the market. Here a stout old lady of heavy build, ornamented with a bonnet like a basket of vegetables, dashes across, followed by her daughter, a rosy-faced, stout-shouldered, masculine young woman. Business is everything to them, and as they pass over the oozy mud they lift their dresses high, high enough to attract the attention of the neighboring men. You follow in their footsteps into the market; at its entrance is a marble-topped stand, over which hangs the title and sign of the Café Rapide, with a painting, illustrative of the title, of many persons devouring their food with dangerous and terrifying celerity. Here you take your seat for a cup of coffee or chocolate, and glance around you.

A man might here study the world. Every race that the world boasts is here, and a good many races that are nowhere else.... The dresses are as varied as the faces; the baskets even are of every race, some stout and portly, others delicate and adorned with ribbons and ornaments; some, again, old, wheezy and decayed, through whose worn ribs might be seen solemn and melancholy cabbages, turnips and potatoes, crammed and jostled together in ruthless imprisonment. The butchers scorn to use all those blandishments that the lower grades of market society make use of to attract purchasers. Like Mahomet, the mountain must come to them. From the ceiling hang endless ropes of spiders' webs, numberless flies, and incalculable dirt. The stalls are deeply worn by the scraping process; in some yawn pits, apparently bottomless; and lastly, the floor of the market is not at all clean, but covered with mud and dirt from the feet of its patrons. Through the crowd lurk some skeleton-dogs, vainly hoping, by some happy accident, to secure a dainty morsel.

At the end of the market lie, sleep, eat and trade a half-dozen Indians. In olden days these Natchez, Choctaws and Creeks were numbered by the thousands, but they are melted away into Mulattoes. The lazy, unstudied attitude of these Red Roses, these daughters of the forest, is not exactly in accordance with the poetic idea one used to drink in, in his earlier days. The Indian females are formless, and the bag that they wear has no pretensions to fitting. When in addition they have hung around them bundles, beads, babies, and other curiosities, they fail to arouse our poetic sentiments.

Still following the drift of the crowd, you enter the Bazaar market, the newest of this batch of old buildings that are collectively honored with the title of market. It is in a tolerably good state of preservation. The architect had high and ambitious views, evidenced by two tin cupolas that rise like domes from the market-house. The flush days of the Bazaar market are fled; no longer are fortunes to be gained there; gloom and melancholy lurk within; many of the shops are boarded up, and even those that are occupied see few purchasers. A string of youthful merchants stretched across the street from the Bazaar to the vegetable market. Though but a dozen or so years of age, they have learned all the "tricks of the trade," and overwhelm you with good bargains, and almost extort your money from you.

At the angle of the vegetable market is the chicken repository. The dead chickens hang downward from the roof; the live ones are cooped up, and chant endless rounds of music. This market is the most cosmopolitan of all. The air is broken by every language—English, French, Italian and German, varied by gombic languages of every shade; languages whose whole vocabulary embraces but a few dozen words, the major part of which are expressive, emphatic and terrific oaths.

Nor are the materials for sale less varied. Piles of cabbages, turnips and strange vegetables adorn each side. Monstrous cheeses smile from every corner; the walls are festooned with bananas, etc.; while fish, bread, flour, and even alligators, have each appropriate tables. The bright sun leaks drowsily through the spider webs, producing a sad, sleepy light; the monotonous cries of the boys, "*cinq à dix sous,*" "two cents apiece, Madame," keeps on as endlessly as Tennyson's brook, and the crowd jostles you with baskets and bundles until you drop into some neighboring stall for a bite, or make your way altogether out of the market.

If you wait a little while until the press of trade slackens somewhat and the market people begin to go home, you will have an opportunity to study the queer habits of the "dagoes"—the Italian fruit and onion dealers, who make up so important and picturesque an element in the market.

A dark-skinned woman is going out of the empty market alone. She wears a soiled, faded calico dress; but in her eye there is *Madame Dufarge* boldness, which attracts the attention. She crumples her dress in her dark fingers, holding it up higher as she crosses the muddy, sloppy street through the rain. When she reaches the curbstone she stamps her bare, brown feet on the banquette—they are wonderfully formed feet—and gives herself a shake to get the mud and water off, to an extent. She gathers and crumples her calico dress in her hands once more and, walking a short distance, disappears down a narrow, dark alley. Thither she is followed by more fastidious feet, through the puddles of water on the old, cracked flagstone pavement, by heaps of garbage and vegetable refuse, damp and decaying, till the entrance of a dingy, crowded courtyard is reached. This courtyard is surrounded on every side by narrow, dreary-looking buildings two stories high. Rickety, crazy steps lead up from the yard to the galleries of the second story. It is a dismal-looking place as the drizzling rain falls on the mouldy posts and patters on the broken flagstones. It seems a fit spot for Poverty to hold her court, or for the phantom forms of disease to lurk. There is a hydrant in this courtyard. Near the base four spouts are let in, which, when open, pour their water into a circular stone basin about eight feet in diameter. The iron column that rises above this basin performs three separate duties. It is a hydrant at the bottom; a lamp-post, supporting a big glass lamp, at the top; and an ornament altogether. While this column and the circular stone basin below present a very handsome appearance, they are in strange keeping with their surroundings, for the yard is filled with tubs, buckets, barrels, hogsheads, crates and coops, all old, besides many other things that in amount seem almost impossible to crowd into a courtyard fifty by sixty feet. There are wet clothes strung on many lines stretched across this yard from building to building; they dismally flap and flutter about in the drizzly rain which is ever falling. The lower story, surrounding the courtyard, contains fourteen rooms, while the upper has a like number. In these dim chambers, twenty-eight in all, fifty families are living and breathing. This is their home through winter and summer, heat and cold—their home, whether pestilence, a terrible unseen spectre stalks about among them, or whether pity from heaven turns away the dire scourge of disease.

Many children are gathered about the dark doors. They look out vaguely at the rain, or talk and quarrel in the many dialects of their dark-skinned parents. Most of these children seem old and pinched about their faces, as though life were for them already exhausted. Dark-visaged men and women, descendants of the old Pelasgic race are gathered in numbers in these twenty-eight rooms. The men have come in off the wharf, where their boats, or their business, have occupied them all day, and are sitting in the doorways, smoking their pipes, while they gloomily look out on the gloomy weather.

The red flannel shirts and blue trousers which they generally wear give these fellows of the dark eye and raven hair a semi-piratical appearance. Their figures recall the time when Lafitte ruled, a king, over fiercer subjects on the sandy islands of Lower Louisiana. The women are inside the rooms, passing backward and forward, performing the drudgery of domestic work, while now and then they address the men in their many rapidly-spoken languages. They have a soft dialect, these women, while a great many of them possess forms and features that beneath the gentle touch of wealth and refinement would have made some even beautiful. But, with all their raven hair, their flashing eyes, and shapely forms, there is a wildness, a hardness of expression in their countenances, as if the haggard band of want had impressed them with an undefinable asperity.

On the upper gallery, out of the rain and the reach of many hungry-looking children, long strips of maccaroni are hanging up near the ceiling to dry. These people inherit from their fathers a fondness for this article; without which they would be like Americans without their wheat bread. Issuing from their rooms are the discordant notes of many of the feathered tribe, the gobbling of turkeys, quacking of ducks, cackling of guinea hens and crowing of cocks.... As night approaches the lingo from these feathered, red-shirted and calico-clad inhabitants is toned down to a subdued hum-drum. The birds of pride and birds of evil tuck their heads under their wings and are silent. The numerous members of the human family are fast preparing to follow their example. The men, women and children devour their scant suppers of maccaroni and unseasonable market stuff, then drop off to their respective corners or huddle among the crates and the coops in the little rooms. Soon no sound is heard save the noise made by the elements. The drizzling rain is still falling from the dull, dark sky; the water off the roof dripping down with a pattering noise on the broken stones, or beating with loud thumps on the bottom of the tin spouts. These people go to bed early, for they have to get up early in the morning. The court yard looks in the darkness as if it had been deserted. Red shirts and faded dresses are waving backward and forward on the lines. The solitary iron lamp post, without a light at the top, stands up dimly as a true sentinel over the place. Fifty families are asleep. In the dark, silent building, sleeping quietly, to awake and go through another day of poverty, privation and toil.

At three in the morning the first sounds of stirring are heard in the twenty-eight rooms. It is dark, but soon a faint streak from a match is seen flickering on the wall; then others; soon almost all of the rooms are dimly lighted up. A figure is seen descending the rickety stairs that lead down to the stones of the yard. It is that of a boy, his dress being the same in which he retired last night. This boy goes up to the lamp-post standing above the circular basin. He has a candle in one hand, while he uses the other hand, and a pair of bare legs, to twist himself up to the lamp at the top of the post. Lighting the candle he comes down and stands on the edge of the basin awhile to rub his sleepy eyes, and recall his faculties to the post of duty.

Soon nearly all the human occupants are up and moving about, putting on the blue trowsers and faded skirts which were thrown aside at the early bedtime.

The fowls get waked up, too, by these indications that their owners are awake, and set up a clatter of indignation at being outdone in this matter of early rising by the human members of the community. At last all the figures have risen up from their various resting places; then the sleepy crowd of men, women and children follow each other down the crazy steps. They form around the iron hydrant in the dim lamp light, like matutinal votaries, who are assembled to perform their mystic rites, and do their devotions before an idol. They throng around the four spouts which pour their water into the circular stone basin. They are all barefooted and bareheaded; some even have bare shoulders, but none are completely nude. These olive-complexioned people roll up their blue trowsers, tuck up their faded skirts and go into the big basin by fours, holding their hands under the running jets of water. They shower their heads and faces till they are wide awake. . . .

The boys then run up-stairs to get the coops of poultry, which they bring down and deposit tenderly on the stone pavement. Then they are off again after the baskets and crates of vegetables, which they bring down and pile in heaps just outside of the big basin. At the first glimpse of day they are going to take these out to the market; but in the meantime they are going to wash and get them clean before offering them for sale. To do this they roll up their blue breeches above the knees and step into the circular basin, whose waters, after having performed the duty for human heads and faces, are now going to cleanse cabbage heads and potatoes. The women pour in piles of parsnips, beets, radishes and potatoes, and the boys manipulate or pedipulate these roots under the water, where all the dirt is trodden off them, and they are taken out looking bright, nice and clean, all ready to be ranged in rows on the market stands. The four spouts of the hydrant are kept running all the time, while the water that brims over the basin runs out into the gutter beyond through overflow conduits.

The men and women are constantly jabbering while this operation is going on, about the prior rights of having their respective lots of vegetables washed, as everybody is anxious to be first at the market. In the meantime the coops of proud and noisy poultry are being carried out by other boys, who run constantly backward and forward from the yard to the market. After a while the jabbering is less loud, for many of their number have their vegetables washed, and the carriers, many of whom are women, have gone out down the alley, most of them staggering under wagon loads of comestibles.

A few old women are still left washing their stuffs in this basin of all uses. Their shrill, garrulous tones are heard till all get through. Then the stone basin, with its iron hydrant, lamppost, and light at the top, is deserted. A few of the oldest crones are left to take care of the very young children. All children who are not mere infants have gone out to work. These shriveled old women keep up for a short time a slight show of converse; a child or two cries as if unable to account for the cessation of the noise, and soon all is quiet. . . .

The courtyard people are only a part of the numbers who sell vegetables in the market. There are many others engaged in the business, who bring their vegetables in various ways and conveyances. There is a large class of people who raise their own vegetables and bring them to this place for sale in carts. At about two or three o'clock in the morning the sounds of many loaded carts are heard jolting on the streets. They travel generally at that pace commonly practiced at fashionable funerals. They creak and rumble in a characteristic manner as they go up the street, for their drivers are ostentatiously plodding and methodical. These drivers look sleepy; the horses and mules look about half asleep; even the carts seem as though they objected to being pulled out of their sheds and dragged through the darkness at that unheard-of hour. Of these drivers, some are men and some are women.

On the arrival of the loads of vegetables at the market, the carts back up to the curbstones, the sleepy drivers descend, and the work of unloading and arranging the vegetables on the stall counters commences. The women with their limp petticoats and dresses, damp with the dew of the morning, gathered about their thick-set limbs, arrange the vegetables to their taste. . . .

In Billingsgate it is said that the "heavenly gift divine—the power of speech"—is a faculty habitually abused. Here the abuse is more flagrant, for not "king's English" alone is subjected to pretty rough handling, but every language spoken on the globe is slanged, docked, or insulted by uncivilized innovations on its original purity. This commingling of languages is swelled to an absolute uproar by sunrise, when the market-goers begin to arrive. Aristocratic old gentlemen with their broadcloth, polished manners and boots puffed in and out; fat females with fat baskets hanging on their fat arms, waddle to and fro; footmen, waiters, maids and small boys come and go away. Nearly all trades, professions, colors and castes are represented with baskets on their arms.

The red-limbed, thick-set woman is at her stand, busily filling the baskets of many customers. Her short, stubby, harsh-looking broom is standing idle up against one of the shelves, waiting till the day is over. Then its harsh, yellow straws will grate once more against the paving stones of the place, as it sweeps the broken cabbage leaves and carrot tops out of the deserted market into the dirty street.

There are several marble-top tables about, in different parts of the market; four-legged stools are standing in rows alongside of these. . . . They are streaked with grease, or the polish is worn off at regular intervals where the stools are placed along side of them. The legs might look better; stray cabbage leaves and other waste material, scattered around their feet, give these legs a half-unclean, negligent appearance that borders on depravity. But then this is the market, and the wilted cabbage leaves are a part of the place. The tall stools, too, have this semi-negligent aspect. They are brightly polished on the top of their seats unavoidably, but their rungs and legs are scratched and scraped by iron shoe-pegs, or just the least bit discolored by mud. With the odors of the aromatic coffee, steaming from the urns, is mingled a peculiar market smell.

The keepers of these stands are semi-neat looking, too. Their shirts are as white as the marble tops of the tables, their buttons as bright as the little cups and saucers, and their countenances fresh and healthy-looking as the steaming dishes of bacon and greens. Their pants show they have been in contact with the grease-spots on the table or *vice versa*. Their shoes have been treading too much about among the wilted cabbage-leaves to lay claim to a respectable appearance. But probably hungry men are not too fastidious, and they don't mind a little grease or a little mud in the gentlemen who sell coffee at "five cents a cup," and the accompaniments accordingly. Most of these coffee-vendors have the power of imitating all the languages spoken in the place, to a certain extent. They make themselves understood to all their customers, and seem thoroughly posted in favorite slang phrases of the would-be fast men who come there to drink coffee. They are acknowledged as the elite of market society by the common consent of their humbler neighbors, of the vegetable and poultry trades; and they act well up to the license of this general acknowledgment. They are condescending, however, to those around them. They seem to feel a pity for those poor vegetable sellers; for some of them were once vegetable men themselves and they can appreciate the position. They are proportionately urbane as their customers are respectable. They pour out their coffee in dignified silence for the poor market men and women who come up and lean their elbows on the marble tops of the tables. When monsieur from the steamboats, or his desk, or his loafing place at the corner, comes up to get his breakfast, the coffee-vendor is all politeness.

Strangers who come into town late at night, bringing into the city with them their rural tastes and appetites, like to get a bite of something early in the morning. So they, too, often patronize the coffee stands. Some of these have a rural lack of assurance which they failed to leave at their homes, and they look very modest when they climb the high stools. They hesitate in answering to the question whether they'll take "*café au lait* or *café noir*"; they believe, however, they'll take "the first." The respectable keeper of the coffee stand has a pitying look in his eye for the ignorance of country people. The stranger of this class gets through, fumbles awkwardly in his pocket for the necessary pay; then gives place to the man of display, who pulls in on his purse here to gratify a taste for the ornamental somewhere else....

Sometimes old rich men come here to get cheap breakfasts; for certainly black coffee, "five cents a cup," and warm beefsteaks, are as nourishing and wholesome as broiled mutton chops, soft boiled eggs, and the thigh of a spring chicken, even if it is the least bit noisy down here, and smells more like a market than a restaurant.

The red-legged woman with the short, harsh broom, and the dark-eyed, raven-haired resident of the courtyard, say that they all have to pay fifteen cents a drawer and twenty cents a corner a day for their stands, besides a city license of ten dollars a year. A drawer is the space between two posts on a shelf, and a corner is a shelf where two of the passage-ways of the market cross each other. When the collector comes around, they dive their hands down into the pockets of their damp, faded dresses, pull out their small change, and silently hand it over. But some of the sellers of vegetables are inspired with a spirit of liberty and independence. They are very jealous of their rights, and this kind don't see money matters in the same light as do most people in the world. They pay up squarely when the collector steps up, but they think forty-five cents a day a very high rent to pay for the intervals of a stall between four posts....

Los Criollos

NEW ORLEANS, DECEMBER 3, 1877.

The common error of interpreting the word "Creole," as signifying a mulatto, quadroon or octoroon of Louisiana, and particularly of New Orleans, is far from being a local one, and dates back through centuries. It is not even confined to the uncultivated classes of the population of the Northern States, but flourishes, curiously enough, even in the South. It exists also in European countries—especially France, England, and Spain—mother-countries of West Indian colonies. Strangest of all, it actually lives in New Orleans, where the word Creole is a term of proud honor among the aristocrats of the South. There are numbers in this cosmopolitan city who have some vague idea that the more lightly-tinted half-breeds are rightfully called Creoles.

I need not dwell upon the prevalence of this error in the North among the mass of the reading public. Ladies at Washington have been known to faint while conversing with Southern Senators at a reception, because the honorable and distinguished gentlemen accidentally observed in the course of the conversation that they were Creoles. Doubtless the remark was made with a most aristocratic feeling of pride; and its result must have been all the more astonishing to the misunderstood Southerners. When a Louisianian says "I am a Creole," he is apt to utter the words with such an intonation as might have been given by an ancient Latin colonist to the proud words, "I am a Roman citizen." For many knightly names survive among the old families of the Crescent City; and many a Creole can trace his ancestry back to the nobility of old France, or to the grandees of Spain in the days of the Conquistadores.

It, therefore, seems odd, indeed, that even among the most ignorant portion of the population of this city, there should be found any person of the opinion that a Creole may be a quadroon or octoroon. But when one considers that the light-tinted, French-speaking colored element of New Orleans,—the relatives and the children of true Creoles,—call themselves Creoles, and desire to be so called, the existence of the fallacy does not appear so extraordinary after all.

Probably the misapplication of the term will continue indefinitely, despite all definitions of popular dictionaries and all explanatory essays in popular encyclopædias, inasmuch as it has been sanctioned by the custom of more than a hundred years. It always differs more or less, however, according to locality.

In the North the error is usually confined to the belief that the almost-white colored residents of New Orleans are Creoles, and that Creoles are indigenous and peculiar to the city. I have frequently, however, encountered it in the aggravated form of a supposition that the word applies to the light-colored women only of New Orleans. In the South there appears to be a widely diffused opinion among the lower classes that the Creoles of New Orleans are "nothing more'n dammed niggers who jabber French." In New Orleans itself I have been told by persons who considered themselves really informed upon the subject, that "a Creole means a New Orleans Frenchman and nothing else." In England the proper signification of the word is generally much better understood than here, but a large class of people hold that it applies to the children of Europeans in the West Indies only, while others contract the application of the term yet further, as signifying only the children of Spanish colonists. With good reason the native Spaniard considers a true Creole as necessarily one of Spanish blood; and the native Frenchman, with thoughts of *la Nouvelle Orleans* in his mind, will often insist that only the French residents of Louisiana are true Creoles....

...I had the good fortune to obtain one of the most remarkable articles ever written upon the subject. It is exhaustive and explicit, was published in a New Orleans journal in 1875, and was written by Professor Alexander Dimitry, a Greek gentleman of New Orleans, who enjoys a wide reputation for his learning and his extraordinary ability as a writer. Dimitry wrote the article not as an article or for publication, but as a letter and in reply to a written inquiry from a friend. The friend, with excellent journalistic judgment, however, at once carried the letter to a newspaper office, where it was gladly published. It gives some curious facts in regard to Creolisms in Louisiana, and I will quote freely from it, as it presents the information desired in a much more explicit and interesting fashion than I could hope to do in an analysis thereof.

After some severe allusions to the inadequateness of the definitions by Webster and Worcester, the Professor quotes authorities as follows:

> "From the Dictionary of the Spanish Language published by the Royal Academy of Madrid in 1762, we learn that the word 'Creole' signified 'one born in either of the Indies, whether the East or the West Indies, of Spanish parents or of parents of other Nations who are not Indians.' This word 'Creole' is one invented by the Spanish conquerors of America and by them made common in Spain to distinguish their European progeny, as we learn from Acosta's *History of the Indies,* in the fourth book and chapter the twenty-fifth. The definition goes on to say: 'This word *creole* in course of time came to apply not only to children born of European parents, but it was also extended to animals, vegetables, and fruits. Hence they had creole horses, creole pears, creole beans, and creole flour to distinguish these no doubt from those which were imported into the colonies from Spain.'
>
> "In the profound work of Covarrubias on the *Origins of the Spanish Language*... we find that 'the word *criollo,* a creole, is an invention of Spanish born parents, to denote their children, begotten and born in America....'"

Mr. Dimitry next quotes from V. de Solorzano, one of the most profound jurists of Spain, a member of the "Supreme Council, and the Board of Policy in Spanish-America." In his Commentaries Solorzano says:

"Who and what are Creoles? It is my duty, as an expounder of law—*como intérprete de derecho*—to say something concerning those who, in the two Indies, and born of Spanish parents, because, in those countries it is the custom to call them Creoles, just as it is customary to call 'Mestizos' those who are born of Spanish fathers and Indian mothers, and 'mullatoes' those born of Spanish fathers and negro mothers. In so much as related to the first—*entiendo los crillos*—I mean the Creoles, there can be no doubt that they are true white Spaniards, and that as such they are entitled to all the rights, honors, and privileges of their Spanish parents, granted by various charters and letters royal to the Colonies of Spain since the days of the conquest of Mexico. The reason of this is clear, because, although begotten (*criados*) in these remote and barbarous regions, they do not share in the accidental dwelling place; but they do in the land of their parents' origin and birth...."

The learned Professor concludes his letter with a very amusing disquisition upon other uses and abuses of the word "Creole," which portion of the epistle I quote almost entire:

"Go back to any file of newspapers, dating even twenty years ago, and you can read as I now read in the columns of the Louisiana *Courier* of the 28th of February, 1830: 'For sale—A likely young *Creole negro,* twenty-seven years of age; is something of a carpenter,' etc.; 'Runaway—A stout *American negro,* with a wen on his neck'; (runaway with a wen on his neck is simply delightful); 'he is a jack-of-all-trades.' Here, you see, we have a stout *American* negro in contrast with a likely *Creole* negro. From what admitted geography of the earth could you suppose that a stout American negro and a likely Creole negro could lawfully have come? Farther on I find: 'Estray—A sorrel *Creole* horse with a white spot on his left forefoot.' Very well for the stray Creole horse. I read a little farther on and I find an '*American* bay horse, with a blaze on his face.' Attracted by this newspaper zoology, and probably urged on by a slight curiosity of knowledge, I pass on with the hope of ascertaining whether I might not in this goodly company find some other respectable quadruped hemmed within the compass of a composing stick. In the columns of the paper, however, I find no advertisement for either a Creole or an American donkey. The fact compelled me to infer with inexorable logic that there were, then, no animals of the kind in Louisiana. Of other specimens of Creolism of which you daily hear we have 'Creole cows,' to distinguish them from the four-hoofed ladies that come from Texas or Kentucky. We have 'Creole chickens,' to distinguish them from the pipped and drooping brothers and sisters that travel in railroads and steamboats from St. Louis and Cincinnati. When the hens have become acclimatized and drop their eggs on Louisiana soil, they become '*Creole* eggs,' by virtue of which the huckster-women will charge you five cents apiece for them, while they will readily give you two '*American* eggs' for the same price. Ask, Why this difference? And the answer is ready: 'Them's none of yer Louisville eggs; them's Creole eggs, laid right here in New Orleans.' Then again, you have 'Creole cabbage'—not so firm and white as Western; but how much more tender in leaf and sweeter in taste. Again, the savory 'Creole onion,' out of the grand soil of Louisiana, instead of the large, tough Connecticuts. The 'creole sugar-cane,' so soft in fiber, and as slender as an asparagus stalk, pitted against the half-saccharine *otaheiti*, or the hard Cuban cane. The oily, yellow 'Creole corn,' for the hominy of the breakfast table, against the white flint of Ohio and Kentucky. The 'Creole rice,' which is more esculent than is the rice of the Nile of Egypt, or that of the banks of the Irawaddy, and safer to the molars than the rice from the pebble fields of South Carolina."

I must not omit to observe that the Professor lays special stress upon the fact of the word having been invented by the *Conquistadores* "as early as the year 1520, and seven years before the period when Chaves, by Imperial schedule and under the sign-manual of Charles V., *had introduced an African on the soil of America.*"

... It only remains to observe that the Creoles of New Orleans and of Louisiana (whatever right any save Spaniards may originally have had to the name), are all those native-born who can trace back their ancestry to European immigrants or to European colonists of the State, whether those were English, Dutch, German, French, Spanish, Italian, Greek, Portuguese, Russian, or Sicilian. But the term is generally understood here as applying to French residents, especially those belonging to old French families, and few others care to claim the name.

34

There is, however, a very select and cultivated circle of citizens in New Orleans who are especially proud of the name, and who unite all possible effort to make it an honor to those who bear it. In this Creole circle the French element indeed prevails; but the circle, nevertheless, embraces Creole citizens of Spanish and Italian, of Greek and Sicilian, of Portuguese and English, of Dutch and of Danish blood. They are the learned, the cultivated, the influential element of Louisiana society. The last remnant of the Louisiana aristocracy survives here, no longer splendid, it is true, with the shimmer of wealth, but yet maintaining loyally the old adherence to chivalrous principle, and the polished culture of the old French oligarchy. Riches in these unfortunate days fall to the portion of a few; and poverty does not exclude from this little Creole *cenacle.* Its atmosphere is European; its tastes are governed by European literature and the art-culture of the Old World. Something of all that was noble and true and brilliant in the almost forgotten life of the dead South lives here still. The *littérateur,* the art-lovers, the *dilettanti,* the thinkers of that South are here gathered together. They seldom appear in literature because literature has been to them, as to the gentlemen of the mother-countries, a source of recreation, a means of cultivating taste and elegance of expression; but there is perhaps a wealth of genius and a power of talent among the Creole Society of New Orleans such as may not be found in any other city of the land. . . .

Some Little Creole Songs

—When I read for the first time Alphonse Daudet's wonderful novel, *Froment jeune et Risler aîné,* which has been excellently translated under the title of *Sidonie,* I was particularly charmed with the refrain of the pretty Creole song, which Sidonie sings at various dramatic passages of the story:

> "Pauvre p'tit Manzel Zizi!
> C'est l'amou', l'amou' qui tourne la tête."

I determined, on coming to New Orleans, that should opportunity offer I would make some efforts to procure the entire song, made famous by this refrain. As yet I have not wholly succeeded; but here is something which makes it appear as if I was not far from success. I have only been able to procure one stanza with the refrain:

Z'autres qu'a di moin, ça yon bonheur;
Et moin va di, ça yon peine:—
D'amour quand porté la chaine,
Adieu, courri tout bonheur!
     Pauvre piti' Mamzel Zizi!
     Pauvre piti' Mamzel Zizi!
     Pauvre piti' Mamzel Zizi!
Li gagnin doulor, doulor, doulor,—
Li gagin doulor dans cœur à li!"

"Others say, it is your happiness;
I say, it is your sorrow:
When we are enchanged by love,
Farewell to all happiness!
     Poor little Miss Zizi!
     Poor little Miss Zizi!
     Poor little Miss Zizi!
She has sorrow, sorrow, sorrow;—
She has sorrow in her heart."

This appears to be an old fragment from either the beginning or from the end of an entire song. I can not venture to aver, however, that it is a part of the same song whose refrain I found preserved in the leaves of *Froment jeune et Rilser aîné*, for a great number of Creole songs, having various airs and differing greatly in their metrical construction, have similarly worded refrains. A very common burthen in these songs is—

"Mo l'aimin vous
Comme cochon aimin la boue!"
"I love you just as a little pig loves the mud!"

This refrain I have found attached, in various forms, to at least half a dozen various ditties. . . .

While on this subject allow me to give you several odd little Creole songs which I have just collected. Some of these are very old. I am told that Bernard Marigny de Mandeville, of famous memory, used to have them sung in his house for the amusement of guests—among whom, perhaps, was Louis Phillippe himself. The airs are very lively and very pretty:

> "'Delaide, mo la reine,
> Chemin-là trop tongue pour aller,—
> Chemin-là monté dans les hauts;
> Tout piti qui mo yé
> M'allé monté là haut dans courant
>> C'est moin, Liron, qui riv.
>> M'allé di yé,
>> Bon soir, mo la reine.
>> C'est moin, Liron, qui rivé."

"Delaide, my queen, the way is too long for me to travel;— that way leads far up yonder. But little as I am, I am going to stem the stream up there. 'I, Liron, am come,' is what I shall say to them. My queen, good night; 'tis I, Liron, who has come."

> "Tous les jours de l'an,
> Tous les jours de l'an,
> Tous les jours de l'an,
> Vous pas vini 'oir moin:
> Mo té couché malade dans lit;
> Mo voyé nouvelles auprés mo la reine;
> Vous pas seulement vini 'oir moin:
> A présent qui mo bien gaillard,
> Cher ami, mo pas besoin 'oir vous."

"Every New Year's day you neglected to visit me. I was lying sick in bed. I sent word to my queen. But you did not even once come to see me. Now that I am quite well, dear friend, I do not want to see you."

The Creoles of the Antilles seem to have felt more pride in the linguistic curiosities of their native isles than the Creoles of Louisiana have manifested regarding their own antiquities. In Trinidad fine collections of Creole legends and proverbs have been made, and an excellent grammar of the dialect published; in Martinique, hymn books, *paroissiens,* and other works are printed in Creole; the fables of La Fontaine and many popular French fairy tales have found Creole translators in the West Indies, while several remarkable pamphlets upon the history and construction of the West-Indian dialects are cited in Parisian catalogues of linguistic publications. But it was not until the French publishers of *Mélusine* showed themselves anxious to cull the flora of Louisiana Creole that the Creoles them-selves made any attempt to collect them. Happily the romantic interest excited throughout the country by George Cable's works stimulated re-search to further exertion, and even provoked the creation of a Franco-Louisianian novel, written by a Creole, and having a considerable portion of its text in patois. Nevertheless nothing has yet been attempted in Louisiana comparable with the labors of MM. Luzel and Sébillot in Bre-tagne; no systematic efforts have been made to collect and preserve the rich oral literature of the Creole parishes. . . .

Among the colored population of the old quarter the Creole survives like some plant that has almost ceased to flower, though the green has not yet departed from its leaves. One can find many scattered petals of folklore, few entire blossoms. Education is slowly but surely stifling the id-iom. The later colored generation is proud of its correct French and its public-school English, and one must now seek out the older inhabitants of the *Carré* in order to hear the songs of other days, or the fables which delighted the children of the old *régime*. Happily all the "colored Creoles" are not insensible to the charm of their maternal dialect, nor abashed when the invading *Amerikain* superciliously terms it "Gombo." There are moth-ers who still teach their children the songs—heirlooms of melody reso-nant with fetich words—threads of tune strung with *grigris* from the Ivory Coast. So likewise, we need not doubt, are transmitted the secrets of that curious natural pharmacy in which colored nurses of Louisiana have mani-fested astounding skill—the secret of fragrant herb medicines which quench the fires of swamp fever, the secret of miraculous cataplasms which re-lieve congestions, the secret odorous *tisanes* which restore vigor to torpid nerves—perhaps also the composition of those love philters hinted at in Creole ballads, and the deadly *ouanga* art as bequeathed to modern Voudooism by the black Locustas of the eighteenth century.

New Orleans in Wet Weather

The dampness of New Orleans upon a wet day impresses one as some-thing phenomenal. You do not know in the North what such dampness is. It descends from the clouds and arises from the soil simultaneously; it exudes from wood-work; it perspires from stone. It is spectral, mysterious, inexplicable. Strong walls and stout doors can not keep it from entering; windows and doors can not exclude it. You might as well try to lock out a ghost. Bolts of steel and barriers of stone are equally unavailing, and the stone moulders, and the steel is smitten with red leprosy. The chill sweat pouring down from the walls soaks into plank floors, and the cunning of the paper-hanger is useless here. Carpets become so thoroughly wet with the invisible rain that they utter soughy, marshy sounds under the foot. Consequently few houses are carpeted within, and those good folks who insist upon carpets soon learn the folly of putting them down on more than one or two of the upper rooms. Matting is the substitute even in aristocratic houses—dry, crisp, neat matting. Paper-hangers and carpet-layers would starve to death here. If you even lay a few sheets of writing paper upon your table at nightfall you will find them quite limp and rebellious of ink by morning. Articles of steel must be carefully laid away in tight drawers. The garments hung upon the wall, the coverings of beds, the well-starched shirts in the bureau seem as if they had been rained upon; the stair carpets become like wet turf; and a mouldy, musty smell pervades the atmosphere.

Fire is the only remedy possible against this invasion of moisture and mildew, and fires are absolutely necessary in all bedrooms almost all through the winter. During the daytime in winter months doors and windows are generally left open, except upon exceptionally cold or rainy days; the fires are allowed to go out, and the winds are invited to come in and keep things dry. But when night falls, chill mists invade the city, and exhalations of dampness rise from the moist earth. This is the case even in clear weather, and the Louisianians would not think of sleeping without a fire in their bedrooms to dry the air and banish the spectre of dampness. Even in the heat of summer the night-dews are often heavy like heavy rain. . . .

On the finest days in the winter months there are early fogs, that seem visible exhalations from the damp soil below the pavements. The gutters smoke whitely in the heavy air, and the face of the morning sun beyond the spectral mists assumes the sickly yellow of an unripe orange. When the long, burning summer comes, these sheeted fogs do not wholly cease to haunt the streets by night, and often long after daybreak; but their ghostly rule is unstable, for at intervals there comes a mighty sea breath from the Spanish Main, blowing over the cane fields and the fruit groves, driving the shadowy haze from the river banks, and filling the streets with bright air and a faint odor of orange flowers. Even in summer, however, fires are kept up in many houses through the night, partly to preserve the furniture against the mouldering damp, and partly owing to a wide-spread belief that Yellow Jack will not enter the room made cheery by a warm hearth.

I suspect that these fogs and night-damps account for the peculiar habits of late rising prevalent here. In the North at 8 o'clock, business is brisk; here, at 8 o'clock, the city has but just given its awakening yawn, rubbed its eyes and lazily stretched itself in bed.

Strange it is to observe the approach of one of these eerie fogs, on some fair night. The blue deeps above glow tenderly beyond the sharp crescent of the moon; the heavens seem transformed to an infinite ocean of liquid turquoise, made living with the palpitating life of the throbbing stars. In this limpid clearness, this mellow, tropical moonlight, objects are plainly visible at a distance of miles; far sounds come to the ear with marvelous distinctness—the clarion calls of the boats, the long, loud panting of the cotton presses, exhaling steamy breath from their tireless lungs of steel. Suddenly sounds become fainter and fainter, as though the atmosphere were made feeble by some unaccountable enchantment; distant objects lose distinctness; the heaven is cloudless, but her lights, low burning and dim, no longer make the night transparent, and a chill falls upon the city, such as augurs the coming of a ghost. Then the ghost appears; the invisible makes itself visible; a vast form of thin white mist seems to clasp the whole night in its deathly embrace; the face of the moon is hidden as with a gray veil, and the spectral fog extinguishes with its chill breath the trembling flames of the stars.

—The subject of dampness seems to me inseparably connected in New Orleans with the ghastlier subject of graveyards. Here at the depth of a foot or two feet one strikes water in digging, so that the labor of digging a grave is even as the labor of digging a well, and the result is the same. Consequently the practice of burying the dead in the ground has been almost abandoned. They are simply placed in dry tombs built above the ground, but nevertheless termed burial vaults. In some of the cemeteries here these buildings have evidently been designed after the beautiful sepulchres of antiquity, such as still line the Street of the Tombs at Pompeii, or as are scattered along the Appian Way without the city of Rome. They are mostly built of brick, cased with white marble, and entered by two small but ponderous doors of black iron. Over the double entranceway is carved the name of the proprietor, in this wise: "Family Tomb of John A——," or "Family Tomb of Richard B——." But, notwithstanding the beautiful designs of various tombs, the glare of the white stone and the gloom of the iron doors form a most dismal and unpleasant contrast.

What impresses one as most peculiar about some of these New Orleans cemeteries is the character of their inclosure—a wall of white stone, honeycombed with tombs. At a short distance the wall suggests the idea of an enormous system of pigeon-holes, the entrance of each pigeon-hole being apparently about two feet square, but really large enough to admit the insertion of the largest coffin. Here and there you see a row of twenty or thirty "pigeon-holes" closed up with lids of white marble and hermetically sealed. These contain coffins and corpses. Most of these horrid holes are, happily, tenantless, and spiders of incredible size and unspeakable audacity sit within and weave their dusty tapestries of clammy silk across the yawning aperture. Irreverent people term these sepulchres "bake-ovens." Fancy being asked by a sexton whether you wished to have the remains of your wife or child deposited in "one of them bake-ovens."

—The French love of the beautiful, the Italian spirit of art, have made this city beautiful; something of Southern Europe lives in the Garden District, with its singing fountains, its box-trees cut into distaffs, its statues and fantastically-trimmed shrubs, its palms and fig trees, and the yellow richness of its banana and orange orchards. . . .

But it is in the very heart of the city, in the center of the business blocks, and hard by the Cotton Exchange, that one encounters the most charming surprise of this sort. Entering a paved archway from Common street, you suddenly find yourself in a double court; and through the second archway beyond gleams a musical fountain, whose marble basin is made verdant with water plants and flowers. Above Hebe stands ever youthful in bronze, pouring nectar into her shapely cup; swan-birds curve stony necks at her feet, and about the lower basin four sinewy Tritons, whose nervous thighs end gracefully in dolphin-tails, blow mightily through marble horns. It is delightful to meet these fragmentary dreams of antique art,—these fancies of that older world which is yet ever young with the youth of immortality,—thus hidden like treasures in the city's bosom. The windows of this central court all look down upon the fountain; and quaint balconies, worthy of Seville or Cordova, jut out overhead at all possible angles. This is Gallia Court, devoted, alas! to office purposes, by lawyers and by doctors. . . .

I must say a word concerning a certain trade and a certain profession which are profitable in this poverty-stricken city. The trade is that of the bootblack. The profession is that of the beggar. . . .

When I left Cincinnati the bootblacking business was in a bad way. There were many bootblacks, and they were being forced into a reduction of prices. Nobody cared to pay more than a nickel for the most perfect possible "shine." But here prices keep up well. The New Orleans bootblack would reject a nickel with scorn. It takes capital to go into the business here. You must be able to buy a wooden platform, a soft-bottomed chair, a stationary blacking-box with raised foot-supports, five or six brushes, the best description of blacking, and a piece of carpet to kneel upon. Then you must pay a rent of eight or ten dollars a month for permission to exercise your calling upon any sidewalk in any busy part of town. The trade is wholly in the hands of men here, mostly colored, and it is said to be profitable in the winter season. Nobody here would think of having his boots blacked unless the bootblack could furnish him with a comfortable chair to sit down upon during the operation.

As for the beggars, I can only say that they seem to be regarded here as a necessary evil, and have become a nuisance in numbers, and an affliction by reason of their persistent impertinence. They follow you along the street, often two at a time, thrusting hats or hands under your nose in the ferocious determination to wring some mark of attention from you. Several have been locked up since I came here,—not, indeed, for begging, but for violently abusing the unfortunate people who dared refuse them alms. . . .

New Orleans Letter

NEW ORLEANS, JANUARY 5, 1878.

. . . Although one can live in New Orleans cheaper, probably, than in any other city of the country, her citizens have long accustomed themselves to eat but twice a day. Excepting the principal hotels, all eating-houses and boarding-places furnish their patrons with but two meals daily—breakfast and dinner; the former about 9 A.M., the latter about 4 P.M. The Creole is satisfied with a light morning meal, a cup of coffee or chocolate, with some fresh bread, and perhaps an egg, for breakfast. His dinner is more substantial, but far less solid and difficult of digestion than what is generally considered a good dinner in the North. If he be poor he can thrive on bread and coffee, with an ounce of *bouillon* at dinner time, or a plate of *gumbo* soup. If he be "comfortably situated" he will perhaps haunt the old fashioned restaurant of the Four Seasons, where for about seventy-five cents he can procure a meal dainty enough to satisfy the most *blasé* appetite—first-class Parisian cookery, with a bottle of claret, a rich cup of black Mocha, and a clear cigar, to aid digestion. For no true French Creole considers his restaurant dinner complete without a fragrant cigar, to be smoked with the fine cup of black coffee. If he should chance to prefer cigarettes, they are brought to him, and it is then amusing to watch how he prepares one. No Creole smoker would put to his lips any but a real Spanish cigarette, and the Spanish cigarette, you know, is loosely rolled, and tucked in at both ends. Your Creole exquisite unrolls it, and empties the tobacco into his left hand; then he pours it into the right hand, and blows away with a whiff the fine dust it has left in the other palm. Then he pours the tobacco into the left palm a second time, blowing the snuff-like dust from his right, and so on, until the tobacco has been thoroughly winnowed. Then he re-rolls it, and smokes it with little dainty gestures of exquisiteness.

But notwithstanding that boarding-houses furnish their guests with only two meals daily, the rates of regular board and lodging are much higher than in the North, where the rooms are more comfortable, and any one of your three daily meals contains more solid nourishment than the whole of a day's diet in New Orleans. For day board alone the regular charge is $5 per week, and, even with a room the reverse of comfortable, your month's expenses can not very well be reduced below $50. There is not much money in the city, wages are low; employment is difficult to procure except during the brief winter season, and the working classes can ill afford to pay such rates; consequently they do not live at the boarding-houses at all, but at the Markets. Fully half of the population of the city, I believe, take their daily meals at the market-houses. Now, one may live comfortably at the market-houses for the small sum of twenty-five cents per day.

Each market-house has its own long, marble-topped coffee-stand, with a dozen fat-bellied sugar-bowls marshaled in shining rows. Here, for five cents you may purchase an excellent cup of coffee, with a plate of doughnuts; and for five cents more a long loaf of sweet and milky-white French bread. That makes a good ten-cent breakfast. Then for dinner fifteen cents will purchase you meat, vegetables, coffee, and bread *ad libitum*. If you are a smoker you must have a good cigar with each light meal; and these two cigars will cost you two and a half cents each. So that your daily expenses for eating and smoking need not exceed thirty cents per day. As for the cigars, I wish to observe that you can procure, in New Orleans, cigars at the rate of two for a nickel, which are incomparably better than the average Northern dime cigar. I can hardly hope to make you believe this statement without tangible proof; but I can swear to it. The five-cent cigar is the high-priced cigar of the average New Orleans smoker. A ten-cent cigar is an extravagance—an outrageous extravagance.

The era of Spanish domination left its mark on the English language peculiar to New Orleans. It has bequeathed us the words *picayune, quartille,* and *la gniape*. The word *picayune* is yet extensively used instead of "nickel," and *quartille* still signifies a half-picayune, or a value of two cents and a half. However, the term is rapidly becoming obsolete, and is seldom used except by some of the old French-speaking negroes, who occasionally ask at a grocery for a *quartille* of sugar, presenting a nickel in payment. The term *la gniape* is in common use, and applies to a local custom which widely prevails with the tradespeople and storekeepers of the foreign and Creole population. It might be translated "the *give-away*," or idiotically rendered by the term "good-will." If you buy a ten-cent loaf of the delicious, cream-white bread for which New Orleans is famous, the baker presents you with a handful of ginger-cakes or a few doughnuts for *la gniape*. If you buy a package of tobacco the storekeeper will perhaps give you a cigar for *la gniape;* the *la gniape* always varying according to the character of the purchase.... That is *la gniape;* and no matter what else you may call for in the way of lunch, the *la gniape* is always thrown in with every cup of coffee purchased.

Writing the word *quartille* has reminded me that the word "quarter" is seldom used in small trading, either in New Orleans or anywhere along the Mississippi. The old fashioned terms "two-bits," "four-bits," "six-bits," are sill in vogue to denote those three fractions of the dollar that you generally designate as the quarter, fifty cents, and seventy-five cents; the "bit" being nominally equivalent to a value of twelve cents and a half. And speaking of cents, it occurs to me that copper coins do not circulate in New Orleans. The cent is valueless, except at the United States Post-office. No one will even accept ten copper cents for ten cents' worth of groceries; payment must be made with silver dimes or with nickels. . . .

Then we have the so-called negro term "pickaninny." Perhaps there are not many of your readers aware that this term is only a slave corruption of the Spanish words *poco niña* or *poco niño,* a little girl, or a little boy. . . .

—I have spoken with enthusiasm of the beauty of New Orleans; I must speak with pain of her decay. The city is fading, mouldering, crumbling— slowly but certainly.

As moulders and crumbles some quaint pleasure-house in the midst of weed-grown gardens once luxuriantly romantic as those which form a background for the warm pictures of the *Decameron,* so moulders this fair, quaint city in the midst of the ruined paradise of Louisiana. So, also, are mouldering all the old cities of the South, for their prosperity had its root of nourishment in the enormous wealth of the planters of cotton and rice and sugar, and that wealth is gone.

I suppose that when the hatreds of the war have burnt themselves out; when the descendants of the ruined planters remember the family misfortunes only as traditions are remembered; when a new social system shall have arisen from the ashes of the old, like the new world of the Scandinavian Edda from the fires of Ragnarok—then shall the old plantations be again made fertile, and the cottonwood cleared away, and the life of these old Southern cities be resurrected. But the new South shall never be as the old. Those once grand residences that are being devoured by mossy decay can never be rebuilt; the old plantations which extended over whole parishes will be parceled out to a hundred farmers from States that are not Southern; and the foreign beauties of New Orleans will never be restored. It is the picturesqueness of the South, the poetry, the traditions, the legends, the superstitions, the quaint faiths, the family prides, the luxuriousness, the splendid indolence and the splendid sins of the old social system which has passed, or which is now passing away forever. It is all this which is dead or dying in New Orleans, and which can hope for no trumpet-call to resurrection. The new South may, perhaps, become far richer than the old South; but there will be no aristocracy, no lives of unbridled luxury, no reckless splendors of hospitality, no mad pursuit of costliest pleasures. The old Southern hospitality has been starved to death, and leaves no trace of its former being save the thin ghost of a romance. . . . This period of decay seems to me the close of the romantic era of Southern history.

You are aware, no doubt, that the city is bankrupt; but without living here one can hardly comprehend the utter hopelessness of her bankruptcy. Her wealth and her strange foreign beauty were created by an aristocracy which has been destroyed beyond a possibility of resurrection, and were nourished by a social system that has become a thing of the dead past. . . . Already I think her beauty is fading and crumbling. Many of her noblest buildings are sinking into ruin; those dear old French houses, so quaintly picturesque with their green verandas, and peaked gables and dormer windows, are falling into dilapidation and are but too often being removed to make place for hideous modern structures. The charming French Opera-house on Bourbon street, where the Creoles supported opera for nearly half a century, is dark and dead and silent. Even Aimée has not sung there for years, and I suppose she could not now fill the dress-circle boxes with the remnant of her old Creole audiences. Sometimes, when passing under the sharply-cut shadows of the building in a night of tropical moonlight, I fancy that a shadowy performance of *Don Giovanni* or *Masaniello* must be going on within for the entertainment of a ghostly audience; and if somebody would but open the doors an instant, one might catch a glimpse of spectral splendor,—of dusky-eyed beauties long dead,—of forgotten faces pale with the sleep of battle-fields,—of silks that should be mouldering in mouldering chests with the fashions of twenty years ago, and of gems secretly given to the keeping of the children of Israel. I think that when a building has that haunted look its demolition is not far distant. The new generation who live in new fashioned dwellings and patronize new fashioned theaters, will tell you that the French quarter is "ugly and unendurable." The old family residences are being rented out as lodging houses by colored women who once, as slaves, waited upon the luxurious tables of their masters in the very rooms now advertised by them as *chambres garnies à louer*. Many of the quaint old streets have been rechristened with new-fashioned and unromantic names. Sometimes at night a sky-reddening fire blazes out over the gables of the old houses, and when the sun rises one sees that old landmarks have disappeared forever. And the last survivors of the old régime,—the old Creole gentlemen who persistently live in the quaint houses amidst a certain quaint poverty, often, alas, vainly striving to keep out the dampness and to "maintain appearances,"—are disappearing one by one from the life of the moulder-

ing city, and are being filed away, like dusty documents, in the marble pigeon-holes of the cemeteries.

New Orleans in Carnival Garb

...A very considerable number of those who visit New Orleans at Car-
nival-time do so quite as much for the sake of seeing the city itself as of
witnessing the great pageant. But during Mardi Gras the place is disguised
by its holiday garb—almost as much so, indeed, as the King of the Carnival: the native picturesqueness of the quainter districts is overlaid and
concealed by the artificial picturesqueness of the occasion. One finds
the streets themselves masked, so much are their salient features concealed by those innumerable wooden frame-works temporarily erected to
provide against the falling of galleries under an unaccustomed burden of
spectators. The romantic charm of the old city is not readily obtained at
such a time; the curious cosmopolitan characteristics that offer themselves
to artistic eyes in other seasons are lost in the afflux of American visitors,
and true local color is fairly drowned out by the colors of Rex....

To see the Queen of the South in her most natural and pleasing mood
one should visit her during that dreamy season called St. Martin's summer,
when the orange blossoms exhale their fragrance, and the winds are still
lukewarm, and the autumn glow bronzes those faint tints which the old-
fashioned edifices wear.... In that season the nights are tepid, vast, wine-
colored, like the Homeric ocean, and vibrant with an infinite variety of
insect music. From the bayous and the low lands arise sounds as of ghostly
violins, phantom flutes, elfish bells; mocking-birds utter their weird and
wonderful pipings, immense beetles fizz by, stridulous crickets work their
invisible buzz-saws, frogs hold tintinnabulary converse—every surface
inch of land or water seems to possess a voice of its own; the water-lilies
speak one unto the other, the shadows cry out. And through the Egyptian uniformity of the landscape the Mississippi serpentines its way with
Nilotic solemnity, so coiling that to dwellers upon its eastern bank the
sun appears, as in the Moslem prophecy, to rise in the west.

Few of the real attractions of New Orleans are likely to be observed by
Carnival visitors, bewildered as they are by the great eddying of people,
the confusion of preparation, the general inappropriateness of the mo-

ment to curious research and romantic investigation. But a Carnival night in New Orleans, during the coming and going of the great display, offers in itself much remarkable material for study—at least to one who can look about him undisturbed by the surging of the enormous crowd. Canal street presents its long deep vista of illumination—monograms of fire, eagles of flame, ladders of light, blaze along the way; and the uncommon breadth of the great thoroughfare, with its starry lines of electric lamps threading the middle, appears to be increased by the luminosity. For eight miles to right and left the city begins to empty its population into the great central highway, through all the tributary streets and alleys, and the force of that human circulation is resistless—to strive against the current is out of the question. The physician or telegraph messenger whom duty summons in an opposite direction at such a time must take to the middle of the street if he hopes to reach his destination. Rising one above another through the glow of illumination, the broad galleries packed with spectators seem like the tiers of an enormous hippodrome. When the human spring-tide has reached its fullest the pageant issues from its hiding-place, and sails by like a grotesque Armada, while the ocean of witnesses ebbs away in its wake.

That Canal street offers, in a large sense, the best view of the procession is beyond dispute; but the strictly *local* picturesqueness of the exhibition may be studied to advantage in the antiquated French by-ways. The Canal street spectacle is imposing, but not unique. Under similar conditions a street of equal breadth in any other great modern city would offer a spectacle of magnificence scarcely inferior. The grotesque silhouettes of the moving panorama are partially lost in such a street—the shadows can not reach the sides of the buildings. But through the queer old streets of the French quarter the Carnival procession must almost squeeze its way, casting eccentric shapes of darkness upon the walls, and lighting its path with torch-light that flings upwards the shadows of projecting galleries, and lends much Rembrandtesqueness to the faces peering down from balconies or dormer-windows.

After the pageant has gone glimmering, and the whirl of the midnight ball is over, day dawns upon a scene of merry wreck. Streets are strewn with fragments of brightly colored paper, tatters of tinsel, remnants of torn decorations; perhaps some gorgeous wagon, or "float," disabled during the great review, may be seen lying abandoned at some point of the route, like a gold-freighted galleon astrand. Last year did not the eyes of early risers behold, glittering upon Canal street, North, the ruined gates of the New Jerusalem? But the city soon rids itself of all these souvenirs—the wrecks and waifs mysteriously vanish, the pictured Carnival journals are devoured by the post-office, the King's standards cease to fill the streets with shadowy flutterings, the intricate paraphernalia of illumination are removed, and the nervous system of New Orleans returns to its normal condition. Only the unsightly skeleton woodwork still shoulders up the galleries to provide against accident upon the 4th of March, which is "Firemen's day." Already the carnival societies are secretly preparing for the display of next year. Ere long the moist and odorous spring will blow in the streets, and the city will gradually settle down into its long and dreamy summer languor; the pulses of its commercial life will beat more slowly with the lengthening of the days, the forest of masts along its eighteen miles of wharves will dwindle as the sultriness thickens, the wilderness of smoking chimneys at its sugar and cotton landings will diminish, and the somnolent and burning season will come, with warm winds and lightnings from the Gulf, with clouds splendid and ponderous as those of geologic eras, when the heavens were heavy with vaporized iron and gold.

The Last of the New Orleans Fencing Masters

Perhaps there is no class of citizens of New Orleans—the Marseilles of the western world—about whom so little is generally known as our Spanish element. I do not refer to those numerous West Indian and foreign residents who speak Spanish—Cubans, Manilla-men, Mexicans, Venezuelans, natives of Honduras, etc.—or even to our original Spanish Creoles, descendants of those colonists who have left us few traces of the ancient Spanish domination besides a few solid specimens of Latin architecture and a few sonorous names by which certain streets and districts are still known. The old Spanish Creole families exist, indeed, but they have become indistinguishable from the French Creoles, whose language, manners, and customs they have adopted. The true Spanish element of modern New Orleans is represented by a community of European immigrants, who preserve among them the various customs and dialects of the mother country, and form an association of about three hundred families. They

49

are more numerous than the Greeks...; more numerous than the Portuguese, who have a large benevolent association; but much fewer than the Italians and Sicilians...Yet, for various reasons, the Spaniards are less publicly visible than the other Latins; they live in the less frequented parts of the city, they pursue special callings, and form special industrial organizations; they have their own trades-unions, their own benevolent associations, their own priests, physicians, and lawyers, and before 1853 they formed an excellent militia corps, the *Cazadores*. This fine body voluntarily disbanded because of the refusal of the governor to permit them to suppress a great anti-Spanish riot, incited by Cuban refugees. The governor wisely preferred to trust the work of suppression to the cooler-blooded and disinterested American militia, justly fearing the consequences of giving rein to the rage of the Spanish soldiery, mostly Asturians, Catalonians, and Biscayans. Since the disbandment of its military organization the Spanish community, though numerically as strong as ever, has almost disappeared from public view.

Whether Catalonians, Biscayans, Gallegos, Asturians, or men from the Balearic Islands, nearly all these Spaniards are inter-associated as brothers of one order, and Catalan is the prevalent dialect. At their meetings, indeed, Castilian is supposed to be the official tongue; but should any discussion of an exciting nature arise, the speakers involuntarily abandon the precise speech of the *Academia* for the rougher and readier argumentative weapon of dialect.

A great number of these men are in business on their own account; those who are not independent are, for the most part, fresh immigrants or elder sons beginning life; and the trade generally followed is tobacco manufacturing. Many Spaniards own factories. So soon as a young man lays by a certain sum, he marries—usually either a Creole of the poorer class or a European woman, Irish, English, or German—and thus it happens that almost every one of our Spaniards above thirty is the head of a large family.

The New Orleans Spaniard has all the self-reliance, the shrewdness, the economy, and the sobriety of the Italian; he has less patience, perhaps, and is more dangerous to provoke; but strangely enough, crimes of violence are almost unheard of among the Spaniards, while they are fearfully common among our Sicilians, who practice vendetta. Moreover, the Spaniard is rarely found among the criminal classes; if he happens, by some extraordinary chance, to get into trouble, it is because he has used his knife or other weapon, not as a skulking assassin but as an open enemy....

There are few Spanish houses in the antiquated portions of the city where a visitor will not observe a certain portrait or photograph—the likeness of a vigorous, keen-eyed man, with a slightly curved nose, long firm lips, facial muscles singularly developed, and a fair beard having that peculiar curl in it which is said to indicate a powerful constitution. The face is a very positive one, though not harsh, and the more you observe it the more its expression pleases. If you should happen to visit a Spanish home in which the photograph is not visible, it is more than probable that it is treasured away in the *armoire* or somewhere else; it has become one of the Spanish *penates*. But a few years ago it was an even more familiar object in Havana, perhaps also in far Madrid; and the Havanese soldiery, the *voluntarios,* the loyalists, the Spanish ladies, were eagerly purchasing copies at the rate of two *pesos* per copy. Thousands upon thousands were placed in Cuban parlors. Still, the original of that picture, photograph, or engraving (for the likeness of the man has been reproduced in many ways) is not a prince, a diplomat, or a soldier, but a private citizen of New Orleans, a member of our Spanish community. His face is now seldom seen on Canal street, but he is still a very active and vigorous man, despite his three-score and ten years. He is a hero, and a titled hero who won his fame by sole virtue of those qualities named in enamel upon the golden cross he is privileged to wear: *Virtus et Honore—* "*Virtus,*" of course, with the good old Roman signification of the word, which is valor.

Señor Don José Llulla, or Pepe Llulla, as he is more affectionately styled by his admirers, is a person whose name has become legendary even in his life-time. While comparatively few are intimate with him, for he is a reserved man, there is scarcely a citizen who does not know him by name, and hardly a New Orleans urchin who could not tell you that "Pepe Llulla is a great duelist who has a cemetery of his own." Although strictly true, this information is apt to create a false impression of some connection between Pepe's duels and Pepe's necropolis; the fact being that none of his enemies repose in the Louisa street Cemetery, which he owns, and that he has never killed enough men to fill a solitary vault. There is, in short, no relationship between the present and the past occupations of the cemetery proprietor; but before speaking of the former, I may attempt to give a brief outline of the career of this really extraordinary character who won his way to fortune and to fame by rare energy and intrepidity.

Pepe was born near Port Mahón, capital of Minorca, one of those Balearic Islands whose inhabitants were celebrated in antiquity for their skill in the use of missile-weapons, and have passed under so many dominations—Carthaginian, Roman, Vandal, Moorish, Spanish, French, and English. . . .

Pepe's imagination was greatly impressed during early boyhood by the recitals of sailors who used to visit his father's home at Port Mahón; and his passion for the sea became so strong as he grew older that it required constant vigilance to keep him from joining some ship's crew by stealth. Finally, when an American captain—John Conklin of Baltimore, I believe—made known in Port Mahón that he wanted an intelligent Spanish lad on his vessel, Pepe's parents deemed it best to allow their son to ship as cabin-boy. He remained several years with the Captain, who became attached to him and attempted to send him to a school to study navigation, in the hope of making a fine sailor of him. But the boy found himself unable to endure the constraints of study, ran away, and shipped as a common seaman. He went with whalers to the Antarctic Zone, and with slavers to the West African coast, and, after voyaging in all parts of the world, entered the service of some merchant company whose vessels plied between New Orleans and Havana. At last he resolved to abandon the sea, and to settle in New Orleans in the employ of a Spaniard named Biosca, proprietor of a ballroom and *café*. Being a very sinewy, determined youth, Pepe was intrusted with the hazardous duty of maintaining order; and, after a few unpleasant little experiences, the disorderly element of the time recognized they had found a master, and the peace of Biosca's establishment ceased to be disturbed.

Pepe soon began to visit the popular fencing-schools of New Orleans. He was already a consummate master in the use of the knife (what thorough Spaniard is not?), but he soon astonished the best *tireurs* by his skill with the foils.

At that time fencing was a fashionable amusement. It was the pride of a Creole gentleman to be known as a fine swordsman. Most of the Creole youths educated in Paris had learned the art under great masters; but even these desired to maintain their skill by frequent visits to the *salles d'armes* at home. Indeed, fencing was something more than a mere amusement; it was almost a necessity. In New Orleans, as in Paris, the passions of society were regulated if not restrained by the duel; and the sword was considered the proper weapon with which gentlemen should settle certain disputes. . . .

The demand for fencing-masters was amply supplied by foreigners and also by some local experts, *maîtres d'armes* whose names are now remembered only by a very few venerable citizens. The most celebrated were L'Alouette, an Alsatian; Montiasse, also an Alsation and Napoleonic veteran; Cazères, of Bordeaux; Baudoin, of Paris; the two brothers Rosière, of Marseilles; Dauphin, a famous expert (killed at last in a shot-gun duel which he had recklessly provoked). Behind these fading figures of the past, three darker ghosts appear: Black Austin, a free negro, who taught the small-sword; Robert Séverin, a fine mulatto, afterward killed in Mexico, and Basile Croquère (I am not sure that I spell the name correctly), also a mulatto, and the most remarkable colored swordsman of Louisiana. . . .

It was under L'Aoulette that Pepe principally studied; and the fencing-master, finding after a time that his pupil excelled him, appointed him his *prevôt* or assistant. In a succession of subsequent encounters the young man proved that, though he might have one or two rivals with the foils, he had no real superior among the *maîtres d'armes*. Then he began to study the use of other varieties of weapons; the saber, with which he became the most expert perhaps in the South; the broad-sword, with which he afterward worsted more than one accomplished English teacher. With the foil, which is only a training weapon and allows of a closer play, fine fencers have been able to make some good points with him; but with the rapier or small sword he was almost invulnerable. With firearms his skill was not less remarkable. Pepe's friends were accustomed to hold a dollar in their fingers or a pipe between their teeth for him to shoot at. Twenty years ago he would often balance an egg on the head of his little son, and invariably break the shell with a Colt-ball at the distance of thirty paces; with a rifle he seldom failed to hit any small object tossed in the air, such as a ball, a cork, or a coin.

L'Alouette and his pupil became very warm friends; their intimacy was only once chilled by an unfortunate accident. At a time when the bowie-knife was still a novel arm in New Orleans, L'Alouette insisted upon a public contest with Llulla, the weapons to be wooden bowies with hickory blades. Pepe had no equal, however, in the use of a knife of any sort; and L'Alouette, finding himself repeatedly touched and never able to make a point, lost his temper and made a violent assault on the young Spaniard, who, parrying the thrust, countered so heavily that the fencing-master was flung senseless to the floor with two ribs fractured. But the friendship of the two men was renewed before long, and continued until L'Alouette's death several years later. Llulla, in whose arms he died, succeed him as a teacher, not only of fencing, but also of the use of fire-arms. He did not, indeed, teach the knife, but he has often given surprising proofs of his skill with it. A gentleman who is quite expert with most weapons, told me that after having succeeded in persuading Pepe to have a sham contest with him only a few years ago, he received the point of Pepe's mock weapon directly in the hollow of his throat almost at the very first pass, and was repeatedly struck in the same place during five or six vain efforts to make a point. None of the serious contests in which Pepe has engaged lasted more than a few moments; he generally disabled his adversary at the very outset of the encounter.

Although remunerative in those days, the profession of fencing-master did not suit Llulla's energetic character. He kept his *salle d'armes*, but hired assistants, and only devoted so much of his own time to teaching as could be spared from more practical duties. He had already laid down the foundation of his fortune, had brought out from Minorca his mother and brother, had married, and commenced to do business on his own account. Few men have attempted as many different things as he has with equal success. He built slaughter-houses and speculated in cattle; he bought up whole fleets of flatboats and sold the material for building purposes (working all day up to his waist in water, and never getting sick in consequence); he bought land on the other side of the river and built cottages upon it; he built a regular Spanish bull-ring and introduced bullfights; he bought a saw-mill and made it pay, and finally purchased the Louisa street cemeteries, after accumulating a capital of probably several hundred thousand dollars. During the war he remained faithful to the Union, declaring that he could not violate his oath of allegiance to the *United States*. . . .

During all those years Pepe kept his fencing-school, but rather as a recreation than as a money-making establishment. He is now the last of the old fencing-masters, and although he has practically retired from public life will not refuse to instruct (*gratis*) pupils introduced to him by personal friends. For nearly half a century he was the confidant and trainer of New Orleans duellists, and figured as second in more than a hundred encounters. The *duello* is now almost obsolete in the South; and

Creole New Orleans is yielding in this respect to the influences of Americanization. It is fully three years since Pepe's services were last called into requisition.

While his formidable reputation as an expert often secured him against difficulties and dangers to which another in his position would have been exposed, it did not save him from the necessity of having some twenty or more affairs of his own. In half a score of these affairs his antagonists weakened at the last moment, either apologizing on the field or failing to appear at all, and that only after having attempted to take every advantage attached to their privilege of the choice of weapons. One individual proposed to fight with poniards in a dark room; another with knives inside a sugar hogshead; another wanted a duel with Colt revolvers, each of the principals to hold one end of the same pocket-handkerchief; another proposed that lots should be drawn for two pistols—one empty, the other loaded; and a Cuban, believing no such weapons procurable in New Orleans, proposed to fight with *machétes;* but, to the horror of the man, Pepe forthwith produced two *machétes,* and proposed to settle the difficulty then and there, a proposal which resulted in the Cuban's sudden disappearance. Only once was Pepe partly thwarted by a proposition of this sort, when some Havanese filibuster proposed that both principals and witnesses should "fight with poisoned pills," lots to be drawn for the pills. Pepe was willing, but the seconds declared they would not take the pills or permit them to be taken. Several of Llulla's duels were undertaken in behalf of friends, while he was actually acting in the *rôle* of second only, and when one of the principals could not fulfill the duties of the moment. On a certain occasion the second of the opposite side, who was a German fencing-master, declared his principal in no condition to fight, and volunteered to take his place. "We accept," replied Llulla instantly, "but in that case you shall deal not with my principal but with me!" Ten seconds later the German lay on the ground with a severely gashed arm and both lungs transpierced. It was seldom, however, that Pepe cared to wound an antagonist so severely; and although he has had duels or difficulties with men of most European nationalities, only two men died at his hands, after having placed him under the necessity of killing or being killed. . . . Since the war Pepe has had no personal difficulties, except those assumed in the cause of Spanish patriotism; but these affairs first made him really famous, and form the most interesting incidents of his singular career.

After having long been the headquarters of the Cuban filibusters, New

Orleans was violently convulsed, in 1853, by the fate of the Lopez expedition, and serious outbreaks occurred, for the results of which the Spanish government subsequently demanded and obtained satisfaction from the United States. It was Pepe Llulla who at that time saved the Spanish Consul's life, by getting him out of the city safely to the plantation of a compatriot. Pepe's own life was then menaced; and though none ventured to attack him in broad daylight, his determination and courage alone saved him from several night-attempts at assassination. After the Lopez riots the anti-Spanish fury died down to be revived again in 1869 by another Cuban tragedy. But in 1869 the United States garrison was strong, and there was no serious rioting. The rage of the Cuban revolutionaries vented itself only in placards, in sanguinary speeches, in cries of *Death to Spain!* and in a few very petty outrages upon defenseless Spaniards. Pepe Llulla challenged one of the authors of the outrages, who, failing to accept, was placarded publicly as a coward.

Then he resolved to take up the cause of Spain in his own person, and covered the city with posters in English, in French, and in Spanish, challenging all Cuban revolutionaries, either in the West Indies or the United States. This challenge was at first accepted by a number, but seemingly by men who did not know the character of Llulla, for these Cuban champions failed to come to time, a few declaring they respected Pepe too much to fight him; yet at the same time a number of efforts were made to assassinate him—some by men who seemed to cross the Gulf for no other purpose.... The Cuban emissaries and others fared no better in 1869. Two men, who concealed themselves in the cemetery at dusk, were unexpectedly confronted with Pepe's pistols, and ordered to run for their lives, which they proceeded to do most expeditiously, leaping over tombs and climbing over walls in their panic. Another party of ruffians met the Spaniard at his own door in the middle of the night, and were ingloriously routed. Once more, hearing that a crowd of rowdies were collecting in the neighborhood after dark with the intention of proceeding to his house, Llulla went out and attacked them single-handed, scattering them in all directions.

At last the Cubans found a champion to oppose to the redoubtable Pepe, an Austrian ex-officer who had entered the Cuban revolutionary service, a soldier of fortune, but a decidedly brave and resolute man. He was a good swordsman but, considering the formidable reputation of his antagonist, chose the pistol as a weapon more likely to equalize the disparity between the two men. The conditions were thirty paces, to advance and fire at will. When the word of command was given, the Spaniard remained motionless as a statue, his face turned away from his antagonist; while the Austrian, reserving his fire, advanced upon him with measured strides. When within a short distance of Llulla he raised his arm to fire, and at that instant the Spaniard, wheeling suddenly, shot him through both lungs. The Austrian was picked up, still breathing, and lingered some months before he died. His fate probably deterred others from following his example, as the Cubans found no second champion.

The spectacle of a solitary man thus defying the whole Cuban revolution, bidding all enemies of Spain to fight or hold their peace; evoked ardent enthusiasm both among the loyalists of Cuba and the Spaniards of New Orleans. Pepe soon found himself surrounded by strong sympathizers, ready to champion the same cause; and telegrams began to pour in from Spaniards in Cuba and elsewhere, letters of congratulation also, and salutations from grandees. . . .

Such telegrams came fluttering in daily like Havanese butterflies, and solicitations for Pepe's photograph were made and acceded to, and pictures of him were sold by thousands in the streets of the great West Indian City. Meanwhile the Cubans held their peace, as bidden. And then came from Madrid a letter of affectionate praise, sealed with the royal seal, and signed with the regent's name, Don Francisco Serrano y Domínguez, el Regente del Reino, and with this letter the Golden Cross of the Order of Charles III (*Carlos Tercero*), and a document conferring knighthood, *libre de gastos,* upon the valiant son who had fought so well for Spain in far-away Louisiana.

But I have yet to mention the most exquisite honor of all. Trust the Spanish heart to devise a worthy reward for what it loves and admires! From Havana came one day a dainty portrait of Pepe Llulla worked seemingly in silk, and surrounded by what appeared to be a wreath of laurels in the same black silk, and underneath, in black letters upon a gold ground, the following honorific inscription: "A DON JOSÉ LLULLA, DECIDIDO SOSTENEDOR DE LA HONRA NATIONAL ENTRE LOS TRAIDORES DE NEW ORLEANS." But that woven black silk was the silk of woman's hair, the lustrous hair of Spanish ladies who had cut off their tresses to wreathe his portrait with! It hangs in the old man's parlor near the portrait of his dead son, the handsome boy who graduated at West Point with honors, and when I beheld it and understood it, the delicious grace of that gift touched me like the discovery of some new and unsuspected beauty in human nature.

Under the Oaks

The "code," as it is called, the duello, was universally recognized in New Orleans before the war, and even to this day duels occur, although growing rarer every year. The man who would not fight "in the days before the war" was regarded as not entitled to the treatment due a gentleman and was socially tabooed, and liable to the grossest insults.

All the efforts of the religious portion of the community to stop duelling proved a failure and aroused the most bitter prejudice. An Article was inserted in the Constitution of the State in 1848, disfranchising duellists. The Creoles complained bitterly of this, which they claimed was an attempt to drive men of courage from the State, and so vigorous was the opposition raised—for nearly all the leading men found themselves disfranchised by this provision—that the anti-duelling article was repealed four years later, and duellists restored to favor again.

In the early Creole days, the rapier or colechemarde was the weapon most in favor in duels, but broadswords and sabres were sometimes used. The Americans introduced the pistol, rifles and shot gun, which made duelling much more fatal. With the rapier, a slight wound was sufficient to satisfy honor, whereas with the shot gun or rifle one of the principals was nearly always seriously wounded. In fact, in a majority of the duels in which the shot gun was used, one or more deaths ensued.

There was no excuse for refusing to "fight." No matter how high your position, you must accept any challenge sent you by a gentleman. Thus, the first American Governor, Claiborne, left the gubernatorial mansion to fight Daniel Clarke, the State representative in Congress, an encounter which resulted in the severe wounding of Clarke. This duel took place at the mouth of Bayou Marechel.

A [particularly notable] story is that of the duel between Major Henry, of Nicaraguan fame, and Major Joe Howell, renowned among all those who remember the old Louisiana traditions for coolness and daring. Howell and Henry had met in a coffee-house at the corner of Canal and St. Charles streets (where Joe Walker now keeps the Crescent Hall), and had had a difficulty which wound up in a challenge to fight that evening at the Half-Way House. It was impossible for the seconds to find out what was the origin of the trouble, Howell himself not recollecting anything about it. It seems that he and Major Henry—a noted brave of the Nicaraguan army—who had served with Walker, had had a *mal-entendu* in Nicaragua, and cherished no friendship for one another. They met, and Henry invited Joe to drink. Both were under the influence of liquor. Unfortunately two newsboys came and commenced to fight. According to the theory of the times, Joe bet on one and Henry backed the other. Henry's newsboy caved in when he then remarked that the fight would have been very different if he and Joe had been engaged instead of the boys. Joe nodded "Yes." "Well, then," put in Nicaragua Henry, "suppose we do have it." Joe whipped out his six-shooter, for short answer. "Hold on, old boy, I'm not ready; let us meet at five o'clock this evening at the Half-Way House; bring your navy; I will have mine." "All right," answered Joe, and the whisky straights, which had been losing some of their lightning by evaporation, instantly disappeared in well-accustomed channels; not, however, before the glasses had violently tinkled against each other. Just then two policemen put in an appearance, and both belligerents were taken to the station. Mutual friends, actuated as much by a desire to see the sequence as by any other Christian motive, soon obtained their release. Henry kept on drinking, and Joe went to sleep, as some great generals have done before him on the eve of mighty battles.

Both parties were known as men of indomitable pluck and desperate courage. Major Henry's reputation was proverbial; further on we will give some particulars of his eventful career. Joe Howell was a brother-in-law of Jefferson Davis, stood six feet seven inches in his boots, was admirably proportioned, and his body was covered with scars caused by wounds inflicted with knife, arrow and bullet.

At 4½ o'clock Joe woke up, took one cocktail, and without the least nervousness or concern bid his friends *au revoir* and jumped into the carriage. Dr. Sam Choppin, acting surgeon on the occasion, followed.

On the way, as is customary in the fulfillment of his duty, Howell's second offered some advice to his man. He told him to endeavor to get the first shot in on his antagonist, to fire low and to cock with his right hand without lowering his pistol.

His answer was, after driving a cloud of smoke from his cigarette: "Tut, tut, my boy, teach your grandmother how to suck eggs!"

The second said no more.

When the grounds were reached 300 persons were found there. All the hacks and cabs had been engaged as soon as the news flashed over the city that these two men were about to meet in mortal combat. Not less than fifty Nicaraguans were there; but these were clustered around Henry, who could be seen some two hundred yards out in the field, resting on one elbow in a dry hollow.

Joe Howell had also many friends among the spectators and gayly chatted with them.

All efforts to settle the affair failed.

"Will you please give me your version of the cause of this difficulty," Howell's second asked.

"It don't matter; we are here to fight," was the sharp answer from Henry's second.

"Well, but brave men don't fight like children, for nothing. We want to know what we are going to fight about; if we are wrong we may apologize, or vice versa."

"We don't know anything about it; but if there is to be an apology, Major Howell must make it."

"But if you are ignorant of the origin and cause of this difficulty how can you point out our wrong?"

"Wait; we will see Major Henry."

And off they went to the ditch where Henry sat leisurely resting.

In less than three minutes the Nicaraguans were back.

"Well?" asked Howell's man.

"Well, Major Henry says, if Joe Howell will apologize it's no fight."

"Apologize for what?" asked the other with some animation.

"Don't know, and don't care," was the laconic reply.

"Then there is no possible way of arranging this matter amicably. Suppose both parties approach each other half way and shake hands without a word? Will you see Major Henry and tell him the proposition comes from our side?"

After some discussion they consented to this, but very reluctantly.

This time the seconds remained fully ten minutes by the side of their principal. There was animated discussion and much gesticulation among them, but they returned and said: "Major Henry says Joe ought to apologize, and then they can shake hands."

"Then it means fight. Load your navy, we will do likewise; ten paces; six barrels loaded; fire at will, and advance."

The line of fire was a narrow path, flanked on either side by a small ditch. Howell stood six feet seven inches in his boots, and, contrary to advice, wore white pants and an alpaca coat, making him a dangerously conspicuous target.

The command was given:

"Gentlemen, are you ready?"

Joe, who was facing the woods, answered firmly, "Ready!" but kept his eye looking steadily along the barrel of his cocked pistol. Henry, in a nonchalant fashion, threw his head on one side, his pistol dangling at his arm, and in a lazy tone said, "Ready." The word was then given: "Fire!" Both raised simultaneously, fired, and missed. Howell cocked with his right thumb and fired again before Henry was ready for his second shot. Howell's ball pierced Henry's left forearm, when Henry again fired and missed. Howell now came in with his third shot, striking Henry in the abdomen. To this Henry responded with a shot which threw up the dirt right at Howell's feet. The latter then advanced one step, and, taking deliberate aim, pulled the trigger. Seeing that Henry was done for, Howell's second rushed up and threw up Joe's pistol with his hand. The shot flew away up in the air, that certainly would then and there have killed Henry.

The other side having cried "Stop!" according to agreement, in case of either party being badly wounded, uttered shrill cries of "Foul! Foul!" and immediately whipped out their revolvers. Then followed a scene of confusion, and for a long time it looked as if a wholesale duel would follow; but the crowd interfered, and prevented the fight. The wounded man was taken to the Half-Way House, where he remained for some weeks before he could be transported to the city.

Major Henry was, what is known in the vernacular of the ordinary novelist, a character. Retiring in disposition, little given to talk, of a melancholy temperament, he gave no external evidence of the power and determination of the man beneath. Those who knew him intimately and who were with him in the most desperate of dangers say that he was one of the few men they knew who had no appreciation of the word fear. He would face what appeared to be almost certain death with an equanimity that was startling. Joining Gen. Walker's filibustering expedition to Nicaragua, as an officer in the battles there, he was noted for his daring and coolness. Without caring whether he was followed or not he would charge single-handed into the enemy's ranks, cutting and shooting, right and left, himself receiving wound after wound. He seemed to bear a charmed life, for, notwithstanding the fact that his body was covered with scars, he received new wounds without blenching, and so great was his vitality that he recovered in a very short time.

He served for many years as an enlisted soldier in the Seventh Regiment Infantry, United States army; was made quartermaster-sergeant of the regiment during the Mexican war on account of gallant conduct, and at the close of the war was promoted to a lieutenancy. In this capacity he was stationed for a long time in the Cherokee Nation, where his taciturn disposition made him very unpopular with the men, but his daring and recklessness in amorous exploits caused him to be quite a favorite with the squaws.

This came very near being the cause of his death, for one night at a ball he found himself suddenly environed by a crowd of Cherokee braves, and when they dispersed he was lying on the ground in a pool of his own blood, with seven stabs in his body. No other man would have recovered, but he did. . . .

During the Nicaraguan war this remarkable fighter distinguished himself on every occasion, and was much admired and respected as a soldier. His temper, however, was not such as would permit him to live in peace with his fellow-officers. He was noted for several brilliant duels during that eventful campaign—among which, one with Col. Jules Dreux, was fought at Messiah. He was major of the regiment of which Dreux was colonel, and they had a misunderstanding. Dreux waived his rank, and they fought with navy revolvers at twelve paces. . . .

But to merely recount the duels that have taken place at New Orleans would fill a large volume. The Oaks, the favorite meeting place of the old days, and which now lie in what is styled the Lower City Park, just back of the cemeteries, between Canal and Esplanade streets, have witnessed hundreds of fatal duels. Since the war dueling has not been quite so much in favor as it was a quarter of a century ago, but hostile meetings are still frequent, and not a few of them have terminated fatally.

Executions

In former years all of nearly all executions were public; but the last one was that of Delisle and Adams, the former a Creole and the latter a Frenchman, who were convicted of murdering a woman in what is now known as the Third district. They saw the woman secrete a bag containing what they thought was specie, and they killed her to obtain possession of it, when, to their consternation, the bag was found to contain pecans. The circumstances surrounding their execution were so horrible that a riot was imminent. It is said that they appeared—to the eyes of the multitude assembled in the neutral ground on Orleans street—on the small gallery extending across the alley or court between the two buildings, the male and female departments, which form the Parish Prison.

Delisle was violent and demonstrative, whilst Adams was subdued and quiet, and wished to precipitate matters. The ropes were adjusted around their necks, Delisle expostulating loudly all the time. The weather was dark and gloomy, a sombre cloud overspread the face of the blue sky, angry flashes of lightning lit up the scene with short lurid darts of flame, followed by the dull, rolling noise of thunder in the distance.

The trap fell, and at the same instant a blinding flash of lightning, almost instantaneously followed by a loud clap of thunder, almost frightened the people into spasms. The rain poured down in torrents, drenching all. Many fled the terrible scene, rendered doubly terrible by the ominous appearance of the heavens. When the fear, which was only momentary with most of those present, had somewhat subsided, the ropes were seen dangling and swaying loosely in the wind, for there was nothing at the lower end.

On the flagging beneath the gallows two forms were seen lying on the pavement; they were the bodies of Delisle and Adams. The former started to crawl away on hands and feet, and the latter lay moaning with pain. His arm was broken. Pity for the two men became predominant in the hearts of the multitude; but the law was inexorable, and its servants were compelled to perform their horrible duty. The two men were picked up and conducted back to their former positions on the scaffold, despite the torrents of rain which fell; and in defiance of what seemed to the terror-stricken people to be an intervention of Providence, they were hung.

The police force at that time was under the command of Steve O'Leary, and he with a detail of fully two hundred men had great difficulty in quieting the mob during the confusion which ensued.

This execution was viewed with so much abhorrence and indignation throughout the city, that the Legislature at its next session passed a law prohibiting public executions.

Up to this time hangman's or execution day was a gala day; for the morbid curiosity so common to human nature then had an opportunity for gratification, and there were but few persons who remained at home. . . .

A number of instances where condemned criminals sought to cheat the hangman by suicide can be cited. One was the case of a German who had murdered a child, and who sought to cut his throat with a piece of tin-plate or spoon; but the most notable and successful attempt was that of a man named Costello. He and a man named Pat Kennedy, both convicted of murder, were doomed to die on the same day. Kennedy had been respited on a previous occasion, although fully prepared then to meet his doom. When Costello was sentenced his execution was fixed for the same day. Several days previous to that fixed for the execution, the clothes which were to be worn by the condemned men were brought to them. In the cuff of Costello's shirt was concealed a small package of strychnine.

On the morning of the execution Costello said to Kennedy: "Are you going to let that howling crowd see you dance on nothing?"

Kennedy did not answer; whereupon Costello tore open the wristband of his shirt and produced a package containing the poison. Facing Kennedy he said: "here you can have half of this; there is enough for two."

Kennedy asked him what he was going to do, when Costello opened his mouth and dropped the contents of the package on his tongue and swallowed it. Kennedy gave the alarm, but too late, for half an hour afterwards Costello was in convulsions and beyond the reach of human skill or science. Kennedy died quietly, confident that his sins had been forgiven. . . .

On June the 16th, 1858, the first private execution under the law of the Legislature took place in the criminal yard of the Parish Prison, and James Nolan, a young man of 22 years, was launched into eternity from the same trap-door, which up to the present day has performed its ghastly offices, and which has ever since been brought into requisition. . . .

On July 29, 1859, James Mullen expiated the crime of murder on the gallows. For weeks previously Mullen used his coffin to sleep in. He passed his time in decorating this, his last home; and on the day of execution had it ornamented with fringe, metallic crosses and other trimmings. . . .

In the spring of 1866 a negro named Plydor was hung for rape in the Parish Prison. In 1870 a Malay named Bazar was on the scaffold, the rope was around his neck, the black-cap had been drawn down over his eyes. The executioner stood in cell No. 9 arrayed in his black domino, with his face covered by the sombre-hued mask. The nervous fingers of the hangman had already grasped the handle of the keen-edged axe, the arm was uplifted and about to fall, when a commutation of sentence stayed proceedings, and Bazar's sentence was commuted to imprisonment for life.

The Creole Doctor: Some Curiosities of Medicine in Louisiana

The Northerner who decides to settle in New Orleans will find after the experience of a few summers in the Louisiana climate that he has become more or less physiologically changed by the struggle of his system with those novel atmospheric conditions to which it was obliged to adapt itself. According to the constitutional peculiarities of the individual, the effects of acclimatization may vary—while some persons suffer considerably, others endure very little positive discomfort; but all are subjected to a certain physical transformation.... The changes in the blood accompanying acclimatization necessarily involve corresponding changes in regard to diet and habits of life; but while the appetite may be maintained by the use of acidulated drinks, or such gentle stimulants as claret-and-water, one's capacity for intense or prolonged exertion steadily diminishes, and finally passes away. Nothing resembling the electrical vim—the almost furious energy—of the Northwestern American will endure under this sun, and yet the physical languor which supervenes may be eventually compensated by increased capacity for rapid menial work.

During this process of enervation the stranger is peculiarly liable to fever, and of fevers (which in epidemic years, all seem to lose their special characteristics and to interblend with the dominant evil) there is a surprising variety. Some, like the *dengue*, seem to bray the muscles as with fingers of iron; in others, the victim may shiver with cold under the heat of a July sun—there are different kinds of remittent, intermittent, and other malarial affections which are easy of treatment, and slow torpid fevers which scorn the power of quinine and so sap the nervous energy as to leave the victim prostrate for months. The acclimated citizen rarely suffers from these maladies; but woe to the incautious and energetic stranger who attempts to live in this sub-tropical and pyrogenic region, indifferent to the danger of excessive fatigue, or the perils of self-exposure to sudden changes of temperature!

...It was during my own struggles with such novel conditions of climate that I first became interested in the subject of Creole medicine—a natural art rapidly becoming obsolete—whose traditions have never been collected, much less published, and whose secrets are being buried every year with some one belonging to the old French-speaking generations of colored nurses and domestics....

My own experiences have not enabled me to make any noteworthy observations of the more purely African features of this somewhat occult art; but they enabled me to know the real skill of colored nurses in dealing with local fevers and other ailments of a less serious character. Among several curious remedies for which I had to thank these mysterious people I will cite only two. The first was a cure for billious fever—which cure was brought to me in a small earthenware jug, piping hot. It was a drink which had a reddish color, and agreeable odor, and an unpleasantly bitter taste. I was told to let the fluid cool before drinking, and not to be frightened at the results, which proved alarming, for dizziness and difficulty of breathing were among them. But the draught restored me to complete health; and I may say that I even felt unusually well for several months subsequently. I wanted to obtain the recipe from the negress who prepared the medicine; but this, to my surprise, she refused to give even in exchange for what I believed to be a rather handsome remuneration. Furthermore she declared the medicine was *bien dangereuse,* that I could not use it without instructions, and that I could not find "the plant." I knew there were at least four ingredients in the preparation; but the color and odor, at least, were not due to any very unfamiliar simples.

The second remedy was a very simple one for inflammation or congestion of the eyes; and was told me by an old colored woman who had the reputation of being a Voudoo, but whom I never suspected of belonging to that confraternity. She was able to comprehend the interest I felt in Creole folklore, and collected for me a number of little songs and proverbs in the patois. Her recipe was this: "Take a fresh Creole egg [egg laid in Louisiana]; separate the yolk carefully from the white, and then beat up the white into a light, fine foam. Then take a strip of cotton or linen about six or eight inches wide; fold up the egg-foam in it so as to form a cataplasm wide enough to cover both eyes, and go to bed with the cataplasm well attached by knotting the ends of the linen or cotton folds about the head." This simple egg poultice, thus left to dry upon the eyes, proved in my case remarkably efficacious, although I cannot imagine that there is any special virtue in albumen. I must also state that I recommended the cataplasm with good results in instances where hot or cold compresses had failed, for some reason or other, to reduce inflammation.

The reluctance of the negress who prepared me the potion above referred to, either to sell or give away the secret, I found to be shared by most of the colored people from whom I attempted to procure the same kind of information. It is really only the Creole gentleman or lady, accustomed to command this class, and habituated to their habits and beliefs, who can obtain their absolute confidence in such matters. The greater number of the recipes cited in this article I could not have obtained but for the aid of Creole friends; and I am especially indebted but for the aid of Creole friends; and I am especially indebted to a scholarly Spanish physician, Dr. Rodolfo Matas, now president of the New Orleans Medical Association, for many valuable facts and suggestions. . . .

Tisanes, or those preparations classified by our Creoles under the general name of teas (*thés*),—being infusions of medicinal herbs obtained by boiling the leaves,—occupy a larger place in Creole medicine than do the tisanes recognized by English or American pharmaceutical science as worthy of classification in dispensatories. There are hundreds of them. Some are too familiar to need more than an allusion,—such as the orange-leaf, lemon-leaf, and sassafras teas. "*Mo pas boi dithe pou fieve lit*" ("I'm not going to drink tea for his fever"), is a Creole proverb referring, not to tea proper, which is not a favorite beverage with our native French-speaking population, but to those warm herb infusions administered in fever. The following recipes are among the most interesting in the little collection I have been able to make of Creole medicine belonging to the first and second divisions of the subject.

Chills and Fever—For this familiar disorder several queer tisanes are recommended: 1. Tea prepared with the leaves of the pimento (pepper plant); 2. Thick black coffee mingled with fresh lemon-juice to be taken three times a day; 3. Snake-root (*serpentaria*) in whiskey—I do not know how strong the infusion is made; 4. Tea made from the leaves of the "*cirier-batard*" (*Myrica gale*), a small cupful to be swallowed three times a day. In addition to these hot drinks, alternated sometimes with draughts of claret or spiced beer, well heated, the patient may be ordered to put cayenne pepper in his shoes every day for nine days. In the absence of quinine or other recognized febrifuges, some of the above remedies are not to be scoffed at. The plant called by our Creoles the *cirier batard* has, moreover, been utilized in various ways by regular medical science, owing to its astringent qualities. Its aromatic properties are said to have a purifying effect upon the air of the swamps which it loves. In North America its geographical range extends from Louisiana to Greenland. The roots of the *Myrica* contain so much tannin that they can be utilized with great success in the manufacture of ink....

Coffee, considered a febrifuge in the domestic medicine of most hot countries, is administered largely in typhoid fever; but the infusion is made with the green berries in whiskey, a dose three times a day. To alleviate the cerebral symptoms, a live pigeon is cut open and the warm, bleeding surfaces applied to the head....

The honeysuckle (*Lonicera caprifolium*) is known to medical practice. The expressed juice of the plant has long been recommended as a remedy for the stings of bees or wasps,—to be rubbed into the puncture. The fruits of all the varieties are said to be emetic and cathartic; and some varieties have been used by physicians in practice. The variety called *periclymenum* has been used in France as a gargle. Is this bit of Creole medicine a colonial inheritance from the mother country?

There are other local remedies for sore throat, of a character altogether too mediæval to allow of their being mentioned in print. I doubt, however, if these are Creole; for I have heard of similar medicine among the peasantry of Europe.

Indigestion introduces us to another tea, very fragrant and soothing, made from bay-leaves and leaves of the mint-plant. A little whiskey is usually added. Sugar water is also recommended.

Melonseed tea is given in jaundice, and also in several other forms of disease. But the great remedy is carrot-juice; the carrots are first scraped, then squeezed through muslin. A cup of this juice is believed to be efficacious in the extreme.

For tetanus cockroach tea is given. I do not know how many cockroaches go to make up the cup; but I find that faith in this remedy is strong among many of the American population of New Orleans. A poultice of boiled cockroaches is placed over the wound. In Louisiana this insect (*Blatta Orientalis*) grows to a positively amazing size; and a very few would make quite a large plaster. Oil of copaiba is also recommended to rub the body with in case of tetanus; but there is nothing especially Creole in the use of the latter remedy. Powdered sulphur, salt, and tallow are likewise used as a mixture to rub the person with; and cockroaches fried in oil with garlic for indigestion.

An immense variety of remedies for diarrhœa are known in Creole medicine; I will name only a few. Tea made with an infusion of pecan husks, pecan bark, and the leaves of the pecan tree steeped in whiskey are very popular. This is doubtless due to the astringent quality of the pecan, rich in tannin. Another remedy consists in a hot drink made by roasting rice, and subsequently pouring boiling water on the grains. Hot water in which toast has been steeped is also given. Flaxseed tea, administered in so many ailments, is recommended likewise. Hot tea made with dandelions is said to be another efficacious cure. Milk and starch intermingled are often taken; also egg-shells ground or powdered, and drunk in water. Finally the banana fruit (used otherwise in a hundred ways by our motley population) is advocated as possessing excellent curative properties. The fruit should be plucked or selected green, cut into thin slices, placed in a vessel, softened to a pap by having boiling tea poured upon it, and then absorbed....

There are Creole remedies for headache, which by reason of their savage simplicity seem worthy of an African origin. These chiefly consist in applications to the forehead, temples or head of fresh leaves, which are changed as soon as the leaf begins to dry or wrinkle up. Leaves of the wild plantain are very popular for this method of cure; fig-leaves, elder-leaves, and orange-leaves are also used. But the orange-leaf is usually smeared with lard before being applied. Another remedy is to pour a little hot water, mixed with laudanum, into the ear. Wild plantain-leaves, dipped in cold water, are very often used also to allay inflammation of the eyes, when the fresh skin of a certain fish, or the excellent egg poultice, is not immediately procurable.

In swelling of the glands of the throat the swollen gland should be well rubbed with tallow; and the tallow smeared on thoroughly melted by holding close to the skin, without actually touching it, the blade of a knife heated in the flame of a lamp or candle. Some say the point of the heated blade only should approach the skin, and that the point should be moved so as to describe a cross immediately over the gland. This seems to be a purely superstitious idea.

In erysipelas a poultice of almond-leaves and rice flour is generally applied to the sore. Almond-leaves, it may be observed, are also considered to possess special virtue and healing qualities in relation to affections of the eyes. . . .

These recipes may serve to convey some idea of the nature and variety of Creole medicine, a subject much larger, however, than this essay can justly indicate. . . . So far as my limited observation enables me to judge, the most valuable part of Creole medicine has been developed by climatic necessities. Febrifuges, indeed, form the most important portion of this domestic medicine; and the art of preparing these, as well as various sudorifics and diet-drinks, seems to have been evolved by an experience not without serious value.

Finally, let me request the reader to observe that I have used the word "Creole" only in its popular sense,—just as we used to say in slave days, a "Creole negro," or as we say to-day, a "Creole egg." Many of these prescriptions and ideas are of negro origin; and but few of them are now ever used by the educated French-speaking people of Louisiana, with the exception of certain tisanes the medical value of which has been latterly recognized by physicians.

The Death of Marie Laveau

Not far from Rampart, on St. Ann street, there is a queer old house, with walls mostly constructed of moss and plaster, and trees all about it,—said to have been constructed by some Spanish builder at a remote epoch in the history of New Orleans. This house was for many years the residence of one of the most famous characters of New Orleans—one who is whispered to have inspired George Cable's remarkable figure of "Palmyre," in "*Old Creole Days,*"[1] and one whose name inspired much superstitious and foolish fear even in recent years,—Marie Laveau, vulgarly styled the "Queen of the Voudous," although her connection with voudouism was very mythical. Marie Laveau died yesterday at the advanced age of ninety-seven years.

Marie was certainly a very wonderful old woman with a very kind heart. Whatever superstitious stories were whispered about her, it is at least cer-

---

[1]Ed. note: Palmyre was actually a character of Cable's novel *The Grandissimes: A Story of Old Creole Life,* on which Hearn had written a review the previous year for the *City Item* (Sept 27, 1880).

tain that she enjoyed the respect and affection of thousands who knew her, of numbers whom she befriended in times of dire distress, of sick folks snatched from the shadow of death and nursed by her to health and strength again with that old Creole skill and knowledge of natural medicines which is now almost a lost art. In her youth she was a very beautiful woman,—one of the most beautiful perhaps, of those famous free women of color, who have almost wholly disappeared within the last twenty years. She was married in St. Louis Cathedral by Père Antoine to Jacques Paris, a carpenter, nearly seventy years ago. Paris strangely disappeared a year after the marriage and was never heard of again. Marie was subsequently married to one Capt. Christophe Glapion, who served under Jackson, in the war of 1815, in the San Domingo battalion. By this marriage Marie became the mother of fifteen children, only one of whom now lives,—a very estimable widow.

It is pretty certain that the strange stories in circulation about Marie Laveau were wholly due to her marvellous skill in the use of native herb medicines, and her ready wit also in aiding those who came to her for advice or relief. Her medicines were almost infallible; her tisanes were elixirs; and her kind heart inspired her to undertake any trouble with the view of alleviating misery or securing the happiness of those in whom she became interested. In the great epidemic of 1853, a committee of citizens was appointed to wait upon her, and beg her to lend her aid to the fever-smitten, numbers of whom she saved. It is also said that whenever Marie could be induced to exercise her influence to save the life of a condemned prisoner she rarely failed; nor were the fruits of her interference ever regretted. No shrewder judge of character could have been found, and when Marie interceded there was generally good ground for mercy.

Of late years numbers of persons, including very prominent citizens, called upon Marie Laveau frequently, in the hope of obtaining certain information from her that would have been invaluable to historians and others. But unfortunately the old woman's memory was failing; and those who had neglected when she most needed and wanted their kindness, found ample cause for regret. There were problems in the history of New Orleans she could have elucidated; there were traditions of extinct families she might have told; there were incidents in the lives of some of the greatest men of the United States she could have related. But it was too late. Her knowledge of all the events of New Orleans for nearly a century died with her; and thousands of strange secrets also which she always kept locked up in her own heart and never could have been induced to reveal under any circumstances. She had seen Aaron Burr, had been kissed by Lafayette, knew Gen. Humbert, and the Louisiana Governors of a hundred years, besides every prominent personage of New Orleans history since Claiborne.

The funeral ceremony was performed by Father Mignot, and the attendance was very large. Marie Laveau, was one of the kindest women who ever lived, and one who probably did more good to a greater number of people here than any other who lived to her great age. What good she did was done unselfishly and what she did not do was not done only because she was not able to do it.

St. John's Eve — Voudouism

St. John's eve is specially devoted to the worship of the Voudous. It is on that night that they congregate at some secret meeting-place on Lake Pontchartrain—changed from time to time—and hold their religious dances and impious ceremonies of worshipping the prince of evil, for, in their theology, the devil is God, and it is to him they pray. Voudouism is rapidly dying out, even among the negroes of Louisiana, but, for all that, a negro is frightened to death if he is "hoodooed," and with reason. The secret magic of the Voudous was nothing more than an acquaintance with a number of subtle vegetable poisons, which they brought with them from Africa, and which caused their victims to fade gradually away, and die of exhaustion.

Every St. John's eve thousands of persons visit the lake ends in the hope of coming upon the Voudous, but few succeed in finding them.

On St. John's eve, last year, the night was dark, and on the eastern sky hung a black cloud, from which now and then burst flashes of lightning, which lit up the road, the bayou and the surrounding swamp with a lurid glow, in fit introduction to what was to follow. The scene on the lake coast from Spanish Fort to Milneburg, was one which cannot easily be forgotten. All along the shore, at intervals scarcely more than 300 yards, groups of men and women could be seen standing around blazing pine-knot fires, their dark copper-colored faces weirdly gilded by the red flames and their black forms thus illuminated appearing gigantic and supernatural against the opaque background of the lake and sky on one side and the mystical darkness just tinged with starlight of the seemingly limitless swamps on the other. Some of the men were stripped to the waist, and all were gesticulating with animation, or seemed to be in waiting for something. Along the road at various intervals were negresses standing by small tables where gombo and coffee were dispensed.

Between Spanish Fort and Milneburg, the shore was crowded with negroes, who seemed to be enjoying themselves laughing, talking and romping like children, but the music which came from the shanty where a dance had evidently been started, sounded like that of an ordinary negro ball.

As soon as the purlieus of Milneburg were left, the way down the Lake shore toward the now brilliant bonfires was difficult, for in the darkness one had to pick his steps. Between the Lake on the one side and the swamp on the other there was a belt of land not more than fifty feet across, and in some places this was diminished by more than half, by the encroachment of Pontchartrain's waves. There was no roadway, but simply a devious by-path which wended around stumps and mud holes in a most irregular manner.

After some ten minutes' walk there came to the ear the faintest sound as of a drum beaten rhythmically, and on listening a chorus of voices could be heard.

Behind, the hundreds of small watchfires along the shore twinkled like stars in the distance, and where they were built upon little points of land they were reflected in the water so brightly the duplication added a peculiar weirdness to the scene.

Pursuing the same path was a party of Creole negroes, the men carrying musical instruments and the women laden with coffeepots and tin buckets of gombo. They were not inclined to talk and, when asked where the Voudou dance was to take place, answered that they knew nothing about it.

Passing around a little willow copse that grew almost in the lake there opened to the view a scene Doré would have delighted to paint. The belt of land here was about 100 feet in width, and in the middle of this little plot was burning a large fire. Grouped around it were some thirty or forty negroes, the rising and falling of the flames giving a grotesqueness to their figures that was as curious as it was entertaining. There shadows stretched out over the rushes and reeds of the swamp, and their faces brought out in effect looked wild enough to satisfy any lover of the wild and mysterious.

Built half over the swamps and half on the land stood a small hut or, to give it all its pretensions, a house of two rooms. It was like most of the fishermen's cabins seen along the Lake, but rather more roomy.

Through the open window there came quite a flood of light, and a song was heard chanted, it seemed by some eight or ten voices.

It was about three-quarters of a mile below Milneburg, and the place was appropriately selected, for certainly no more dismal and dreary spot could have been found. Citywards the swamp, with its funereal cypress, stretched in gloomy perspective, while in front, lapping the rushes and stumps, the ripples in the Lake came in, the water appearing almost black from the vegetable matter held in suspension.

Near the fire were two or three tables laden with gombo and dishes of rice, while on the embers hissed pots of coffee.

When the group near them was approached they gave evidence of uneasiness at the appearance of the party, there being no white persons present.

A few words in Creole patois made the negroes feel more at ease, and when a cup of coffee was purchased they ceased to look suspiciously on the new arrivals.

The music in the house began with renewed vigor at this time, and there was by general consent a movement thither. It was nearly midnight.

The wide gallery on the front was soon thronged, and it was noticed but few were allowed to enter the large room which formed the eastern side of the building. The door was closed, and a stout young negress guarded it on the inside.

A few words from Chief Bachemin in creole proved an *open sesame,* and the door was opened just wide enough to permit the party to enter one at a time. With their entrance the music ceased and all eyes were turned upon the new comers.

A bright mulatto man came forward and, in good English, said that if the gentlemen desired to remain they would have to obey the orders that had been given. It would spoil the charm if they did not take off their coats.

Accordingly the coats were removed.

Seated on the floor with their legs crossed beneath them were about twenty-five negro men and women, the men in their shirt sleeves, and the women with their heads adorned with the traditional head handkerchief or *tignon.*

In the centre of the floor there was spread a small tablecloth, at the corners of which two tallow candles were placed, being held in position by a bed of their own grease.

As a centre-piece, on the cloth, there was a shallow Indian basket filled with weeds, or, as they call them, *herbes.* Around the basket were diminutive piles of white beans and corn, and just outside of these a number of small bones, whether human or not could not be told. Some curiously wrought bunches of feathers were the next ornamentations near the edge of the cloth, and outside of all several saucers with small cakes in them.

The only person enjoying the aristocratic privilege of a chair was a bright *café au lait* woman of about forty-eight, who sat in one corner of the room looking on the scene before her with an air of dignity. She said but little, but beside her two old and wrinkled negresses whispered to her continually. She was of extremely handsome figure, and her features showed that she was not of the class known in old times as field hands. She was evidently raised about the plantation house. She was neatly attired in a blue calico dotted with white, and on her head a brilliant *tignon* was gracefully tied.

On inquiry it was learned that her name was Malvina Latour, and that she was the queen.

As soon as the visitors had squatted down in their places against the wall an old negro man, whose wool was white with years, began scraping on a two-stringed sort of a fiddle. The instrument had a long neck, and its body was not more than three inches in diameter, being covered with brightly mottled snake skin. This was the signal to two young mulattoes beside him, who commenced to beat with their thumbs on little drums made of gourds and covered with sheepskin.

These tam-tams gave forth a short, hollow note of peculiar sound, and were fit accompaniments of the primitive fiddle. As if to inspire those present with the earnestness of the occasion, the old darkey rolled his eyes around the room and then, stamping his foot three times, exclaimed: "*A présent commencez!*"

Rising and stepping out toward the middle of the floor a tall and sinewy negro called the attention of all to him. He looked a Hercules, and his face was anything but attractive.

Nervous with restrained emotion, he commenced at first in a low voice,

which gradually became louder and louder, a song, one stanza of which
ran as follows:

> Mallé couri dan déser,
> Mallé marché dan savane,
> Mallé marché su piquan d'oré —
> Mallé oir ça ya di moin!

> Sangé moin dan l'abitation ci la la?
> Mo gagnain soutchien la Louisiane,
> Mallé oir ça ya di moin!

Which can be translated as follows:

> I will wander into the desert,
> I will march through the prairie,
> I will walk upon the golden thorn—
> Who is there who can stop me?

> To change me from this plantation?
> I have the support of Louisiana—
> Who is there who can resist me?

As he sang he seemed to grow in stature and his eyes began to roll in a
sort of wild frenzy. There was ferocity in every word, boldness and defiance
in every gesture.

Keeping time to his song the tam-tams and fiddle gave a weird and sav-
agely monotonous accompaniment that it was easy to believe was not unlike the savage music of Africa.

When it became time for all to join in the refrain he waved his arms,
and then from every throat went up:

"*Mallé oir ça ya di moin!*"

He had hardly ended the fourth stanza before two women, uttering a
loud cry, joined their leader on the floor, and these three began a march
around the room. As the song progressed, an emaciated young negro
stepped out, and amid the shouts of all, fell in behind the others.

The last addition to the wild dancers was most affected of all, and in a
sort of delirium he picked up two of the candles and marched on with
them in his hand. When he arrived opposite the queen she gave him something to drink out of a bottle. After swallowing some he retained a mouth-
ful which, with a peculiar blowing sound, he spurted in a mist from his

lips, holding the candle so as to catch the vapor. As it was alcohol it blazed up, and this attempt at necromancy was hailed with a shout.

Then commenced the regular Voudou dance with all its twistings and contortions. Two of the women fell exhausted to the floor in a frenzy and frothing at the mouth, and the emaciated young man was carried out of the room unconscious.

The Last of the Voudoos

In the death of Jean Montanet, at the age of nearly a hundred years, New Orleans lost, at the end of August, the most extraordinary African character that ever obtained celebrity within her limits. Jean Montanet, or Jean La Ficelle, or Jean Latanié, or Jean Racine, or Jean Grisgris, or Jean Macaque, or Jean Bayou, or "Voudoo John" or "Bayou John," or "Doctor John," might well have been termed "The Last of the Voudoos"; not that the strange association with which he was affiliated has ceased to exist with his death, but that he was the last really important figure of a long line of wizards or witches whose African titles were recognized, and who exercised an influence over the colored population. Swarthy occultists will doubtless continue to elect their "queens" and high-priests through years to come, but the influence of the public school is gradually dissipating all faith in witchcraft, and no black heirophant now remains capable of manifesting such mystic knowledge or of inspiring such respect as Voudoo John exhibited and compelled. There will never be another "Rose," another "Marie," much less another Jean Bayou.

It may reasonably be doubted whether any other negro of African birth who lived in the South had a more extraordinary career than that of Jean Montanet. He was a native of Senegal, and claimed to have been a prince's son, in proof of which he was wont to call attention to a number of parallel scars on his cheek, extending in curves from the edge of either temple to the corner of the lips. This fact seems to me partly confirmatory of his statement, as Berenger-Feraud dwells at some length on the fact that the Bambaras, who are probably the finest negro race in Senegal, all wear such disfigurations. The scars are made by gashing the cheeks during infancy, and are considered a sign of race. Three parallel scars mark the freemen of the tribe; four distinguish their captives or slaves. Now Jean's face had, I am told, three scars, which would prove him a free-born Bambara, or at least a member of some free tribe allied to the Bambaras, and living upon their territory. At all events, Jean possessed physical characteristics answering to those by which the French ethnologists in Senegal distinguish the Bambaras. He was of middle height, very strongly built, with broad shoulders, well-developed muscles, an inky black skin, retreating forehead, small bright eyes, a very flat nose, and a wooly beard, gray only during the last few years of this long life. He had a resonant voice and a very authoritative manner.

At an early age he was kidnapped by Spanish slavers, who sold him at some Spanish port, whence he was ultimately shipped to Cuba. His West-Indian master taught him to be an excellent cook, ultimately became attached to him, and made him a present of his freedom. Jean soon afterward engaged on some Spanish vessel as ship's cook, and in the exercise of this calling voyaged considerably in both hemispheres. Finally tiring of the sea, he left his ship at New Orleans, and began life on shore as a cotton-roller. His physical strength gave him considerable advantage above his fellow-blacks; and his employers also discovered that he wielded some peculiar occult influence over the negroes, which made him valuable as an overseer or gang leader. Jean, in short, possessed the mysterious *obi* power, the existence of which has been recognized in most slave-holding communities, and with which many a West-Indian planter has been compelled by force of circumstances to effect a compromise. Accordingly Jean was permitted many liberties which other blacks, although free, would never have presumed to take. Soon it became rumored that he was a seer of no small powers, and that he could tell the future by the marks upon bales of cotton. I have never been able to learn the details of this queer method of telling fortunes; but Jean became so successful in the exercise of it that thousands of colored people flocked to him for predictions and counsel, and even white people, moved by curiosity or by doubt, paid him to prophesy for them. Finally he became wealthy enough to abandon the levee and purchase a large tract of property on the Bayou road, where he built a house. His land extended from Prieur street on the Bayou road as far as Roman, covering the greater portion of an extensive square, now well built up. In those days it was a marshy green plain, with a few scattered habitations.

At his new home Jean continued the practice of fortune-telling, but combined it with the profession of Creole medicine, and of arts still more mysterious. By-and-by his reputation became so great that he was able to demand and obtain immense fees. People of both races and both sexes thronged to see him—many coming even from far-away Creole towns in the parishes—and well-dressed women, closely veiled, often knocked at his door. Parties paid from ten to twenty dollars for advice, for herb medicines, for recipes to make the hair grow, for cataplasms supposed to possess mysterious virtues, but really made with scraps of shoe-leather triturated into paste, for advice what ticket to buy in the Havana lottery, for aid to recover stolen goods, for love powders, for counsel in family troubles, for charms by which to obtain revenge upon an enemy. Once Jean received a fee of fifty dollars for a potion. "It was water," he said to a Creole confidant, "with some common herbs boiled in it. I hurt nobody; but if folks want to give me fifty dollars, I take the fifty dollars every time!" His office furniture consisted of a table, a chair, a picture of the Virgin Mary, an elephant's tusk, some shells which he said were African shells and enabled him to read the future, and a pack of cards in each of which a small hole had been burned. About his person he always carried two small bones wrapped around with a black string, which bones he really appeared to revere as fetiches. Wax candles were burned during his performances; and as he bought a whole box of them every few days during "flush times," one can imagine how large the number of his clients must have been. They poured money into his hands so generously that he became worth at least $50,000!

Then, indeed, did this possible son of a Bambara prince begin to live more grandly than any black potentate of Senegal. He had his carriage and pair, worthy of a planter, and his blooded saddle-horse, which he rode well, attired in a gaudy Spanish costume, and seated upon an elaborately decorated Mexican saddle. At home, where he ate and drank only the best—scorning claret worth less than a dollar the *litre*—he continued to find his simple furniture good enough for him; but he had at least fifteen wives—a harem worthy of Boubakar-Segou. White folks might have called them by a less honorific name, but Jean declared them his legitimate spouses according to African ritual. One of the curious features in modern slavery was the ownership of blacks by freedmen of their own color, and these negro slave-holders were usually savage and merciless masters.

Jean was not; but it was by right of slave purchase that he obtained most of his wives, who bore him children in great multitude. Finally he managed to woo and win a white woman of the lowest class, who might have been, after a fashion, the Sultana-Vilidé of this Seraglio. On grand occasions Jean used to distribute largess among the colored population of his neighborhood in the shape of food—bowls of *gombo* or dishes of *jimbalaya*. He did it for popularity's sake in those days, perhaps; but in after-years, during the great epidemics, he did it for charity, even when so much reduced in circumstances that he was himself obliged to cook the food to be given away.

But Jean's greatness did not fail to entail certain cares. He did not know what to do with his money. He had no faith in banks, and had seen too much of the darker side of life to have much faith in human nature. For many years he kept his money under-ground, burying or taking it up at night only, occasionally concealing large sums so well that he could never find them again himself; and now, after many years, people still believe there are treasures entombed somewhere in the neighborhood of Prieur street and Bayou road. All business negotiations of a serious character caused him much worry, and as he found many willing to take advantage of his ignorance, he probably felt small remorse for certain questionable actions of his own. He was notoriously bad pay, and part of his property was seized at last to cover a debt. Then, in an evil hour, he asked a man without scruples to teach him how to write, believing that financial misfortunes were mostly due to ignorance of the alphabet. After he had learned to write his name, he was innocent enough one day to place his signature by request at the bottom of a blank sheet of paper, and, lo! his real estate passed from his possession in some horribly mysterious way. Still he had some money left, and made heroic efforts to retrieve his fortunes. He bought other property, and he invested desperately to lottery tickets. The lottery craze finally came upon him, and had far more to do with his ultimate ruin than his losses in the grocery, the shoemaker's shop, and other establishments into which he had put several thousand dollars as the silent partner of people who cheated him. He might certainly have continued to make a good living, since people still sent for him to cure them with his herbs, or went to see him to have their fortunes told; but all his earnings were wasted in tempting fortune. After a score of seizures and a long succession of evictions, he was at last obliged to seek hospitality from some of his numerous children; and of all he had once owned nothing remained to him but his African shells, his elephant's tusk, and the sewing machine table that had served him to tell fortunes and to burn wax candles upon. Even these, I think, were attached a day or two before his death, which occurred at the house of the daughter by the white wife, an intelligent mulatto with many children of her own.

Jean's ideas of religion were primitive in the extreme. The conversion of the chief tribes of Senegal to Islam occurred in recent years, and it is probable that at the time he was captured by slavers his people were still in a condition little above gross fetichism. If during his years of servitude in a Catholic colony he had imbibed some notions of Romish Christianity, it is certain at least that the Christian ideas were always subordinated to the African—just as the image of the Virgin Mary was used by him merely as an auxiliary fetich in his witchcraft, and was considered as possessing much less power than the "elephant's toof." He was in many respects a humbug; but he may have sincerely believed in the efficacy of certain superstitious rites of his own. He stated that he had a Master whom he was bound to obey; that he could read the will of this Master in the twinkling of the stars; and often of clear nights the neighbors used to watch him standing alone at some street corner staring at the welkin, pulling his woolly beard, and talking in an unknown language to some imaginary being. Whenever Jean indulged in this freak, people knew that he needed money badly, and would probably try to borrow a dollar or two from some one in the vicinity next day.

Testimony to his remarkable skill in the use of herbs could be gathered from nearly every one now living who became well acquainted with him. During the epidemic of 1878, which uprooted the old belief in the total immunity of negroes and colored people from yellow fever, two of Jean's children were "taken down." "I have no money," he said, "but I can cure my children," which he proceeded to do with the aid of some weeds plucked from the edge of the Prieur street gutters. One of the herbs, I am told, was what our Creoles call the "parasol." "The children were playing on the *banquette* next day," said my informant.

Montanet, even in the most unlucky part of his career, retained the superstitious reverence of colored people in all parts of the city. When he made his appearance even on the American side of Canal street to doctor some sick person, there was always much subdued excitement among the colored folks, who whispered and stared a great deal, but were careful not to raise their voices when they said, "Dar's Hoodoo John!" That an unlettered African slave should have been able to achieve what Jean Bayou achieved in a civilized city, and to earn the wealth and the reputation that he enjoyed during many years of his life, might be cited as a singular evidence of modern popular credulity, but it is also proof that Jean was not an ordinary man in point of natural intelligence.

The Garden of Paradise

If there be any particular spot of this continent where natural beauty might justify dreamers to claim an American site for the primitive Garden of Paradise, that spot is the Teche country of Louisiana.... [There] groves of giant oaks are such as Martin pictured in his illustrations to *Paradise Lost;* and his fairy Eve might have mirrored her white body in the smoothness of that sinuous bayou not less perfectly than in the waters of a Paradisaical pond. Where the wild bushes and the cypresses do not crowd to the bank in promiscuous herds of green, the prairie dips its mossy softness into the water. The first general impression of the Teche scenery is that of sailing through some enormous garden;—but the Spanish moss gradually and fantastically dissipates that idea.

It is the moss that forms the *theme* of the scenery—if a musical word may be used descriptively. It constitutes the character of the landscape. It is omnipresent and omnipotent in effect. It streams from the heads and limbs of the oaks; from the many-elbowed cypress skeletons it hangs like decaying rags of green. It creates suggestions of gibbets and of corpses, of rotten rigging, of the tattered sails of ships "drifting with the dead to shores where all is dumb." Under the sunlight it has also countless pleasant forms—the tresses of slumbering dryads, the draperies flung out upon some vast woodland-holiday by skill of merry elves. Under the moon, losing its green, every form of goblinry, every fancy of ghastliness, every grimness of witchcraft, every horror of death, are mocked by it. A weird and wonderful morning seems to droop over the plains;—all the woods and the groves, the lily-kissed pools, the shadow-reflecting bayous,—appear to lament some incalculable bereavement, some vast and awful death. It is as though this land were yet weeping for Pan,—as though all the forests and streams had not ceased after more than a thousand years to lament the passing away of the sylvan gods and nymphs of the antique world.

Circling, coiling, curving, curling, the bayou moves without a ripple through wildernesses of wildly fantastic beauty—through land worth a surface-covering of golden coin,—through forlorn cypress woods, weeping their moss into the shadowed water,—through fields of cane,—through vistas of evergreens dying away into blue dreaminess,—under orange-trees holding out their yellow riches to passing boats,—close by fallen trunks drowned in the waveless current and alligators hard to be distinguished from the dead-gray bark. At long intervals a white town dozing under green shadows. Land,—and the streets sleep beneath the sun, full of flower-fragrance, and the nuptial incense of orange-groves. There is hardly a stir; the songs of birds drown the voices of men; the shadows of the trees scarcely waver. And the great dreaminess of the land makes itself master of thought and speech,—mesmerizes you,—caresses with tender treachery,—soothes with irresistible languor,—woos with unutterable sweetness. . . . Afterward when you have returned into the vast metropolis, into the dust and the turmoil and the roar of traffic and the smoke of industry and the iron cares of life,—that mesmerism will not have utterly passed away, nor the perfume of that poppied land wholly evaporated from the brain. The songs of the birds will still be heard by you—faint as fairy flutes, and in dreams the golden Teche will curve for you once more under wondrous festoons of green, under wizard appareled groves, through deep enchantments of perennial summer; and you will awake to feel the great sweet dreaminess come back upon you again—a moment only, but a moment that makes dim the eyes as with mists of a tropical morning.

Saint Maló: A Lacustrine Village in Louisiana

For nearly fifty years there has existed in the southeastern swamp lands of Louisiana a certain strange settlement of Malay fishermen—Tagalas from the Philippine Islands. The place of their lacustrine village is not precisely mentioned upon maps, and the world in general ignored until a few days ago the bare fact of their amphibious existence. Even the United States mail service has never found its way thither, and even in the great city of New Orleans, less than a hundred miles distant, the people were far better informed about the Carboniferous Era than concerning the

swampy affairs of this Manila village. Occasionally vague echoes of its mysterious life were borne to the civilized center, but these were scarcely of a character to tempt investigation or encourage belief. Some voluble Italian luggermen once came to town with a short cargo of oysters, and a long story regarding a ghastly "Chinese" colony in the reedy swamps south of Lake Borgne. For many years the inhabitants of the Oriental settlement had lived in peace and harmony without the presence of a single woman, but finally had managed to import an oblique-eyed beauty from beyond the Yellow Sea. Thereupon arose the first dissensions, provoking much shedding of blood. And at last the elders of the people had restored calm and fraternal feeling by sentencing the woman to be hewn in pieces and flung to the alligators of the bayou.

Possible the story is; probable it is not. Partly for the purpose of investigating it, . . . the *Times-Democrat* of New Orleans chartered and fitted out an Italian lugger for a trip to the unexplored region in question—to the fishing station of Saint Malό. And a strange voyage it was. Even the Italian sailors knew not whither they were going, none of them had ever beheld the Manila village, or were aware of its location.

Starting from Spanish Fort northeastwardly across Lake Pontchartrain, after the first few miles sailed one already observes a change in the vegetation of the receding banks. The shore itself sinks, the lowland bristles with rushes and marsh grasses waving in the wind. A little further on and the water becomes deeply clouded with sap green—the myriad floating seeds of swamp vegetation. Banks dwindle away into thin lines; the greenish-yellow of the reeds changes into misty blue. Then it is all water and sky, motionless blue and heaving lazulite, until the reedy waste of Point-aux-Herbes thrusts its picturesque lighthouse far out into the lake. Above the wilderness of swamp grass and bulrushes this graceful building rises upon an openwork of wooden piles. Seven miles of absolute desolation separate the lighthouse keeper from his nearest neighbor. Nevertheless, there is a good piano there for the girls to play upon, comfortably furnished rooms, a good library. The pet cat has lost an eye in fighting with a moccasin, and it is prudent before descending from the balcony into the swamp about the house to reconnoiter for snakes.

Still northeast. The sun is sinking above the rushy bank line; the west is crimsoning like iron losing its white heat. Against the ruddy light a cross is visible. There is a cemetery in the swamp. Those are the forgotten graves of lighthouse keepers. Our boat is spreading her pinions for flight through the Rigolets, that sinuous waterway leading to Lake Borgne. We pass by the defenseless walls of Fort Pike, a stronghold without a history, picturesque enough, but almost worthless against modern artillery. There is a solitary sergeant in charge, and a dog. Perhaps the taciturnity of the man is due to his long solitude, the vast silence of the land weighing down upon him. At last appears the twinkling light of the United States custom-house, and the enormous skeleton of the Rigolets bridge. The custom-house rises on stilts out of the sedge-grass....

On the eastern side of the Rigolets, Lake Borgne has scalloped out its grass-fringed bed in the form of a gigantic clover leaf—a shallow and treacherous sea, from which all fishing-vessels scurry in wild terror when a storm begins to darken. No lugger can live in those short chopping waves when Gulf winds are mad. To read the Manila settlement one must steer due south until the waving bulrushes again appear, this time behind muddy shoals of immense breadth. The chart announces depths varying from six inches to three and a half feet. For a while we grope about blindly along the banks. Suddenly the mouth of a bayou appears—"Saint Maló Pass." With the aid of poles the vessel manages to shamble over a mud-bar, and forthwith rocks in forty feet of green water. We reached Saint Maló upon a leaden-colored day, and the scenery in its gray ghastliness recalled to us the weird landscape painted with words by Edgar Poe—"Silence: a Fragment."

Out of the shuddering reeds and banneretted grass on either side rise the fantastic houses of the Malay fishermen, poised upon slender supports above the marsh, like cranes or bitterns watching for scaly prey. Hard by the slimy mouth of the bayou extends a strange wharf, as ruined and rotted and unearthly as the timbers of the spectral ship in the "Rime of the

Ancient Mariner." Odd craft huddle together beside it, fishing-nets make cobwebby drapery about the skeleton timber-work. Green are the banks, green the water is, green also with fungi every beam and plank and board and shingle of the houses upon stilts. All are built in true Manila style, with immense hat-shaped eaves and balconies, but in wood; for it had been found that palmetto and woven cane could not withstand the violence of the climate. Nevertheless, all this wood had to be shipped to the bayou from a considerable distance, for large trees do not grow in the salty swamp. The highest point of land as far as the "Devil's Elbow," three or four miles away, and even beyond it, is only six inches above low-water mark, and the men who built those houses were compelled to stand upon ladders, or other wood frame-work, while driving down the piles, lest the quagmire should swallow them up. . . .

Here is the home of the mosquito, and every window throughout all the marsh country must be closed with wire netting. . . . Wood-worms are busy undermining the supports of the dwellings, and wood-ticks attack the beams and joistings. A marvelous variety of creatures haunt the surrounding swamp—reptiles, insects, and birds. The *prie-dieu*—"pray-god"— utters its soprano note; water-hens and plovers call across the marsh. Numberless snakes hide among the reeds, having little to fear save from the wild-cats, which attack them with savage recklessness. Rarely a bear or a deer finds its way near the bayou. There are many otters and musk-rats, minks and raccoons and rabbits. Buzzards float in the sky, and occasionally a bald-eagle sails before the sun.

Such is the land: its human inhabitants are not less strange, wild, picturesque. Most of them are cinnamon-colored men; a few are glossily yellow, like that bronze into which a small portion of gold is worked by the moulder. Their features are irregular without being actually repulsive; some have the cheek-bones very prominent, and the eyes of several are set slightly aslant. The hair is generally intensely black and straight, but with some individuals it is curly and browner. In Manila there are several varieties of the Malay race, and these Louisiana settlers represent more than one type. None of them appeared tall; the greater number were undersized, but all well knit, and supple as fresh-water eels. Their hands and feet were small; their movements quick and easy, but sailorly likewise, as of men accustomed to walk upon rocking decks in rough weather. They speak the Spanish language; and a Malay dialect is also used among them. There is only one white man in the settlement—the ship-carpenter, whom all the Malays address as "Maestro." He has learned to speak their Oriental dialect, and has conferred upon several the sacrament of baptism according to the Catholic rite; for some of these men were not Christians at the time of their advent into Louisiana. There is but one black man in this lake village—a Portuguese negro, perhaps a Brazilian maroon. The Maestro told us that communication is still kept up with Manila, and money often sent there to aid friends in emigrating. Such emigrants usually ship as seamen on board some Spanish vessel bound for American ports, and desert at the first opportunity. It is said that the colony was founded by deserters—perhaps also by desperate refugees from Spanish justice.

Justice within the colony itself, however, is of a curiously primitive kind; for there are neither magistrates nor sheriffs, neither prisons nor police. Although the region is included within the parish of St. Bernard, no Louisiana official has ever visited it; never has the tax-gatherer attempted to wend thither his unwelcome way. In the busy season a hundred fierce men are gathered together in this waste and watery place, and there must be a law unto themselves. If a really grave quarrel arises, the trouble is submitted to the arbitration of the oldest Malay in the colony, Padre Carpio, and his decisions are usually accepted without a murmur. Should a man, on the other hand, needlessly seek to provoke a difficulty, he is liable to be imprisoned within a fish-car, and left there until cold and hunger have tamed his rage, or the rising tide forces him to terms. Naturally all these men are Catholics; but a priest rarely visits them, for it costs a considerable sum to bring the ghostly father into the heart of the swamp that he may celebrate mass under the smoky rafters of Hilario's house—under the strings of dry fish.

There is no woman in the settlement, nor has the treble of a female voice been heard along the bayou for many a long year. Men who have families keep them at New Orleans, or at Proctorville, or at La Chinche; it would seem cruel to ask any woman to dwell in such a desolation, without comfort and without protection, during the long absence of the fishing-boats. Only two instances of a woman dwelling there are preserved, like beloved traditions, in the memory of the inhabitants. The first of these departed upon her husband's death; the second left the village after a desperate attempt had been made to murder her spouse. In the dead of night the man was unexpectedly assailed; his wife and little boy helped to defend him. The assailant was overcome, tied hand and foot with fish-lines, and fastened to a stake deep driven into the swamp. Next morning they found him dead: the mosquitoes and *tappanoes* had filled the office of executioner. No excitement was manifested; the Maestro dug a grave deep in the soft gray mud, and fixed above it a rude wooden cross, which still shows its silhouette against the sky just above the reeds.

Such was the narrative which El Maestro related to us with a strange mixture of religious compassion for the unabsolved soul, and marvelous profanity expressed in four different languages. "Only mosquitoes live there now," he added, indicating the decaying edifice where the dead man had dwelt.

But for the possession of modern fire-arms and one most ancient clock, the lake-dwellers of Saint Malô would seem to have as little in common with the civilization of the nineteenth century as had the inhabitants of the Swiss lacustrine settlements of the Bronze Epoch. Here time is measured rather by the number of alligator-skins sent to market, or the most striking incidents of successive fishing seasons, than by ordinary reckoning; and did not the Maestro keep a chalk record of the days of the week, none might know Sunday from Monday. There is absolutely no furniture in the place; not a chair, a table, or a bed can be found in all the dwellings of this aquatic village. Mattresses there are, filled with dry "Spanish beard"; but these are laid upon tiers of enormous shelves braced against the walls, where the weary fishermen slumber at night among barrels of flour and folded sails and smoked fish. Even the clothes (purchased at New Orleans or Proctorville) become as quaint and curiously tinted in that moist atmosphere as the houses of the village, and the broad hats take a greenish and grotesque aspect in odd harmony with the appearance of the ancient roofs. All the art treasures of the colony consist of a circus poster immemorially old, which is preserved with much reverence, and two photographs jealously guarded in the Maestro's sea-chest. These represent a sturdy young woman with Creole eyes, and a grim-looking Frenchman with wintry beard—the wife and father of the ship-carpenter. He pointed to them with a display of feeling made strongly pathetic by contrast with the wild character of the man, and his eyes, keen and hard as those of an eagle, softened a little as he kissed the old man's portrait, and murmured, "*Mon cher vieux père.*"

And nevertheless this life in the wilderness of reeds is connected mysteriously with New Orleans, where the headquarters of the Manila men's benevolent society are—*La Union Philippina*. A fisherman dies; he is buried under the rustling reeds, and a pine cross planted above his grave; but when the flesh has rotted from the bones, these are taken up and carried by some lugger to the metropolis, where they are shelved away in those curious niche tombs which recall the Roman *columbaria.*

How, then, comes it that in spite of this connection with civilized life the Malay settlement of Lake Borgne has been so long unknown? Perhaps because of the natural reticence of the people. There is still in the oldest portion of the oldest quarter of New Orleans a certain Manila restaurant hidden away in a court, and supported almost wholly by the patronage of Spanish West Indian sailors. Few people belonging to the business circles of New Orleans knew of its existence. The *menu* is printed in Spanish and English; the fare is cheap and good. Now it is kept by Chinese, for the Manila man and his oblique-eyed wife, comely as any figure upon a Japanese vase, have gone away. Doubtless his ears, like sea-shells, were haunted by the moaning of the sea, and the Gulf winds called to him by night, so that he could not remain.

The most intelligent person in Saint Malô is a Malay half-breed, Valentine. He is an attractive figure, a supple dwarfish lad almost as broad as tall, brown as old copper, with a singularly bright eye. He was educated in the great city, but actually abandoned a fine situation in the office of a judge to return to his swarthy father in the weird swamps. The old man is still there—Thomas de los Santos. He married a white woman, by whom he had two children, this boy and a daughter, Winnie, who is dead. Valentine is the best pirogue oarsman in the settlement, and a boat bears his name. But opposite the house of Thomas de los Santos rides another graceful boat, rarely used, and whitely christened with the name of the dead Winnie. Latin names prevail in the nomenclature of boats and men: Marcellino, Francesco, Serafino, Florenzo, Victorio, Paosto, Hilario, Marcetto, are common baptismal names. The solitary Creole appellation Aristide offers an anomaly. There are luggers and sloops bearing equally romantic names: *Manrico de Aragón, Maravilla, Joven Impératriz.* Spanish piety has baptized several others with sacred words and names of martyrs.

Of the thirteen or fourteen large edifices on piles, the most picturesque is perhaps that of Carpio—old Carpio, who deserts the place once a year to play monte in Mexico. His home consists of three wood edifices so arranged that the outer two advance like wings, and the wharf is placed in front of the central structure. Smoked fish black with age hang from the roof, chickens squeak upon the floor, pigs grunt under the planking.

Small, squat, swart, dry, and grimy as his smoked fish is old Carpio, but his eye is bright and quick as a lizard's. . . .

There is no liquor in the settlement, and these hardy fishers and alligator-hunters seem none the worse therefor. Their flesh is as hard as oak-wood and sickness rarely affects them, although they know little of comfort, and live largely upon raw fish, seasoned with vinegar and oil. There is but one chimney—a wooden structure—in the village, fires are hardly ever lighted, and in the winter the cold and the damp would soon undermine feeble constitutions.

A sunset viewed from the balcony of the Maestro's house seemed to us enchantment. The steel blue of the western horizon heated into furnace yellow, then cooled off into red splendors of astounding warmth and transparency. The bayou blushed crimson, the green of the marsh pools, of the shivering reeds, of the decaying timber-work, took fairy bronze tints, and then, immense with marsh mist, the orange-vermilion face of the sun peered luridly for the last time through the tall grasses upon the bank. Night came with marvelous choruses of frogs; the whole lowland throbbed and laughed with the wild music—a swamp-hymn deeper and mightier than even the surge sounds heard from the Rigolets bank: the world seemed to shake with it! . . .

Rod and Gun

Both hunting and fishing are favorite amusements in New Orleans. No city in the Union can offer such advantages as the Crescent City in this respect. Surrounded as it is on all sides by an uninhabited swamp, such game as ducks and snipe, and all varieties of fish, both fresh and salt water, are to be caught within the city limits.

A favorite sport is alligator hunting. There are not as many alligators in the suburbs of New Orleans as there were before the skins of the mighty saurians became commercial commodity, and hunters went to work to kill them as a profession; but there are still enough to furnish the sportsman with plenty of good game. You will have no difficulty in finding as many alligators as you want in the innumerable bayous and lakes just back of Algiers. The discovery will do you little good, however, unless you know exactly how to hunt the alligator. Hunt them by night in a pirogue—a boat hewn from a solid log—paddled by a skilled swamper. The boat glides noiselessly through the water. A torch throws a glare of light ahead and shows you the sparkling eyes of the alligator. Fire straight at it, and if you are any marksman the game is bagged, and the "bull," after frothing the water, will roll with its white belly upward.

The scene is impressive, and will fix itself indelibly in your memory. A small canoe, propelled by the paddle of a brawny African, is gliding noiselessly through the water, stagnant and covered with a thick, green scum. The mournful decaying cypresses, fit emblems of death, dip their gray moss-threads in the water. All around is gloom and melancholy, desolation and darkness, but ahead upon the stygian waters flickers here and there a star. It is the eye of an alligator; and as you get nearer you discern the ugly head of the repulsive animal. Doré never drew anything more striking than this picture would be.

There is no game, however, more constant and more attractive than the duck. The Gulf coast and the shores of Lake Pontchartrain are his natural winter home. Here everything is offered him and in profusion, seaweed, insects, aquatic plants in such abundance, that the greedy bird often falls a victim to his gluttony.

When, last winter, one of the lagoons, deemed by the *jeunesse de la chasse* an especially good place for ducks, was found covered with several hundred of these dead bodies, a cry of indignation went up against the professional hunters, who were charged with having, Borgia-like, poisoned the ducks in order to spoil the sport of the amateur, until it was discovered that the ducks had actually choked themselves to death with seaweed—there was so much of it.

Of the ducks which frequent the waters of Louisiana, there is an endless variety; buffle-heads, canvas-backs, harlequins, mallards or French, the largest, choicest and most hunted, pentails, teal—fishy and not often palatable—spoonbills, grey ducks, widgeons, wood ducks and perhaps a half a hundred more.

And you can hunt them in as many different ways. Many sportsmen have little hunting lodges of palmetto leaves and swamp grass scattered among some favorite lagoons, and looking so much like the surrounding marsh that even the most suspicious and knowing of the web-footed race would never detect them. To this cabin the hunter repairs over night, while the ducks are snoring way in the bulrushes, and here reclining comfortably upon a bed of straw he waits patiently until daylight offers him a good shot.

Decoys are generally used to attract the wary birds, and every good hunter has a bag of them. As soon as these wooden ducks are sent swimming in the water a flock of their brethren of the air swoop down among them, gobbling and quacking; and just as they alight upon the water, and before they have time to discover the character of the decoys, fire is opened upon them with deadly effect.

Knowing Nimrods have their own boats, decoys, etc., and a paddler in readiness upon their arrival. Frequently they take with them two live tame (puddle) ducks, which they put down in the water and tie by the leg to a bush nearby, which proves a decoy dangerous to the most wary of the veterans of the lagoons, who learn, towards the end of the season, how to distinguish between wooden ducks and live ducks. A good sportsman thus equipped on a fair day will get fifty to seventy-five shots.

On the prairies near Opelousas and Vermillionville, La., there are innumerable small ponds to be found, in which, during the winter months, are to be seen great numbers of ducks. No trees or cover of any kind to conceal the sportsman exists, and the hunter procures an old ox trained for the purpose, and to stand fire. Getting on the off side of the ox—that is, placing the ox between the ducks and himself—the sportsman is enabled to get within gunshot of the game quite easily. He gives a loud whoop when the ducks take to wing, and then gives them both barrels; and should the ducks be teal or of the smaller varieties, he will get out of a large flock some twenty-five to fifty ducks.

Fire hunting is also very successful with the ducks. A lighted torch attracts them as a candle does the moths, and they are so dazzled and bewitched that they allow the hunters to approach within very close range of them.

Still another mode of catching the ducks—one much used of old in the Chandeleurs, and still occasionally employed there—is by means of nets, stretched at nightfall from bay to bay and point to point, directly in the course of the ducks' flight, and into which they plunge in their rapid flight to some favorite lagoon, and are caught. . . .

On the prairie, west of New Orleans, nearly all varieties of grouse, generally called Creole quails in Louisiana, are to be found—the heather cock or pine grouse, very much like the Alpleauerhahn, a fine table bird with a slight pine flavor, which adds to its gamey taste, the ruffled grouse, and the prairie hen—but grouse hunting not being as exciting as hunting ducks is thus less popular.

Within one hundred miles from New Orleans, on any of the railroads, bear, turkey, squirrel-deer and quail can be found, and on application to any of the gun stores in the city the location will be given you, when to go, and all the information in regard to outfit, etc., etc.

Fishing

Fishing is in equal favor, and during the season every train takes out large parties of fishermen. Along the line of the Mobile road there are many places where good sport can be had.... The first place that merits the reputation it has so long had is Chef Menteur, twenty miles from the city, on the route to Mobile. The sportsmen, upon arrival there, can call upon any of the professional fishermen in the neighborhood—there are two or three living immediately at the station—and secure a boat and meals for $1. A negro guide or paddler will charge about $1.50 for a day's work, and this is all the expense. Trout and red fish abound at the mouth of the Chef, and bite well. Sheephead and croakers are also plentiful, and along the edges of the bayous there the perch bite almost as fast as the hook, is dropped into the water. The accommodations are good, and the amateur will be well repaid for his visit. The next place is Miller's Bayou, twenty-seven miles from here, on the same road. Here Mrs. Miller, the widow of the famous professional hunter, keeps a lodge, where one can make his headquarters comfortably. A good boat, with meals, costs only $1, and if the sportsman does not know how to paddle a pirogue or row a skiff, a guide can be had for $1.50 per day, who will carry him to the best places. In Lake Catherine—only 200 yards from Mrs. Miller's house—redfish and sheephead are abundant. The next favorite place is Lookout Station, about thirty-seven miles from the city. At this spot are erected the fishing and hunting boxes of the wealthy private clubs, and a visitor must carry all his accommodations with him, as none can be had on the spot....

On the western shore of Lake Pontchartrain is the Tangipahoa River, which can only be reached by sailboat from here; at least, that portion of it where the fishing is superb.

It is, to use an old fisherman's phrase, "the boss place around these diggings," for green trout. In low tides artificial baits work well here. The mouth of the river enters the lake about thirty-five miles north-northeast from the West End, and a party starting in a sailboat the evening before reaches the spot in time to make a good catch and get back the next afternoon. There are no accommodations there, so that everything will have to be taken on board before starting.

Coming nearer home we have Bayou Laurier, about four and a half miles to the westward of West End, where sheephead, trout, perch and sacalait can be found. Of late, however, fishermen have been in the habit of gill netting here, and the fish are not as abundant as they should be. One need not expect to find any quarters there. Next is Bayou Labarre, two and a half miles from West End, which is of the same character as Bayou Laurier, and then nearer is Bayou Tchoupitoulas, a sister stream to the others. A skiff or sailboat is taken to reach the above.

Across the river there is Harvey's Canal, to be reached by the ferry at Louisiana avenue, a well known resort of the largest perch. A boat and a man to pull one down the canal to Bayou Barataria costs $2.50 a day. Below the city is the Ship Island Canal, twelve miles from the slaughter-house. It runs from a spot close to the river out into Lake Borgne, and at its mouth redfish, sheephead, trout and croakers abound.

Bait for all of our fish can readily be had. They consist of minnows and shrimp, and crab, if the two former are not at hand. All of them will take either of the above greedily.

The outfit can be as expensive as one likes. For $2.55 a very handsome get-up can be had consisting of jointed rod, hooks, sinkers, floats and fifty yards of excellent line. For seventy-five cents a cheaper outfit can be had, a Japan pole taking the place of the more costly jointed rod.

With these data before him, the seeker after a quiet day cannot go wrong.

The Gulf of Mexico, the Mississippi river, the lakes and bayous, abound in fish of the greatest Variety. . . .

To give an idea of the mode of fishing, let us select representative specimens of the two varieties of fish, fresh and salt water, such as the red fish and green trout.

The redfish belongs to one of the divisions of the drum species. Of this species the common drumfish is the largest found in Southern waters, while the familiar little croaker is the smallest cousin of the family. The species is named from a singular noise made by all those fish, which is a weak croak in the diminutive croaker, while when uttered by the larger specimens it is precisely similar to a distant drum-beat. . . .

The greatest size attained by the redfish is a matter of dispute. The largest probably ever seen near New Orleans was a specimen captured in East Bay, a few miles from the South Pass lighthouse, in the latter part of April, 1876. The dimensions of this, as nearly as could be estimated after a close inspection, were—length over four and a half feet, breadth about one foot and weight certainly over seventy-five pounds. This fish was captured by a veteran professional, who called it "a long ways the biggest red fish" he ever saw. Such of these fish as are caught out in deep water average a larger size than those captured in the numerous bayous and indentations of our coast. Usually a thirty pounder is considered a pretty fair specimen of the fish in any waters....

The colors of the redfish are at times very brilliant, and are always very variable, being affected by the same causes which change the hues of many other fish....At times the coloring of the male is simply magnificent, and the crimson of the back merges into rich golden lines along the sides. Following the same rule as that set down in the creation of other fishes, the female is much less prominently and distinctly marked than is the male. The fishes of both sexes have a jet black spot on each side near the tail, while occasional specimens have been caught with several of these spots on them in a line from the pectoral fins to the tail. Some of our amateur fishermen have decided this to be the fish from whose mouth the Apostles obtained pieces of money. It is stated that when these ancient fishermen picked up the fishes by the tails and shook the money from their mouths they left the noted black spot on the tail of each fish as a mark for succeeding generations of fish to reverentially note and praise....

Green trout is a misnomer for the splendid fish which is so called in New Orleans. Our famous "green trout" are not trout at all—in fact, they are in no wise connected with any of the genus *salmo* save in being members of the fish kind. In the ponds and streams of other Southern States it lives under the more appropriate cognomen of pond bass, and is esteemed properly as the finest fresh-water fish of the Southern States. It is found in abundance in the mill ponds, beaver ponds, and clear streams of the Gulf States, but attains its greatest size and beauty in the bayous and lakes of Lower Louisiana, from which waters specimens of the fish weighing over six pounds are sometimes taken....

In the clear waters of the currentless bayous, the green trout acquires its greatest beauty in coloring and markings. In common with a great many other species of fish, this has the chameleon-like power of modifying, even almost entirely changing, the hues of its skin. Whether this modification is effected by the fish's volition or by the surroundings, it is impossible to determine. However, in the fishing season proper, when the hues of the fish are nearest perfection, they reach and retain their greatest vividness in bright clear water. When this same water is made turbid by a recent heavy rain-fall, or by an influx from the river, the fish rapidly loses its rich hues. Its back turns to a dull brown, the stripe becomes almost indistinct or entirely disappears, and the bright white of its belly takes a slight tinge of yellow. The markings, in fact, undergo as great a change as that noticed by the angler between a fish which is just landed flapping on the hook, and the same fish when dead a few hours afterward.

Angling for green trout is carried on in various ways, according to the tastes and ideas of the different followers of this fine sport. The fish is a ready biter at live baits, or baits made to counterfeit life on a line skillfully handled. They will rarely ever bite at a dead bait, and will scarcely ever rise to the cast of an unskillful angler, whatever bait he uses. In the bayous west of the city they are caught by 'Cadien fishermen in the following manner: The fisherman has a long rod, on the end of which is a short line baited with a little bit of red flannel and a small bunch of mallard or teal feathers tied on two or three small hooks. The fisherman sits in the bow of a pirogue; another man in the stern of the same boat slowly and noiselessly propels the craft with a paddle. The two, having started out before sunrise, go slowly down a favorite bayou, which is partially covered with plats of duckweed or water-lily. The fisherman occasionally bobs his bait in the clear spaces among the water-grasses, while all along the bayou can be heard the snapping of the trout, goggle-eyes and perch as they capture their prey of minnows, dragon-flies or aquatic insects. Before the fisherman in the bow of the pirogue returns, numbers of snaps will also have been made at his "bob," which the fish apparently mistakes for some clumsy insect and, striking at it, is taken in. In this manner an humble fisherman often captures several dozens of splendid green trout in a single morning. On a cloudy day the sport pursued in the manner noted may be carried on all day, but in bright, clear weather it only lasts for a few hours in the morning and may be enjoyed for an hour late in the evening. The following is the most sportsmanlike manner of capturing green trout.

The angler has a slender and supple rod about fifteen feet in length, with a line about one foot shorter, or of such a length that he can swing the bait back to his right hand without the necessity of reaching for it and frightening the fish by useless movement. The line should be delicate and strong, and should have a small float on it, the hook baited with active live minnows, which are not always easily procured, but when obtained are the most killing baits. The angler, quietly walking *near* the edge of the bayou, stream or pond in which he may be fishing, throws as noiselessly and with as much dexterity as possible into the most likely places, and according to his skill (taking it for granted that fish are in the water) will be repaid. In this manner the skillful angler enjoys right royal sport, and takes into little account such petty annoyances as mosquitoes, deer ticks and red bugs when he surveys the accumulating trophies of a faithful rod. . . .

PART II

From the Land of Dreams

SKETCHES

When Hearn joined the staff of New Orleans's struggling *Daily City Item*, its editor wisely gave him free reign to indulge his literary fancy. Soon he was drawing on local topics to produce whimsical essays of a kind never before seen in the Crescent City. He even illustrated them with his own simple and folksy woodcuts. Readers were delighted. Circulation soared.

If Hearn's "sketches" had a purpose it was simply to entertain. But by sharing his distinctive vision of the city he put words to feelings many local residents shared but had not articulated. In this way, he helped shape how New Orleanians viewed themselves and their world. His repertoire of local idiosyncrasies lives on in scores of books and films on New Orleans today.

Voices of Dawn

A dreadful sound is in his ears. —Job XV, 21.

There have never been so many fruit-peddlers and viand-peddlers of all sorts as at the present time—an encouraging sign of prosperity and the active circulation of money.

With the first glow of sunlight the street resounds with their cries; and, really, the famous *Book of London Cries* contains nothing more curious than some of these vocal advertisements—these musical announcements, sung by Italians, negroes, Frenchmen, and Spaniards. The vendor of fowls pokes in his head at every open window with cries of "Chick-EN, Madamma, Chick-EN!" And the seller of "Lem-ONS—fine Lem-ONS!" follows in his footsteps. The peddlers of "Ap-PULLS!" of "Straw-BARE-eries!" and "Black-Brees!"—all own sonorous voices. There is a handsome Italian with a somewhat ferocious pair of black eyes who sells various oddities, and has adopted the word "lagniappe" for his war-cry—pronouncing it Italianwise.

He advances noiselessly to open windows and doors, plunges his blazing black glance into the interior, and suddenly queries in a deep bass, like a clap of thunder, "LAGNIAPPA, Madam-a!—la gniap-PA!" Then there is the Cantelope Man, whose cry is being imitated by all the children:

"Cantel-lope-ah!
Fresh and fine,
Jus from the vine,
Only a dime!"

There are also two peddlers, the precise meaning of whose cries we have never been able to determine. One shouts, or seems to shout, "A-a-a-a-ah! SHE got." Just what "SHE got" we have not yet been able to determine; but we fancy it must be disagreeable, as the crier's rival always shouts— "I-I-I!—I want nothing!" with a tremendous emphasis on the I. There is another fellow who seems to shout something which is not exactly proper for modest ears to hear; but he is really only announcing that he has fine potatoes for sale. Then there is the Clothespole Man, whose musical, quavering cry is heard at the distance of miles on a clear day, "Clo-ho-ho-ho-ho–ho-ho-ho-se-poles!" As a trilling tenor his is simply marvelous. The "Coaly-coaly" Man, a merry little Gascon, is too well known as a singer to need any criticism; but he is almost ubiquitous. There is also the fig-seller, who crieth in such a manner that his "Fresh figs!" seems to be "Ice crags!" And the fan-sellers, who intend to call, "Cheap fans!" but who really seem to yell "Jap-ans!" and "Chapped hands!" Then there is the seller of "Tow-wells" and the sellers of "Ochre-A" who appear to deal in but one first-class quality of paint, if we dare believe the mendacious sounds which reach our ears; neither must we forget the vendors of "Tom-ate-toes!" Whose toes? We should like to know.

These are new cries with perhaps three exceptions;—with the old cries added to the list—the "calas" and the "plaisir" and other Creole calls, we might "spread out" over another column. If any one has a little leisure and a little turn for amusement, he can certainly have plenty of fun while listening to the voices of the peddlers entering his room together with the first liquid gold of sunrise.

Char-Coal

Black—coalle—coaly!
Coaly-coaly; coaly-coaly; coal-coal-coal.
Coaly-coaly!
Coal-ee! Nice!
Coaly-co-o-oal!
Cha'coal!
Twenty-five! Whew!
O charoc-oh-oh-oh-oh-oh-lee!
Oh-lee!
Oh-lee-e!
[You get some coal in your mout', young
 fellow, if you don't keep it sheet.]
Pretty coalee-oh-ee!
Char-coal!
Cha-ah-ah-ahr-coal!
Coaly-coaly!
Charbon! Du charbon, Madame! Bon
 charbon? Point! Ai-ai! *Tonnerre de Dieu!*
Char-r-r-r-r-r-rbon!
A-a-a-a-a-w! High ya-a-ah! High-yah!

Vingt-cinq! Nice coalee! Coalee!
Coaly-coal-coal!
Pretty coaly!
Charbon de Paris!
De Paris, Madame; de Paris!

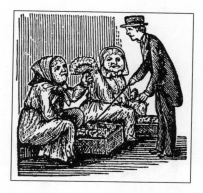

The Flower Sellers

They sit forever under the shadows—silver-tressed and ancient—calmly weaving their flowers into rainbow-tinted gifts for youth and beauty.

And I, gazing upon them impassibly weaving the bright blossoms together, dream of the ancient Norns of Scandinavian legends—

Weaving the warp and woof of human destinies;—measuring terms of life as the stems of flowers are measured;—

Mystically mingling Evil with Good; Joy with Sorrow; Love with Grief;—tints of Passion with tints of Melancholy,—even as in a bouquet the hues of a hundred flowers are blended into one rich design.   Evanescent as the beauty of Woman are the colors of the flowers;—volatile their drowsy-sweet odors as the perfume of youth.

And thou, O reader, when though receivest, from the wrinkled hands of the Norns, who measure the lives of summer blossoms, an odorous gift for the ivory hand of thy living idol,—

Knowest thou that the gift is in itself a voiceless symbol of the fragility of all which thou worshippest?

Fair girl, a mightier Norn than that grey woman who silently weaves her flowers in the sun, has measured the golden thread of thy life:—

Though sweeter than the presence of Esther, bathed six months in palm-oil and rich odors before entering the chamber of the King—thy youth will pass like the breath of a flower;—

Though thy lips be as those of the Shulamitess, they will wither and crisp and wrinkle like the petals of a scarlet blossom;—

And as a flower between the leaves of a book, thou shalt be pressed between the marble covers of that ponderous volume in which Death, who is, alas! strong as Love, keeps the weird record of his deeds.

Cakes and Candy

She buyeth little cakes and selleth them to the little children.

Sometimes, ... she maketh them herself, and great be the cunning skill wherewith she prepareth the little dainties.

Then whenever little boys and girls get five cents to spare, they go to spend it at the cake-stand.

Children are the only customers—it is childhood supporting age.

Some of these ancient women have been selling dainties to little ones through two generations.

Many of the infants who trotted to them with five cents in their dimpled fingers are now grown-up men and women.

Others have now children of their own, and these too toddle to the good old woman with their nickels.

So that the old woman knoweth much of the history of families and the vicissitudes thereof.

During the epidemic of 1878, the business was not good. Little ones who used to buy suddenly ceased to come. And many came no more.

And the aged woman, sitting in the sun, smiled not as was her wont, and spake less than usual.

Wondering what had become of her little darlings.

Of many of them she never heard again:—and never will hear, and she wonders still.

So that, asking her one day where was little fair hair baby, whom we had not seen since last summer, she answered only—*Bon Dieu, li connais!*

Washerwomen

The washerwoman is a creature of which there are various species.

There is the washerwoman who works very cheap; but who never gives you back your own socks or undershirts; and the exchange is invariably to your disadvantage.

There is the washerwoman who makes it a rule of life to wash off all the buttons of your shirts and pull all the strings off your drawers and never dreams of putting them on again. This washerwoman charges like sixty.

There is the washerwoman who puts the thinnest kind of starch in your shirts, so that they become limp rags after being worn an hour. This kind of washerwoman gets rich fast. She has an eye to business.

Then there is the washerwoman who promises to bring your clothes at a certain hour, and never does so under any possible circumstance.

But there is also the good, honest, industrious, prompt, and motherly or sisterly washerwoman who puts buttons on your shirts and darns up your socks and does not charge extra therefor.

We looked for such a washerwoman for ten years before we found her. Now we wouldn't give her up for a small fortune.

If washerwomen have their faults, it must be remembered they have their trials and afflictions. Many of them have been spoiled by bad treatment.

There is no sort of thieving so contemptible as to beat one's washerwoman; but we doubt if any other class of working-people are so much victimized.

It is pretty rough to labor hard all the week, working until one is ready to drop down with fatigue; obliged to watch changes of weather; obliged sometimes when a clothes-line breaks to do all the work over again; obliged to furnish one's own soap and starch and blueing;—

And then to carry the work to those who ordered it,—all nice and clean and pretty,—expecting to receive the just reward of one's labor;—

But, on the contrary, to receive nothing but lying promises and sometimes even hard words;—

And then to go home hungry; and to sit down and cry because there is not a cent in the house!

No wonder the poor women often say it is better to be a slave than a washerwoman.

No wonder that washerwomen should sometimes feel disgusted with their work, and cease all effort to try and please, and tear off buttons and pull off drawer strings with rage and fury.

It isn't their fault if they are not always angels.

Des Perches

Daily he goeth out beyond the limits of the city into lonesome and swampy places where copperheads and rattlesnakes abound.

And there he cutteth him clothes-poles, wherewith he marcheth through the city in the burning glare of the sun; singing a refrain simple in words but weird in music.

A long and lamentable sobbing cry, as of one in exceeding great pain and anguish.

So sorrowful in sooth that the sorrow of the city drowneth the sound and sense of the words,—the words chanted in ancient Creole patois—

And we, listening to the cry, gave ourselves up to solemn meditation;

Dreaming of the cries of anguish that arise when a clothes-line, heavily burdened with its snowy freight, falleth upon the mud;

And the poor little woman sitteth down and crieth till her eyes are red, ere she findeth courage to commence all over again, and mend the clothes-line.

It is to avoid these things that men should buy clothes-poles.

Des perches!

And hearing the ancient negro once more lifting up his voice, we also remembered.

That often in the dead waste and middle of the night, while meandering about the black backyard,

We were suddenly and violently smitten on the nostrils by the treacherous clothespole, hidden between lines of white sheets and shirts that waved their empty arms like spectres.

Also, we remembered how the wet linen fell upon our sacred person; and how we tried to lift up the clothes-pole again but could not;—

For the cunning of the washerwoman was not given to us.

But notwithstanding these things we do bless the clothes-poles, and him that sells them, remembering the service they do to the indispensable washerwoman.

Des perches — des perches!

Shine?

The bootblacks, notably those posted on our big thoroughfares, always address passers-by according to a graduated scale of estimation of rank and wealth, made up from exterior observation. It runs up *crescendo* in about this fashion:

To a seedy-looking man—"Shine?"

To an energetic, simply-dressed man—"Shine, Mister?"

To a tolerably well-dressed man—"Shine 'em up, Captain?"

To a well-dressed man—"Shine this morning, Colonel?"

To a very well-dressed man—"Will you give me a chance this morning, General?"

The Man with the Small Electric Machine

Br-r-r-r-r-r-r-r-r-r-r-r-r-r-r-r-r-r-r-r-r!!

—"Want to try it, sir. Take hold of these two handles. Lower down, please! Now! Tell me when to stop."

Br-r-r-r-r-r-r-r-r-r-r-r-r-r-r-r-r-r-r-r!

—"One hundred and eighty-six,—seventy-five above the average!"

Then the man goes away, thinking he has done very fine, and looking proud of himself.

The machine sometimes runs only to a certain figure, say 150. Almost anybody can hold on till the needle goes clear round. Then the man shuts off the current, pretending he is going to put on more force.

The visitor holds on again, and is told that he has stood an electric pressure of three hundred.

Then the same thing is done again until he believes that he has stood nine hundred!

Everybody is told that he goes above the average.

No average people ever visit the Man with the Single Electric Machine. They are all giants and giantesses,—all people of mark.

Everybody is flattered and pleased until they pay a visit to the man who has a Big Electric Machine, which one must be a hippopotamus to vanquish, and then they find that they are not so far above average as they supposed.

Under the Electric Light

A sound as of the boiling of a prodigious pot, the bubbling of a witches' cauldron, under the electric light. Such was the music of the insect orchestra at the West End last evening.

It was worth the price of the trip alone to behold the spectacle,—a veritable realization of the swarm of flies that afflicted the land of Egypt.

The insects hung about the lights like thin clouds about the face of the moon. The sky was actually obscured at intervals. But the little creatures did not bite. They only uttered their wailing music, and formed a living canopy above the heads of the people, like the canopy formed by the enchanted birds above the head of Soliman in Arabic tradition.

They entered Micholet's restaurant uninvited, and pounced like Harpies upon the viands, spoiling what they could not carry away.

Whether the wind brought them or the lights or the music, we can not positively say; but at ten o'clock they disappeared as if by magic.

It seems not improbable that the electric lights exercise a certain fascination upon them, and perhaps also the sound of music; for mosquitoes have a fine ear for harmony.

At all events they came to the fort together with the crowd of human visitors, and thinned away as the people began to withdraw, after having enjoyed the evening as much as anybody, and secured all the privileges and pleasures and luxuries of the resort without paying therefor. The phenomenon was certainly a most curious one.

— —! — —!! Mosquitoes!!!

The mosquito is the most cunning of all living things which fly. She sees by night even better than by day. She knows by heart all the holes in every mosquito curtain in the largest hotels. She is a first class judge of dry goods, and distinguishes afar off the quality and thickness of socks and stockings. She poketh her little bill through the finest material that modern machinery can spin.

We say "she" because our tormentors are females; the male mosquitoes are respectable, well behaved boys who remain where they are born. Only feminine malice can explain the ingenious capacity for torment possessed by the mosquito which plays vampire both by night and by day.

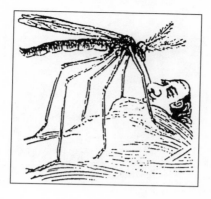

When a mosquito lights softly with a subdued scream of triumph on the end of your nose, or any other end, she always keeps one leg hoisted high in air, so as to be ready to flee at a moment's notice. It is only when she puts that leg down that you have any chance of ending her pernicious existence.

Another matter in which biting mosquitoes show their feminine characteristics is their dislike of tobacco.

But they also possess feminine patience, and will wait hours for a smoker to finish his pipe. Then they will take ample revenge.

Nevertheless mosquitoes have their uses.

If it were not for mosquitoes we should all become terribly lazy in this climate. We should waste our time snoring upon sofas or lolling in easy chairs, or gossiping about trivial things, or dreaming vain dreams, or longing after things which belong to our neighbours, or feeling dissatisfied with our lot, instead of humping ourselves and scooting around and making money. Idleness is the mother of all vices; and mosquitoes know this as well as anybody, and not being lazy themselves they will not suffer us to be lazy.

It is for this reason that they hum around only in summer when everything is lazy and drowsy,—especially on one of those quiet summer days when everything is so silent that one can hear the cocks crowing to each other at long distances, and answering each other like sentries in the old cities of Spanish-America. For in winter time the cold forces us to make ourselves useful as well as ornamental.

And so, even while we curse, let us also bless the mosquitoes, for making us move about and root around, instead of dreaming our lives away.

The Festive

He maketh ghostly noises in the dead waste and middle of the night.

He hath a passion for the green and crimson of beautifully bound books, and after he has passed over them they look as if they had been sprinkled with a shower of vitriol.

He loveth to commit suicide by drowning himself in bowls of cream or stifling himself in other eatables or drinkables.

When trod upon he explodeth with a great noise.

In this semi-tropical climate he sometimes attaineth to the dimensions of a No. 12 shoe.

He haunteth printing offices, and fatteneth upon the contents of the editor's paste-pot, and upon the bindings of newspaper files.

He haunteth kitchens and occasionally getteth himself baked and boiled.

Five hundred thousand means have been invented for his destruction; but none availeth.

If a house be burnt down to the ground he will momentarily disappear; but when the house is rebuilt, he cometh back again.

His virtues are these: He amuseth young kittens, who practice mouse-hunting with him. Also he is the deadly enemy of the *cimex lectularius*. He is used for medicinal purposes.

But none care to recognize his good qualities, because of the mischievous and disgusting propensities, and all creatures wage unrelenting war against him, and nevertheless he continueth to propagate his species and to drown himself in cream.

The Wolfish Dog

The dog days approach and the dogs continue to abandon themselves to midnight orgies with a sense of perfect security.

The dog ordinance is not put into execution except in the case of fine aristocratic dogs belonging to rich people.

Those fine dogs are all well brought up and know how to mind their own business. It is the nasty, snarling, mongrel, vulgar dog which ought to be looked after—the dog which never minds his own business and is always poking his nose into other people's affairs.

The currish and vulgar dog shows his wolfish instincts at night, when he and his brethren render certain streets like unto the streets of Constantinople. Woe be to the wayfarer who walks without a big stick in such neighborhoods after dark. The dogs circle about him in packs and threaten to tear him limb from limb. . . .

The Go-at

The go-at, like other quadruped of the domesticated kind, possess some vices and many virtues.

His name is derived from the former; his value from the latter. It is his habit to go-at unsuspicious people whose presence is distasteful to him; and his head, when used as a battering ram, is found to be extremely hard.

His virtues consist in the capacity of his stomach, in which he resembles the cassowary; and a nanny-goat has a peculiar power of extracting rich milk from brown paper, oyster cans, sawdust, old blacking-boxes, wearing apparel, straw hats, rags, garbage, old bonnets, and newspapers.

A nanny-goat well furnished with brown paper and oyster cans will give more milk than a creole cow.

Everybody that is poor has a goat because it costs nothing to keep them; and they pay well nevertheless for the privilege of being kept.

They represented in other days a peculiar New Orleans industry. There were goatherds here who used to make a good living by selling goats' milk.

Goats are usually good natured in this city, except toward wicked boys and wicked dogs. These do not like goats.

But they are not often troubled with scruples of conscience. They will eat up a thousand-dollar garden with as much ease and nonchalance as they would a roll of grocery wrapping paper.

Consequently goats are regarded by owners of luxuriant shrubberies and gardens with a sinister and suspicious eye.

Goats are valuable to a community in spite of certain odoriferous peculiarities; and it would be much better if there were fewer cats and dogs and more goats.

Cats pretend to catch mice and rats; but they sleep all day and scream like lost souls all night, and do other nasty things which goats never do, and it costs a great deal to keep them in beefsteak and other grub. They are, moreover, ridiculously fastidious about their provisions.

One good rat-trap is worth more than 100 cats.

Dogs are good sometimes; but they are more often bad. They get mad sometimes and bite people; and they go on sprees all night long, and get into disgraceful fights on the street corners.

Goats go at people only under certain justifiable circumstances, and the consequence is not hydrophobia, but merely an inability on the part of the victim to set down with comfort for a few days.

They eat whatever they can get and are thankful for it, and they help poor people to live through hard times. They are not beautiful; but they are good, practical creatures, which only need a little mild discipline to keep them within the bonds of usefulness and virtue. They do not get fits, like cats, or diseases like dogs; for, living like anchorites, they are blessed with constitutions of advancement and the stomachs of ostriches.

God bless the go-at!

The Alligators

None discover aught of beauty in them; yet they were once worshiped as gods.

They were not of this world, in truth, but of another—the Antediluvian world of monsters and dragons and vast swamps broader than continents— where there were frogs larger than oxen, and ferns two hundred feet high, and alligators longer than the serpent slain by the army of Regulus.

The Ichthyosaurus, the Pterodactyl, the Megatherium, the Plesiosaurus— have passed away with the Antediluvian world.

This strange being, with its dull cuirass marked like the trunks of the primeval tree-ferns, still endures—although new strata have been formed since the birth of his species—although the monstrous vegetation of the swamps in which his ancestors crawled has been transformed to beds of coal!

Alligator, crocodile, or cayman—it matters little—they alike belong to the age before which history began.

And looking upon them, must not one dream of the sacred Ganges and the most ancient Nile—of South American rivers that flow by dead palaces buried in the vegetation of virgin forests—of dead civilizations—of Karnac and Thebes and Crocodilopolis—of catacombs and broken-limbed colossi—of empires and of races that have been swallowed up by Time? The world has changed, but the Giant Lizard changes not.

Wet Enough For You?

The sun showed his face yesterday; and the people of New Orleans began to think that the world was coming to an end.

But even as they were trying to accustom their eyes to the light, it became dark again, and the floodgates of heaven were reopened.

So that people talked about rain-areas and barometers and colds and rheumatisms even worse than before.

And the rain it raineth every day.

Web-Footed

The above represents the physiological changes which will probably make themselves manifest in the pedal extremities of our people, if this weather continues. Nature adapts animals to their surroundings. Animals that inhabit swamps are web-footed. Let us prepare ourselves to become web-footed.

A Creole Type

It is a little curious how the old Creole element preserves its ancient customs and manners in the very heart of the changes that are going on about it. At half-past nine or ten o'clock the American city is all alive—a blaze of gas and a whirl of pleasure. The old French town is asleep; the streets are deserted; and the shadow of a pedestrian makes a moving black speck against the moonlight on the pavement only at long intervals. Creoledom wakes up as slowly and cautiously as possible; and has not fairly begun to enter upon the business of the day until the sun has warmed the streets. The comparatively new generation of American citizens, when brought into contact with this older population, is utterly unable to understand the difference of character; and shuns as much as possible the transaction of business with it—which contents the Creoles perfectly well. They seem to tolerate those who understand them, and to abominate those who do not, and propose to live in the good old way as long as possible—marrying and giving in marriage, aiding one another in a good brotherly way, and keeping themselves to themselves. If there is one virtue they possess remarkably, it is the virtue of minding their own affairs—which, alas! cannot always be said of all other people who dwell in New Orleans.

Nothing, perhaps, can be funnier than the contrast of character brought out by the attempt of a stiff-mannered stranger to do business with a typical Creole, especially if the latter be of the fair sex. Let us imagine, for example, the episode of renting a house to a foreigner—somebody whom chance or curiosity has prompted to seek quarters in the old-fashioned part of the city. The stranger is a little phlegmatic; the woman is as much the opposite as any human being could well be—a little dark, tropically dark, but quite attractive, with magnetic eyes, an electric tongue, and an utter indifference to those ordinary feelings which prompt landladies to play the agreeable;—proud as a queen, and quite as determined to show her own individuality as the stranger is to conceal his own. She has a nice little house; and the stranger would like to rent it. She would also like to rent it; but only according to her own original idea of conditions, and she would never think of concealing her inmost feelings on the subject. She is determined that nobody shall impose upon her, and that fact she proposes to explain very forcibly forthwith; the stranger appears to be a good sort of man, but appearances are so deceitful in this wicked world!

She—"Ah, yes monsieur, I have a nice little house. Let me beg of you to wait a moment until I open the other door, so that you can enter my parlor."

He—"But what is the rent of the house?"

She (in a voice sweeter than the sweetest honey)—"One minute!—this way, monsieur—come in; be seated, if you please."

He—"But what is the rent of—"

She (shutting the door, and placing herself before it like a statue of animated bronze, and suddenly changing the sweet voice for a deep and extraordinarily vibrant alto)—"Ah, now, monsieur, let us at once understand one another. I have a nice little house. Good! You want a nice little house. Good! Let us understand one another. In the first place, I do not rent my house to everybody, monsieur. Oh, no, no, NO!!" (*crescendo*).

He—"But what is the rent of—"

She—(imperiously terrifying him into silence with a flash of her black eyes)—"Do not interrupt me, monsieur. Three things I require from a tenant. Do you know what the first is? No?–then I will tell you. Cash, Cash, Cash! (*crescendo*)—right here in my hand—in advance—ah, yes, all the time in advance."

He (very timidly)—"Yes, certainly—I know—of course!—I expected;—but what is—"

She (in a voice like the deepest tone of a passionately agitated harp)—"Attends, donc, monsieur. The second thing which I require from a tenant is a guarantee that he will stay. Ah, yes! I am not one of those who rent houses for a week, or a month, or six months. Mon Dieu, non! I must have people who STAY, STAY, STAY (*pianissimo*); and they must stay a long, long time. You must not come to me if you want a house only for—"

He (with a last and desperate effort, which happens to be partially successful)—"O madam, I want to stay for a number of years in the house, if I take it; but I cannot take it until I have seen it."

She—"You shall see it, monsieur, you shall see it (parenthetically). Now the third thing which I require from a tenant is absolute cleanliness, absolute, absolute! No spitting on the walls, no dirt upon the doors, no grease upon the planking, no cochonnerie in the yard. You understand me, monsieur? Yes!—you shall see the house: these are the keys."

He—"But what is the rent of—"

She (frightening him into motionlessness by a sudden gypsy-like gesture)—"Ah, monsieur, but I cannot trust you with these keys. No; my servant shall go with you. I cannot have all the doors of my house left open. No; I have had too much experience. My servant shall go with you. She shall bring me back my keys. Marie! come here! Go, monsieur, see the house!"

He (resignedly)—"Thanks, but may I ask what is—"

She (with a superb gesture of withering disgust and another of terrible determination)—"Do you not know, sir, that I would rather shut the house up until the last day of the world than rent it to the canaille! Ah! the canaille! Monsieur! Ah! the canaille, the canaille!"

(These last words, with an inexpressible look of horror upon her face, which would make the stranger laugh if he were not afraid to laugh.)

He—"And the rent is—"

She (sweetly as a rose-fed nightingale)—"Twenty-five dollaire to a responsible party, monsieur."

The stranger is by this time fairly mesmerized. He has listened to a sermon, heard an oration, received a reproof, watched a most marvelous piece of natural acting by a beautiful woman, and felt his own will and purpose completely crushed out of him by the superior vitality and will-power of this wonderful creature, whose gestures, graceful as a bayadère's, seemed to weave a spell of magnetism about him. He sees the house; pays faithfully in advance; gives proper recommendations; and never forgets the three requisites which his landlady taught him as forcibly as though she had burned the words into his brain with a red-hot iron.

Complaint of a Creole Boarding-House Keeper

O la canaille! la canaille! All time after dis I will make dem to pay in advance.

De first dat I have, say he vas a capitaine. I know not if he vas a capitaine; but he vas a misérable. After he have eat and sleep here six week and not pay me, I tell him, "Monsieur, I must money have."

He say: "Madame, you take me for tief?"

I say: "Monsieur, it is right dat you pay; I have wait long time assez."

He den say: "I learn you how to speak me in a manner so much insolent. *Now*, I not pay you till when I be ready, and I not hurry myself."

"Go out from my house!" I say.

"I go out, madame, from your dirty house when it me please"—dat how he speak me. And I could not force him to part till when I had take all de furniture out from his room. He owe me not more as seventy dollaire!

...After, I have one Frenchman, I tink him well elevated—le coco. He nail his valise on de floor for make me tink heavy; and he dispar one night—owing me forty-nine dollaire! I find noting in his valise only one *syringe*.

...After, I have two married. Dey pay me enough well, until when de woman run away wit some older man. Her husban' stay till when he owe me eighty dollaire. After, he go too; and write me letter as dis:

"Madame, I cheat you of eighty dollaire; and I not wish only I could cheat you of eighty thousand dollaire. It was for cause of you dat my wife have run away."

After, I find out she not was his wife.

...Den I have a sick man. He fall on de banquette in face of my house, and I take him in to nurse. When dat he get well he tell me he vas one professor of langedge. He eat and sleep here four mont; and first he pay a little. He complain much from noise. He vas what you call nerveaux—so like I was oblige for to make my daughter walk witout shoes in naked foots; and we to to speak in dumb and deaf language by fear of make him trouble. He smoke in de bed and burn de cover; also he break de pot and de cradle-chair, and after, de window, an' de armoir an' de—vat you call de pendule;—he let fall ink on de carpet, and he spit tobacc' on de wall, and he vomit in de bed. But I noting say, as he not 'ave baggage;—ainsi, wen he owe me forty dollare I not want turn him out for dat I get my money more late. When at de end I tell him to go out, he tell me he have receive a checque and pay me on Monday. But I nevaire see him after. He owe me one hundred and sixty-seven dollare—and seventy cent vat I lend him for medicine to buy.

...After, I have one woman, species of camel (espèce de chameau) and one doctor, her husband,—Monsieur! all dat was of abominable (tout ce qu'il y avait d'abominable). She pretend to be—and you call dat?—sage femme; and he is not so much doctor as my cat; but for all dey doctor me for two hundred and fifty dollare, and I not ever obtain of it not one sou.

...After, I have tree familee—all vat vas of rough and ugly; for one mont I not receive of rent. So I serve to dem notice of quit. But dey tell me dey not me pay nevaire, and not quit until when I make law-suit. Eh bien, de rent of de house vas not more as fifty dollare, and de law cost me perhaps one affair of more like one hundred dollare. Ainsi, I quit de house, an' leave dem all dere to do like dey would please. But before dat I could leave, dey steal me two buckets, and one stove, and one broom, and one clock, and one iron, and one coffee-mill, and one hen, and one leetle cat vat I much vas fond of, and one plate, and some linen of womans vat to me not belong.

The Boarder's Reply

Est-ce que vous vous fichez de moi? 'cré nom! No: I not no more pay my rent in advance, because dat I have not of fait in permanence of businesses in Orleans.

Wen I am first come I take myself a room in de Rue Bourgoigne. Dey have in first floor one bear, one parrot, and two macacs and several of cats of Malta; and wen dat I enter myself to pay my rent, I see all dat to move itself about inside. De woman was of color—vat you call one mulatresse—and I pay in advance—like one animal!

After vat I have live in de house six week, I not to her owe noting, but she me owe one affaire of ten piastres more as my rent vat I ever pay in advance;—for dat she me come near every day for borrow one quarter of piastres or one half of dollaire, or two dollaire or until even tree dollaire, and she smile and make so many funny bêtises dat I not could her noting refuse. After dat I be dere two mont, she owe me two mont of room in more as I have her pay in advance.

After a little of time I not see more de little beasts;—she have sell de macacs and de bear for herself obtain money. And I vas well content dat de parrots not dere vas more;—it vas true little demons vas not allow to nobody to repose himself.

One night I not come home until twelve past, and I not hear noting of noise. After I enter into my room, and I find noting inside—no bed, no chaise, no armoire—noting only my linen-dirty and my blue trouser-old. All de house empty; all de rooms naked—personne in its inside. She not have not pay her rent—so, by consequence, dey seize demselves de furniture and have clean out de house—of such way as I find myself have to sleep on one floor much hard and all vat dere vas of dirty. And never again I not noting see of de woman of color vat owe to me near twenty of dollaire.

... But I stay in de house, for one oder woman of color enter in morning; and she have much of furnitures. I explique myself to her, and she tell me in Creole—"To s'ré resté 'vec moue, mo to donné belle chamb' garni asteur, pou' même prix." And I myself dere install. She ask me dat I pay in advance; and I not like for refuse, like I not have time for look for more rooms. C'est égal, say to myself I.

Sometime she clean well my room; and sometime she not it clean not of all. Sometime she permit to strange mens of color dat dey enter my room; and dey permit demselves to lie upon my bed wen dat I was out in way to make a walk. I not was content; but could noting do, for dat I have pay in advance.

One day she desire to buy a miroir, and she ask me dat I pay, for dat she not have of money; and she tell me her husband me pay wen he have de Saturday next arrive. I so pay, like one kind of beast vat I be; and before dat come de Saturday, one sheriff take all vat vas in all de house; and I not vas able, never already, to obtain vat she me owe. Also I since inform myself for as she had noting of one husband.

. . . I be myself disgusted; and I take myself room in house of one white woman, de vat me ask dat I pay in advance. After, she not me well treat. She take from out my room one cradle-chair and much more of furniture, de vat she say vas not put inside but for ornament. She have children vat tear my book, and one locataire steal my trouser, and one steal tobacco, and one steal my soap. Never I could myself keep a little of soap. I have dere one essuiemains for more as two week.

I pay first of mont after. Second of mont I come home, and I see a—vat you call vente à l'encan; and one woman come to have take away my book—one affair of fifty book. Never can I arrive to procure again de money to me, nor even to find where live de woman vat have take my book.

. . . One time of more I pay in advance. De lady was of France, and she had de face beautiful and de heart good. She not me treat but too much well. I have rest in her house forever; but I not rest long. I pay my rent ever de fifteen of mont. I pay de fifteen of Avril. De sixteen, she die quick of vat you call mort subite. Never I see in it-not-matter-what-oder-country of tings pareille. Not again do I be so much beast for in advance to pay.

A Kentucky Colonel Renting Rooms

"Ah, one thing more—de name of monsieur?"

"Colonel Zachariah Mart—"

"Alors, alors, it must dat monsieur pay to me of advance."

"But why in thunderation did n't you tell me at first?"

"Ah, because monsieur did not tell to me vat he be one Colonel. I not have, monsieur, of fait' in peoples military. Dere vas one Captain vat swindle me of sixty dollaire, one Major vat cheat me of fifty dollaire, one Doctor Military of t'irty-nine dollaire, one Colonel of one hoondred and elefen dollaire. And dere vas one General vat ask me de oder day—"

"Yes, ma'am; but that don't apply to the Kaintucky—"

"Attendez donc, monsieur, until I be finish! De General say he nevaire pay of advance, but only all de tree mont. And den I tell him I not can do. He go way; so after I hear vat he owe tree hundred and ninety-seven dol—"

"But d——! —excuse me, ma'am! I'll shell out for a month in advance!"

"One mont! Den, monsieur, I not ever can believe dat you ever have be one Colonel!"

"Well! I'll be Jehovahly—...!!!"

"Pauline! en haut-là! Descendez donc pour m'araranger cette affaire. Je suit tout embaralifocotée!!!

The Restless Boarder

He come to me fust of de mont, an' say, "Madame, I must another room; I not can live in dat for de noise abominable vat make dose infants." And I reply him, "Monsieur, choose youssef vat room mos' you like."

Den he tell me to get him arrange one room on t'ird floor. I get room right morning. Evening he say, "Madame, I not can take dat room; I take back oder." So I change him de tings once more.

Next week he say, "Madame, I must anoder room obtain; I not can suffer more de noise of devils vat dose infants make." So I arrange room on fourt floor. In de evening he tell me his mind be change—dat he not more want dat oder room. So I have all for to move back again.

After, he come to me de tirdeent and say, "Madame, you get to me one oder room, dat for I not leave de house. No more can I suffer de noise infernal and ootrajeous vat make dose infants detestable." I say, "Monsieur, take vonce vat room you deseer, and leave me tranquille."

He den take room on front floor; but in middle night he go down gentle de stair and put all tings updownside, and go back in ole room. Den in de morning he tell my domestique to him aid, an' for more as five hour dey walk up de stair an' down de stair carr'ing much of valise an' of trunk an' of ole pantalons an' of washing-basin an' of pillow—and of pot. De vat me disguss.

At de end all at sudden he take oder room, and dere install him well— vat I much surprise. But not more be I surprise ven dat I see him go out from de house, away, an' one negro vat carry him de valise. And much be I content for dat I see it.

But I not long content.

De morning after I see a procession vat enter de house one time more—de negro, de valise, and he, and one boy vat carry him de tobacco-pot and boots. So he go up de stair, and put back himself to his ole room. Not ever in-no-matter-vat-place see I such tings.

Den he come to me an' say, "Madame, so some one ask after me, tell dem dat I am one mad." "Certainlee," I reply, "I will so dem tell, for dat it be true." But I not understand vat he mean precise until one hour more. Den come to house one man who ask if dat he vas not live here.

"Ah, oui," I say, "he live here, but he is one mad."

"So it is," he reply, "I tink; for as he come to pay me one mont advance, and never not again come back. So you give to him back his monis."

Den I be sorry for dat I tell he vas one mad; for dat I see he not one mad at all;—but only one devel vat desire torment all person vitout paying for his vickedness. So I give to him de money, also one notice of quit. He take money, but notice of quit he not take; and I not can yet guess how for dat I be get rid him.

Furnished Rooms

I not understan' for vat some peoples ask of prizes so much elevate for dere garneesh room—I much mistruss myself of such peoples;—I believe dey all be of vat mos' vicked.

Firs', I go for ask prize of room in my street of de ——, for dat I observe of sign "Room garneesh" at door. Dey to me show one room well garneesh on t'ird floor—not big more as one cell of monk, an' I ask of dem de prize. Dey tell me de prize be t'irty dollaire by week. So dat I find myself much astonish, and I ask for see one oder of room. So dey show to me one oder of room on second floor; an' I ask de prize—ven dey tell to me forty-tree dollaire by week. It be one room of behind; so I demand for dat I see one room of before for curiosité. Den dey tell me vat de room of before be fifty dollaire for me, but for any oder one seexty dollaire by week. So I begin to take dem for mads; and dey ask me if I not deseer to see one room of de firs' floor, an' I say, "No—deveel! Vat for I see one sacré room vat cos' one hoondred dollaire?—better as I buy to myself one hoondred dollaire of mustard!" "Not one hoondred of dollaire," dey tell—"not more as one seventy-five dollaire."

And ven dat I save myself from de house away, dey laugh like all vat be of mos' idiot. Seventy-five of dollaire! Seventy-five tousand of deveels!

After I go see again more of house, and I fine myself all astound. For de room vat I see of mos' good market dey ask seexteen dollaire by week— it be vat you call one attique. Oder rooms not be more as seventee, eightee, one hoondred dollaire by mont—always in advance to pay. Vat mos' I have not understan' be dat I not see one room rent in all of house—not even one. It make me to tink vat dey not ever be rent, and of more, vat de peoples not vant dat dey be rent,—even for dat dey have sign "Room garneesh." And I tink dey all vat be of mos' vicked—for dat how can dey make for pay rent vit room empties vitout as dey be not honeste? It is so as I tink, and I tink also dat de poleeses not ought—but de poleeses! de poleeses!—to vat good dat I talk of de poleeses!

Ghosteses

MIDNIGHT IN AN ULTRA-CANAL PENSION.

You not know vat be dat noise of foots up de stair. Dat be de ole man vat die in my house ago ten year.

I see him now in my t'ought, 'sleep in ze berceuse; afraid to go to his room for cause of vat you call *farfadet*—goblin and ghosteses.

He was very, very old, and he see always of tings vat not exist. He be much torment by goblin and ghosteses vat valk all roun' de house in de night; an' he say it vas one curssed house and one cursed city. He tell me dat people dressed like vas dress since one hoondred year come in his room in de middle of de night; dat he lock de door but not could dem keep out; dat dey sit silent and make at him face horrible and not speak and not make shadow on de floor.

Den he commence to us avake. In de middle of de night he knock at mine door and say,—"Monsieur, mount to my room for dat dere be one man dead in my chamber." So I mount and look and not see no man dead. "He go himself away," say de ole man, "for dat he hear you on stair. But he have make stop my clock and my vatch." And I see dat de clock and de vatch not more march,—I not know how.

After dat he often tell me vat dere be in his bed dead vomans; and dat dead beoples him look at trough de vindow. So he become afraid more to bed go, and ven he mount he not himself sleep, but valk all night on de gallery, one lantern in his hand, and shoes all vat be of mos' heavy for drive away ghosteses—ta-ta—tatatatata—all de long of de night. Much also he sing in de night and swear for dat dis be one curssed country of ghosteses. Also he swear at proprietor of house; for dat he not chase ghosteses.

So it arrive at las' dat not person in de house could himself to sleep go, and dat all de vorld begin to demselves much fatigue. Den dey construct one goblin of vatermelon and inside one candle light; and dey it put on stick and one sheet of bed to make look like fantome. So it come to arrive dat ven de ole man march himself he see one goblin march more horrible dan he have before ever see. So he let fall his lantern—vat cost tirteen dollar—, and try to descend stair for me avake for dat I chase him de goblin. But he fall de top to bottom of stair, and make himself much of hurt. Never again he not speak and soon he be dead, and no person much sorry himself. But it vas much vicked!

It ten year since he be dead; but all de night he march like he march oder time. No one afraid; de ghost of de ole man not make much hurt to personne!

A Creole Journal

I read to you of my journal-book—how he do:

Jan. 1—Mon cher, lend to me one little affaire of ten dollaire, and I pay de 1st, wit good intress. Ah! you be good friend. I be possess of money; but for now I have of de expenses large.

Feb. 1—Mon ami, I much sorry for dat I not can you pay to-day; but soon I you pay wit grand intress. One mus' not ever angry himself for ten dollaire.

March 1—Mon bonhomme, I not can you pay, unto wen as I have of money. You be too much of impatient. I much sorry for dat I ever ask of you money.

April 1—Monsieur, I not have ever suppose dat you like more one miserable ten dollaire as my friendship. I not ever more ask of you one faveur, I not like you speak me so.

May 1—For wat you lend me money like one Imbecile? I more like owe one tousand dollaire as ten—for dat I more be respected. I be tramped upon for dat I owe one dirty ten dollaire. You be pay some one day.

June 1—You are one Insolent! If suppose for dat I do owe to you one miserable dollaire! Is it dat you are one beggar and have of hunger, for dat am I to be ask all time? You take me a one Imbecile? Not have I tell you I pay wen I can? I not will myself suffer more to be insult for one dirty dollaire.

July 1—To-morrow I can you pay. I hope to ask dat you do me one little faveur—to ask dat friend to you dat he give me one place like collecteur or secretaire.

August 1—I not pay until I can one place obtain wen.

September 1—I not pay until wen sugar come in de market...

December 1—I not pay ever at all. I not you noting owe. I not suffer dat I be eternal ask for money. I not speak you not more. Go to devvel for you ten dollaire, for dat I not slap you de visage.

Ultra-Canal

"Is the old man in?"

"Ah! De ole man! He not been live here since more as tree year. He have lef all his furnizer here; but I not know vat him become. I tin vat he lose himself."

"Lose himself?"

"Yes, I tink he lose to himself. Monsieur not speak Français? No? *Eh bien* I make try you explain, zough I not good English speak."

"You see, he have to him ze brain attack, I zink, of recent. He lose all vat to him belong. Some time he lose coat, some time pant, some time shirt,—

all time night-key. I vas oblige for him order more as tirteen night-key, for vat I make him to pay. He live in one kind of dream—*il s'embêtait*—he embeast himself much—he seem all day like vat you call *sonambule.*"

"Yes, yes! Well?"

"*Eh bien!*—some time he put on tree pair pant. Some time on hot day he put him on ze overcoat. One day I see him try to put on to him ze pant for ze shirt. He have put to him ze arm in ze leg of ze pant; an' he swear *sacre rouchi* for dat he not could put on—"

"Yes, I understand. But what has become of him?"

"*Attendez un peu.* I tell one. One oder day he not have any clothes on, an' he try to find his key, an' he swear at tailor for *sacre charogne* for dat he not have made him pocket vat he can easy find. He forget vat he not be dress. Den he lose to him money all time vat make him angry much. One time he take by mistake coat vat not to him belong, and take it to tailor for dat he put tail to it; an' he has to pay to de oder man, of wich he spoil de coat."

"Yes. But where is —"

"Vait—I explain you. He lose everyting—handchef, towl, pockbook, monee, key—all time. One domestique he employ only for find vat he los'; and domestique run himself away, for dat he not more can so hard work endure."

"But, for God's sake, what has become of him?"

"Monsieur, I not can you tell. He go out one morning, and I not have hear or see of him after. His furniser an' all be in my house. He have pay of advance. He owe me notings. He have not ever come back. No one have see or hear. I be satisfy vat himself he lose—like as he lose every oder ting—vat he lose never more find. Vell, he lose to himself. He never more himself find. *Que voulez-vous?*

An Ultra-Canal Talk

(Stranger approaches an ancient Creole house, rings the bell, and beholds the landlady. Landlady says something. Stranger loquitur in surprise:)

"He is dead?"

"Oh, oui, monsieur; 'e ees det, and dere is not person sorry. 'E vas all vat vas of most troublesome. All ze time vat 'e liv, I have troubles vit peoples vat come to see 'im. For everybody know 'im to be one mad, who like to spend his money in foolishness and bêtises. After his son die he not have nobody for 'im look after. So dey come to sell to 'im litograph, vich dey make 'im to believe to be oil painting by great master; an' 'e pay one, two, tree hoondred dollare for litograph vich cost no more as fifty cent. Ven I tell 'im no buy, 'e tell me I vas one ignorant and one imbecile vich have not appreciation of art. After, ven 'e fin' out not oil painting, 'e call zem cursed camel—two-hump camel, an' heap of robber (tas de voleurs) and charogne; an' 'e wish dem all blast by ze feefty tousand flames of hell. So zat 'e not talk of oder tings—only of robbers and liars and assassinses.

"Ven zey could not more sell to 'im play-bills as oil-painting of great master, zey sell to 'im of daub as great water-color picser. 'E pay seventee dollare for vat cos' not more as tree cent each. Ze frames wort perhaps six dollare! At las' 'e fine out how zey 'im swindle; an' 'e talk of robber an' murderer an' camel of two hump. And 'e say dis country ze most curssed country vat exist—all vat be of mos' canaille and racaille and charongne.

"Ven as dey not could no more to 'im sell picser, zey sell to 'im vat you call céamique, old cup and saucer and dish vat wort not more as ten cent and vat dey tell 'im from China come. 'E pay t'irty dollare, as dey tell 'im very 'ard for find. But 'e find one day undaire bottom of cup one word like 'BIRMINGHAM'; and 'e swear so dreadful vat I 'ave me de finger in de ear to put. After 'e not talk more but of tief and liar, and of assassin and of infames and infant of ze devill and children of 'ell—vich 'e wish open and swallow zis sacré charogne de pays. And 'e also say more vat I not you dare racount.

"Also dey sell to 'im boots vat sole vat of paper was made and coat vat was glued together, anot ever could 'im prevent to pay fiftee dollaire for ze coat an' ten dollaire for ze boot. Sixtee dollaire! And ven zat ze boot go into pieces an' ze coat tomble into rag, 'e could not enough to swear in such manner zat people hear 'im more as tree block. Ze same night 'e swear all night so as no one could fall 'imself to sleep. 'E said tings so terrible zat I stuff to me de ears wit cotton; but all same I hear 'im swear until ze sun get 'imself up.

"After, dey sell 'im furniser, armoire, table, bed, chair for mahogany—vat was pine covered wit sometings. 'E pay tree hoondred dollaire! Ze table was only glueded and one day it burst ven he dere put to 'im de elbow; and ze bed also only glueded together. 'E go to law, but ze oder peoples much vas rich, and 'e lose five hoondred dollaire wit lawyer an' 'e soon tire of law.

"After zey sell to 'im vine vat not vas vine and fisky vat not vas fisky an' 'e pay like one millionaire zough 'e not have much of money. Not ever could I prevent 'im to buy or to be swindle."

"Did he say anything before he died?"

"I tink so! 'E not sick—never sick at all. 'E die sitting in ze berceuse. For 'e vas very old, very, very much old. And some one came to sell to 'im sometings. 'E try to get up; but not could, and 'e not let me to help 'im. So I not help 'im; and 'e say, 'Mon bon Dieu, have me mercy—Oh, le tas de canaille! Pray you for me! Oh, les sacrés voleurs! Lord have me pity!—Charogne de pays!—I believe me in de heaven for ze good! Oh, de cursed wretch!—Holy angel 'elp me up!—Oh, ze camel of two hump!—Oh, mon Dieu, miséricorde!—zis be one infame country of assassin and robbaire!' So 'e pray an' so 'e swear. So 'e die wit—'Charogne de pays!' And ven ve sell of 'im ze picsers for vat 'e pay one fortune, dey bring not more as tree dollaire an' t'irdeen cent. But 'e 'ave near one hoondred years ven dat 'e be det. I tink 'e ought have to be det."

Why Crabs Are Boiled Alive

And for why you not have of crab? Because one must dem boil 'live? It is all vat is of most beast to tell so. How you make for dem kill so you not dem boil? You not can cut dem de head off, for dat dey have not of head. You not can break to dem de back, for dat dey not be only all back. You not can dem bleed until dey die, for dat dey not have blood. You not can stick to dem troo de brain, for dat dey be same like you—dey not have of brain.

Creole Servant Girls

Creole colored servants are very peculiar. They are usually intelligent, active, shrewd, capable. They generally perform well whatever they undertake. They are too intelligent to be dishonest, knowing the probable consequences. They comprehend a look, an expression, as well as an order; they will fulfill a wish before it is expressed. They see everything, and hear everything, and say nothing. They are consummate actresses, and can deceive even the elect. They can ape humility, simulate affection, pretend ignorance, and feign sorrow so that the imitation is really better than the reality would be, and serves the same purpose. They can tell a lie with the prettiest grace imaginable, or tell a truth in such a manner that it appears to be a lie. They read character with astonishing quickness, and once acquainted with the disposition of their employer will always anticipate his humors and make themselves pliable to his least wish. They are the most admirable waiting-machines which ever existed;—absolutely heartless, without a particle of affection or real respect for an employer or his children, yet simulating love and respect so well that no possible fault can be found with them. Once initiated into the ways of a household, it is seldom necessary to give them an order. They know everything that is required, and everything is done. If regularly paid and well treated, they will remain in a family for a generation. They demand a great deal of liberty when not actually employed, and will not remain in a house when they are not wholly free after working hours to go out or in as they please. They know everything that is going on, and a great deal more than they have any business to know. If they consider their employer discreet, they will furnish him unasked with the strangest secret news. They possess family histories capable of doing infinite mischief, but seldom make use of them, except among each other. To strangers they are absolutely deaf and blind—neither bribes nor promises will extort information from them when asked by persons they do not know. They can keep people at a distance without offending; and become familiar to any extent without making themselves disagreeable. They can be superlatively vicious, and yet appear to be supremely virtuous. They can also be dangerous enemies—

and there is no denying the fact that their enmity is to be dreaded. They speak several languages, and sing weird songs. They will do anything that any imagination can conceive for money; and are very friendly, indeed, as long as the money holds out. They are actually very cleanly, oddly superstitious, and very diligent. They have a way of working very hard without appearing to work, and of doing little or no work while appearing to be working themselves to death. Their virtues are simply the result of a great natural shrewdness, which appears to have been handed down from old times, with the Latin blood that beats in the veins of French-speaking quadroons and mulattresses. They will not steal; but they have no moral scruples when the infringement of morality does not involve public disgrace and legal punishment. They do not like American or English-speaking people; and it is probable that none but Creoles know how to manage them. The type is fast disappearing; but it certainly affords one of the most extraordinary studies of human nature possible to conceive.

The Creole Character

It was not a difficult job to put up a wooden awning about the corner grocery—two stout Irishmen would have done it in twenty-four hours; but the corner grocery man was a Creole, and he hired four Creole carpenters. So they took three weeks to do it, and they have not done it yet. Ce pas baptême katin, travail comme ça; and they did not propose to work themselves to death. Life was too short. We went round the corner to look at them. Beautifully did they saw the boards and with exquisite grace did they hammer the nails—vrais poseurs they were; and then they wiped their brows and sighed, and rolled up cigarettes and went into the grocery to get a light. There they met Aristide and Jules and Albert and Alcée and Alcibiade, and they all took a drink and cracked awful jokes together. Then the carpenters went out again, and climbed upon the half-finished awning, and grinned at a swarthy young woman passing, who had a graceful air of deportment and a complexion like a statue of bronze. Then they laughed at one another; and it began to rain, so they went down and smoked some cigarettes, until it was time for dinner. After dinner they worked very slowly, deliberately, and artistically for ten minutes, until a mad dog came running down the street, which they chased for half a mile with surprising energy and astounding strength of purpose.

And when they came back they recounted their heroic deeds to an admiring crowd in the grocery, and to the washerwoman round the corner, and the Italian fruit-woman over the way, and the wife of the rival grocery-keeper on the other side, and the two lazy policemen on the beat, and the cook of the neighboring boarding-house, and the confectioner at the southeast corner, and the shoemaker at the northwest corner, and the butcher at the southwest corner, and the coal woman just round the northeast corner, and the coal woman just round the northeast corner. Then they got ready to work; and commenced to hammer away to the air—

> "Madame Caba,
> Tiyon vous tombe;
> Madame Caba,
> Tiyon vous tombe;
> Ah, la reine,
> Piye la su' moi;
> Madame Caba
> Piye la su' moi;
> Madame Caba
> Chandelle 'te teigne," etc."

Then it got dark, and they took another drink and went home. And it was even so next day also, and the next, and so for twenty-three days; and that awning still remains in a wild and savage condition of incompleteness.

All Saints!

As All Saints' Day approaches, a little village of peasant and lemonade stands grows up in the neighborhood of the cemeteries; and those who take charge of the tombs are busy laying in a great stock of shells and sand.

"Want any sand, sir?—any shells?"—a boy asks, as he passes by with his wheel-barrow.

And the stranger shakes his head, muttering,—"No: *my* dead are not here!"

The abrupt question makes him dream, perhaps, of a cemetery beyond the great waste of waters, where there are tombs inscribed with the same name as his own.

Or, perhaps, the query may seem like a reproach: "What!—hast thou no dead loves?—no tombs to decorate?—no graves to weep over?"

And dreamingly, he mutters to himself: "My dead ones are nameless;—my heart is their place of burial;—not with whispering shells and white sand can I make love-offerings, but only with those living thoughts and words which are as incense offered up to the memory of what has been loved and lost."

"Sand, sir? shells?" Life in the midst of death; activity in the shadow of the eternal rest; speculation upon human affection; profit upon grief;—is it not the great melodrama of all human life upon a small scale that we watch at the gates of the cemetery?

Does Climate Affect the Character of People?

If climate can affect the physiological conditions of man and change the ponderable or physical, why may it not the imponderable or moral? Character like climate ranges latitudinally, and we find greater homogeneousness in peoples from the East to West than from North to South.

One great and striking peculiarity of southern nations is their want of unanimity. Why? is beyond our ethnological research; but, that they usually are at variance is proved by the history of the Greeks, Italians, Spaniards, French—look back at the revolutions in France since '93—the Mexicans, and, to close the list, behold the Louisianians! With the greatest possible need for unanimity, dissentions rage, with reason and common sense urging the necessity of concert of action, we see three or four tickets in the field. With vital necessity for prompt action, we dally with circumstances and foolishly expect to win. With craft, unanimity, vigilance, and mercilessness personified in one party against us, we let the golden moments glide by, in stubborn determination to carry out our own individual views.

Why is this? Is it that we as a people are unworthy to be freemen, and fit only to be slaves to some tyrant power—its hewers of wood and drawers of water? Or is it that as Southerners we have received from Pandora's box the fatal gift of dissension and upon fate rests the blame? If it be possible to unite, let there be union for the common good.

The City of Dreams

Latterly it has been said that if New Orleans has any special mania which distinguishes it from other cities, it is the mania of "talking to one's self." It were useless to deny so widely recognized a fact as the propensity of people in New Orleans to perambulate their native streets conversing only with themselves. And strangers visiting us have said: "The people of New Orleans are inclined to madness; they converse continually with themselves, which is a sign of insanity." Is it that the people are being driven mad by stupid legislation and business losses and outrageous taxes? God only knows! But they do talk either to themselves or to viewless beings or to the sleepy shadows that fling jagged bits of darkness across the streets on sunny days.

They are comparatively many, these lovers of solitary musing; and usually seek the quiet of the most deserted streets—those streets to which the Secret Police of the East give the ominous name of *dead streets*. Perhaps one might say as well, *streets of the dead*.

At one time we took a special interest in watching those wandering and murmuring spirits. They are of various ages; but most generally advanced in years. The action of the younger men or women is usually quick and nervous; that of the older, slow and meditative. The former often speak angrily as if brooding over some wrong; the latter, rather in sorrow than in anger. All of which is quite natural and to be expected from those who talk to themselves.

What do they talk about?

That is a matter not always easy to find out. The hard echo of a brisk footstep on the pavement, even the sudden fluttering of a leafy shadow, seems often sufficient to break the reverie; the speaker looks about him like one awakened from a dream, gazes with a half-timid kind of suspicion at those who pass by, as if fearing to have been overheard; and walks off at a quicker gait. To study the character of these people perfectly, one must wear rubber shoes.

It would be cruel to wear India-rubber shoes for such a purpose; it would also be despicable. Therefore we cannot fully answer the question— What are they talking about?

But occasionally the most innocent passer-by cannot fail to catch a word or two—sometimes strangely full of meaning, sometimes meaning-less. We have heard such words. Occasionally vast sums of money were mentioned—billions, quintillions!—a sure sign that the speaker was finan-cially stripped, and had little hope of favors from the goddess Fortuna. Sometimes we heard odd curses—men cursing themselves, and others, nameless places and nameless people, unknown memories and unknown misfortunes. Sometimes they spoke cheerfully, and laughed to themselves softly;—but this was seldom, very, very seldom.

Before the epidemic we fancied that the majority of these conversa-tions with airy nothings were upon the subject of money. Indeed most of the fragmentary mutterings which reached us seemed related to dreams of wealth—wild, vague, and fantastic—such dreams as are dreamed by those who have lost all and hope for nothing, but who seek consolation in the splendor of dreams of the Impossible.

Then came the burning summer with its burning scourges of fever;— under the raw, merciless, dizzy sunlight, and the pitilessly clear infinite of warm blue above, the mutterers still wandered the silent streets, seeking out the bits of shadow, as Arabs oases in a world of yellow sand;—and they talked more than ever to themselves and to the shadows, to the vast void above and to the whispering trees that drooped in the mighty heat.

So the months rolled dryly and fiercely by; the sun rose each day with the same glory of angry heat; and the sky glowed each evening with the glare of molten brass. And the talkers became fewer; but they seemed to talk much more than they ever had before done. They talked to the black streamers that fluttered weirdly at the handles of muffled bells, and to ghostly white things hung to cottage doors, and to the long processions that rumbled ominously toward the Places of Tombs.

Sometimes it seemed that one heard a sound of sobbing—stifled sob-bing; as if a man were swallowing a bitter grief with bitter determination—

but this was perhaps imaginary; for there were so many strange sounds in that strange summer that no one could well trust his ears.

The summer waned; and yet it seemed at last as though the number of those who talked to invisible things became greater. They *did* become greater in number. There was no doubt of it remaining before the first cold wind came from the far North, boisterous and wild as though suddenly freed from some Arctic enchanter. And the numbers of the mysterious ones waxed greater.

Then at intervals their words fell upon our ears; and it seemed that the character of them had undergone a change—no longer expressing ideas of wealth. They had ceased to speak in our hearing of money. They spoke of the dead—and muttered remembered words uttered by other tongues—and asked information from waving shadows and white walls regarding people that God only knows anything about.

Perhaps they remembered that the only witnesses of some last interview were the same white walls and waving shadows. And the shadows lay there at just the same angle—well, perhaps, the angle was a little sharper—and they were waving just as dreamily as then. And perhaps a time might come in which all Shadows that have been must answer all questions put to them.

Seeing and hearing these things, we somehow ceased to marvel that some people dwelling in the city of New Orleans should speak mysteriously and hold audible converse with their own thoughts; forasmuch as we, also, dreaming among the shadows, spoke aloud to our own hearts, until awakened by an echo of unanswered words.

A Dream of Kites

Looking out into the clear blue of the night from one of those jutting balconies which constitute a summer luxury in the Creole city, the eye sometimes marks the thin black threads which the telegraph wires draw sharply against the sky. We observed last evening the infinitely extending lines of the vast web which the Electric Spider has spun about the world; and the innumerable wrecks of kites fluttering thereupon, like the bodies of gaudy flies—strange lines of tattered objects extending far into the horizon and tracking out the course of the electric messengers beyond the point at which the slender threads cease to remain visible.

How fantastic the forms of these poor tattered wrecks, when the uniform tint of night robs them of their color, and only defines their silhouettes against the sky!—some swinging to and fro wearily, like thin bodies of malefactors mummified by sunheat upon their gibbets—some wildly fluttering as in the agony of despair and death—some dancing grotesquely upon their perches like flying goblins—some like impaled birds, with death-stiffened wings, motionlessly attached to their wire snare, and glaring with painted eyes upon the scene below as in a stupor of astonishment at their untimely fate.

All these represented the destruction of childish ambitions—each the wreck of some boyish pleasure. Many were doubtless wept for, and dreamed of afterward regretfully on wet pillows. And stretching away into the paler blue of the horizon we looked upon the interminable hues of irregular dots they made against it and remembered that each little dot represented some little pang.

Then it was natural that we should meditate a little upon the vanity of the ways in which these childish losses had been borne. The little owners of the poor kites had hearts whose fibre differed more than that of the kites themselves. Some might weep, but some doubtless laughed with childish heroism, and soon forgot their loss; some doubtless thought the world was all askew, and that telegraph wires ought never to have been invented; some, considering critically the question of cause and effect, resolved as young philosophers to profit by their experience, and seek similar pleasures thereafter where telegraph wires ensnared not; while some, perhaps, profited not at all, but only made new kites and abandoned them to the roguish wind, which again traitorously delivered them up to the insatiable enemies of kites and birds.

Is it not said that the child is the father of the man?

And as we sat there in the silence with stars burning in the purple deeps of the summer night above us, we dreamed of the kites which children of a larger growth fly in the face of heaven—toys of love and faith—toys of ambition and of folly—toys of grotesque resolve and flattering ideals—toys of vain dreams and vain expectation—the kites of human Hope, gaudy-colored or gray, richly tinseled or humbly simple—rising and soaring and tossing on the fickle winds of the world, only to become entangled at last in that mighty web of indissoluble and everlasting threads which the Weird sisters spin for all of us.

The Tale of a Fan

Pah! it is too devilishly hot to write anything about anything practical and serious—let us dream dreams.

We picked up a little fan in a street-car the other day—a Japanese fabric, with bursts of blue sky upon it, and grotesque foliage sharply cut against a horizon of white paper, and wonderful clouds as pink as Love, and birds of form as unfamiliar as the extinct wonders of ornithology resurrected by Cuvieresque art. Where did those Japanese get their exquisite taste for color and tint-contrasts?—Is their sky so divinely blue?—Are their sunsets so virginally carnation?—Are the breasts of their maidens and the milky peaks of their mountains so white?

But the fairy colors were less strongly suggestive than something impalpable, invisible, indescribable, yet voluptuously enchanting which clung to the fan spirit-wise—a tender little scent—a mischievous perfume—a titillating, tantalizing aroma—an odor inspirational as of the sacred gums whose incense intoxicates the priests of oracles. Did you ever lay your hand upon a pillow covered with the living supple silk of a woman's hair? Well, the intoxicating odor of that hair is something not to be forgotten: if we might try to imagine what the ambrosial odors of paradise are, we dare not compare to anything else;—the odor of youth in its pliancy, flexibility, rounded softness, delicious coolness, dove-daintiness, delightful plasticity—all that suggests slenderness graceful as a Venetian wineglass, and suppleness as downy-soft as the necks of swans.

Naturally that little aroma itself provoked fantacies;—as we looked at the fan we could almost evoke the spirit of a hand and arm, of phantom ivory, the glimmer of a ghostly ring, the shimmer of spectral lace about the wrist;—but nothing more. Yet it seemed to us that even odors might be analyzed; that perhaps in some future age men might describe persons they had never seen by such individual aromas, just as in the Arabian tale one describes minutely a maimed camel and its burthen which he has never beheld.

There are blond and brunette odors;—the white rose is sweet, but the ruddy is sweeter; the perfume of pallid flowers may be potent, as that of the tuberose whose intensity sickens with surfeit of pleasures, but the odors of deeply tinted flowers are passionate and satiate not, quenching desire only to rekindle it.

There are human blossoms more delicious than any rose's heart nestling in pink. There is a sharp, tart, invigorating, penetrating, tropical sweetness in brunette perfumes; blond odors are either faint as those of a Chinese yellow rose, or fiercely ravishing as that of the white jessamine—so bewitching for the moment, but which few can endure all night in the sleeping-room, making the heart of the sleeper faint.

Now the odor of the fan was not a blond odor;—it was sharply sweet as new-mown hay in autumn, keenly pleasant as a clear breeze blowing over sea foam:—what were frankincense and spikenard and cinnamon and all the odors of the merchant compared with it?—what could have been compared with it, indeed, save the smell of the garments of the young Shulamitess or the whispering robes of the Queen of Sheba? And these were brunettes.

The strength of living perfumes evidences the comparative intensity of the life exhaling them. Strong sweet odors bespeak the vigor of youth in blossom. Intensity of life in the brunette is usually coincident with nervous activity and slender elegance.—Young, slenderly graceful, with dark eyes and hair, skin probably a Spanish olive!—did such an one lose a little Japanese fan in car No.——— of the C. C. R. R. during the slumberous heat of Wednesday morning?

Les Coulisses *(The French Opera)*

Surely it cannot have been a poet who first inspired the popular mind with that widely spread and deeply erroneous belief that "behind the scenes" all is hollow mockery and emptiness and unsightliness;—that the comeliness of the pliant limbs which move to music before the starry row of shielded lights is due to a judicious distribution of sawdust; and that our visions of fair faces are created by the magic contained in pots of ointment and boxes of pearl powder of which the hiding places are known only to those duly initiated into the awful mysteries of the Green Room.

No; the Curtain is assuredly the Veil which hides from unromantic eyes the mysteries of a veritable Fairy-World—not a fairyland so clearly and sharply outlined as the artistic fantasies of Christmas picture-books, but a fairyland of misty landscapes and dim shadows and bright shapes moving through the vagueness of mystery. There is really a world of stronger enchantment behind than before the scenes; all that movement of white limbs and fair faces—that shifting of shadowy fields and plains, those changing visions of mountain and wold, of towers that disappear as in tales of knight-errantry, and cottages transformed into palaces as in the "Arabian Nights"—is but a small part of the great wizard-work nightly wrought by invisible hands behind the Curtain. And when, through devious corridors and dimly-lighted ways—between rows of chambers through whose doors one catches sudden glimpses of the elves attiring in purple and silver, in scarlet and gold, for the gaslight holiday among canvas woods and flowing brooks of muslin, mystic, wonderful—thou shalt arrive within the jagged borders of the Unknown World itself to behold the Circles of bright seats curving afar off in atmospheres of artificial light, and the Inhabitants of those Circles become themselves involuntary Actors for the amusement of the lesser audience, then verily doth the charm begin. . . .

Strange! How the mind wanders in this strange place! Yet is easier to dream of two thousand years ago than to recollect that thou livest in the material present—that only a painted ceiling lies between thy vision and the amethystine heaven of stars above, and that only a wall of plastered brick separates thee from the streets of New Orleans or the gardens westward where the bananas are nodding their heads under the moon. For the genii of this inner world are weaving their spells about thee. . . .

There is an earthquake of applauding, the Circles of seats are again hidden, and this world of canvas and paint is tumbling about thy ears. The spell is broken for a moment by Beings garbed in the everyday attire of the nineteenth century, who have devoted themselves to the work of destruction and reconstruction to whom dreamers are an abomination and idlers behind the scenes a vexation of spirit. Va t'en, inseq' de bois de lit!

Aye, thou mayest well start!—thou hast seen her before. Where?—when? In a little French store, not very, very far from the old Creole Opera House. This enchantment of the place has transformed her into a fairy. Ah, thou marvelest that she can be so pretty; nor Shakespeare's Viola nor Gautier's Graciosa were fairer to look upon than this dream of white grace and pliant comeliness in the garb of dead centuries. And yet another and another Creole girl—familiar faces to the dwellers in the Quaint Places of New Orleans. What is the secret of that strange enchantment which teaches us that the modest everyday robe of black merino may be but the chrysalis-shell within which God's own butterflies are hidden?

Suddenly through the motley rout of princes and princesses, of captains and conspirators, of soldiers and priests, of courtiers and dukes, there comes a vision of white fairies; these be the Damosels of the Pirouette. Thou mayest watch them unobserved; for the other beings heed them not; Cophetua-like, the King in his coronation robes is waltzing with a pretty Peasant Girl; and like Christina of Spain, the Queen is tê-à-tête with a soldier. The dancers give the impression of something aerial, ethereal, volatile—something which rests and flies but walks not—some species of splendid fly with wings half-open. The vulgar Idea of Sawdust vanishes before the reality of those slender and pliant limbs. They are preparing for the dance with a series of little exercises which provoke a number of charming images and call out all the supple graces of the figure; it is Atalanta preparing to pursue Hippomenes; it is a butterfly shaking its wings; it is a white bird pluming itself with noiseless skill. But when the Terpsichorean flight is over, and the theatre shakes with applause; while the dancers shrink panting and exhausted into some shadowy hiding-place, breathing more hurriedly than a wrestler after a long bout—thou wilt feel grateful to the humane spirits who break the applause with kindly hisses, and rebuke the ignorance which seeks only its own pleasure in cries of encore.

And the Asmodean Prompter who moves the dramatic strings that agitate all these Puppets of mimic passion, whose sonorous tones penetrate all the recesses of the mysterious scenery without being heard before the footlights, resumes his faithful task; the story of harmony and tragedy is continued by the orchestra and the singers, while a Babel of many tongues is heard among the wooden rocks and the canvas trees and the silent rivers of muslin. But little canst thou reck of the mimic opera. That is for those who sit in the outer circles. The music of the many-toned Opera of Life envelops and absorbs the soul of the stranger—teaching him that the acting behind the Curtain is not all a mimicry of the Real, but in truth a melodrama of visible, tangible, sentient life, which must endure through many thousand scenes until that Shadow, who is stronger than Love, shall put out the lights, and ring down the vast and sable curtain. And thus dreaming, thou findest thyself again in the streets, whitened by the moon! Lights, fairies, kings, and captains are gone. Ah! Thou hast not been dreaming, friend; but the hearts of those who have beheld Fairyland are heavy.

French Opera

Toilets, perfumes, opera-glasses, librettoes, oysters, and wine, refreshments, and many other things.

Greatly rejoiced are these who deal in all those pretty things which add to the beauty of women under the gaslight.

Also those who fortify the stomach with good things late in the night and early in the morning.

Also the vendors of music.

Likewise the dealers in kid gloves.

Furthermore the owners of hacks and carriages.

Thus doth opera cause money to circulate and purses to grow fat.

Down Among the Dives: A Midnight Sketch

Dives, the very name sounds harsh to ears polite, and yet there are dives, and many of them, in this beautiful city of ours.

How the name originated is a mystery and yet it is full of meaning. What more appropriate word could be applied to those disreputable dens where bad men and worse women spend their days and nights? Those who have taken the fatal plunge, dove deep through the tide of propriety; deep, so deep into the perdition of inebriety and crime, that it is almost an impossibility to ever again rise to the surface.

In places of this kind it is often the misfortune of a reporter to lie thrown; but true to his instincts he takes advantage of his opportunities and never fails to note an item that would interest the reading public.

Last night, in company with an official escort, our reporter was piloted through narrow streets and alleys, over broken bridges and dilapidated banquettes. The streets were deserted, the houses dull and dreary looking. Not a ray of light, not a sign of life, all was darkness. A stately looking mansion, at last, was reached, and the musical sound of a bell announced to the inmates that visitors awaited without.

Keen eyes looked through the window lattice, the door was opened, a flood of light fell upon the pavement and the party entered the dive.

The parlor looked like a hospital for ancient and infirm furniture; the solitary picture on the wall appeared lonesome, and even the small statuette of George Washington, on the chimney piece, was minus a hand, evidently lost in a hard fought battle with some mercenary landlord.

The inmates, poor unfortunate women, crowded around the fire in the hearth, and looked as miserable as could well be imagined, for they did not attempt to deceive the officers with forced smiles, or try to conceal their sufferings.

One more step down the ladder of sin and the sound of a cornet mingled with sullen tones of the bass viol proclaimed a dance of some description.

What a sight! A long narrow room, a temporary bar erected in one corner, a crowd of negro men and women; and the orchestra suffices for a description of the ball room. The music strikes up, then men choose their partners, and the dance begins. Wilder and wilder grows the music, and the dancers freely respond to the strains, until heated up and waltzing around the room they appear like demons. How they turn and twist, kick and roll about and scream, even the spectators are inspired by the strange wild music, and mingle with the dancers. At last all is over, the music dies out with one long, low wail as if loath to leave the revelers, and for a moment the dance is discontinued.

This is the bright side of the dives—now for the dark. As the midnight orgies continue, the minds of the revelers by degrees become inflamed, from the frequent potations of the fiery beverage, and they are then seen as a set of fiery demons. Their dances become more weird, and weird and strange to say, while going through their contortions, no shouts escape from their lips. As this drunken revelry goes on a creaking noise is heard in the rear; a sudden cessation in the sport occurs, and all eyes are riveted to the spot whence the noise emanates.

Following the creak, a panel door in the rear opens; momentary darkness is seen beyond, then appears an unsuspecting stranger who, lured by the enticing eyes of an octoroon cyprien, is ushered in the room. This victim, pulled in by a secret entrance in the rear, has, through the wily ways of this saffron enchantress, been induced to become paralyzed by drink. Unable any longer to be judge of his actions, he is but a puppet in the hands of the Amazonian houri.

The grey dawn breaks, and in an unfrequented thoroughfare, the policeman coming on his beat, notices an object in a gutter; a closer investigation proves it to be the unsuspecting stranger, who, lured by the fascinations of the charmer, has been robbed of all his wealth, and thrown into the street. The detectives are placed upon the track, and after long and diligent search they at last find that one more unfortunate had been robbed down amongst the dives.

Fire!

The time used to be in New Orleans when people dressed up to go to a fire. It was an occasion for toilettes. But that has passed away, just like the pretty custom prevalent formerly with young Creole ladies of taking an evening walk without any other head-dress than their own beautiful hair, decorated with flowers.

Still, if you want to see real excitement at a fire to-day, it is in the Second District where you can see it. There, where everybody knows everybody else, and a fire breaks out in one of those funny little stores which line the old fashioned street, the whole population of the quarter seems to turn out *en masse*. And there is none of the roughness which often characterizes an American crowd. Everybody is accommodating—a good-natured curiosity mingled with an audibly expressed sentiment of anxiety and regret animates the throng.

When the fire is out, it is pleasant to hear the voices of the fire-men singing in the night, as they pass through the deserted streets in solid column.

It is the signal that the danger is over; the welcome news that all is well. "Sleep on, good folks!—pleasant dreams!—we are taking care of the good old city!"

Sometimes perhaps they do not sing. There is only a hurried trampling of feet. Their voices are lowered when they speak. And people feel anxious, and look out of the windows into the darkness. It is all well for the city. The fire is out. But the fire of a young life has gone out with it. Some brave boy has died at his post under the red rain of fire. And the singers can not sing, because their hearts are heavy.

That Piano Organ

The Man with the Piano Organ is the new sensation.

In the French quarter the multitude of children, servants, and people of all descriptions who throng about the organ is astonishing to behold.

They are more attracted, perhaps, by the puppets who move inside a glass house to the sound of the music than by the music itself.

The man with the Piano Organ has a pretty little wife who travels about with him, and who speaks Italian, French, and German with equal facility.

And they seem to be more or less of philosophers, these strangers, possessing a serious aspect while all about them are laughing at the puppets,—unconscious that they themselves are after all but puppets on a

larger scale, who dance to the music of all the passion and follies and hopes which agitate mankind.

Unconscious that the little puppets within the glass house are but silent mockeries of the large puppets outside.

Unconscious that the organ-player compels them to behold a satire upon themselves, and makes them also pay to see it.

And the lesson was well worth paying for, if it were properly appreciated.

A Creole Courtyard

An atmosphere of tranquillity and quiet happiness seemed to envelop the old house, which had formerly belonged to a rich planter. Like many of the Creole houses, the façade presented a commonplace and unattractive aspect. The great green doors of the arched entrance were closed; and the green shutters of the balconied windows were half shut, like sleepy eyes lazily gazing upon the busy street below or the cottony patches of light clouds which floated slowly, slowly across the deep blue of the sky above. But beyond the gates lay a little Paradise. The great court, deep and broad, was framed in tropical green; vines embraced the white pillars of the piazza, and creeping plants climbed up the tinted walls to peer into the upper windows with their flower-eyes of flaming scarlet. Banana-trees nodded sleepily their plumes of emerald green at the farther end of the garden; vines smothered the windows of the dining-room, and formed a bower of cool green about the hospitable door; an aged fig-tree, whose gnarled arms trembled under the weight of honeyed fruit, shadowed the square of bright lawn which formed a natural carpet in the midst; and at intervals were stationed along the walks in large porcelain vases—like barbaric sentinels in sentry-boxes—gorgeous broad-leaved things, with leaves fantastic and barbed and flowers brilliant as hummingbirds. A fountain murmured faintly near the entrance of the western piazza; and there came from the shadows of the fig-tree the sweet and plaintive cooing of amorous doves. Without, cotton-floats might rumble, and street-cars vulgarly jingle their bells; but these were mere echoes of the harsh outer world which disturbed not the delicious quiet within—where sat, in old-fashioned chairs, good old-fashioned people who spoke the tongue of other times, and observed many quaint and knightly courtesies forgotten in this material era. Without, roared the Iron Age, the angry waves of American traffic; within, one heard only the murmur of the languid fountain, the sound of deeply musical voices conversing in the languages of Paris and Madrid, the playful chatter of dark-haired children lisping in sweet and many-voweled Creole, and through it all, the soft, caressing coo of doves. Without, it was the year 1879; within, it was the epoch of the Spanish Domination. A guitar lay upon the rustic bench near the fountain, where it had evidently been forgotten, and a silk fan beside it; a European periodical, with graceful etchings, hung upon the back of a rocking-chair at the door, through which one caught glimpses of a snowy table bearing bottles of good Bordeaux, and inhaled the odor of rich West India tobacco. And yet some people wonder that some other people never care to cross Canal Street.

The Accursed Fig Tree

And seeing a certain fig tree by the wayside, He came to it, and found nothing on it but leaves only, and He saith to it: May no fruit grow on thee henceforward forever. And immediately the fig tree withered away. And the disciples seeing it wondered, saying: How is the fig tree presently withered away?—Matt. xxi., 19–20.

Perhaps some of our readers have noticed in the vicinity of the Presbyterian Church on South Street, a vigorous old fig tree, whose apparent lustiness annually offers a strange contrast to its unfruitfulness. It is not, however, wholly barren; for every summer the ground is strewn with its immature fruit; but no mortal eye has ever yet beheld a ripe fig upon that tree. Its crop yearly miscarries; and while the other fig trees groan under the weight of their luscious bearing, this mysterious tree beareth leaves only, or fruit bitter as the waters of Mara. For the tree has been cursed with an everlasting curse. And a friend of the writer, one who loveth the traditions of New Orleans, and whose mind is richly stored with legends of the old French and Spanish dominations, hath told us the story of the perpetual curse in these words:

"It was at one time my fortune to know a certain quaint old Creole gentleman, one of the old school;—a man of memories, who loved much to narrate the legends of the old French families, and who would have been a veritable mine of riches for the antiquary or the historian. With that reserve peculiar to the Creoles, however, the old gentleman seldom permitted strangers to approach him familiarly; and I know not by what curious luck it happened that to me—not a Creole,—he exhibited so much kindly feeling, and confided to me so many precious traditions.

"And one day it came to pass that he told me a strange legend concerning a certain fig tree near the church on South Street, a mysterious tree, which seems in very truth blighted by an undying curse.

"You may recollect that a great portion of good land in this city at one time belonged to the Jesuits, and was afterwards taken from them, after much queer litigation in which some lawyers made themselves great names. This land, the old gentleman told me, extended from the river west to a certain point in the heart of the city;—but unfortunately upon that day I happened to be in an unusual hurry, and contrary to my wont, omitted to note down the dates and localities of his narrative.

"The priests were finally dispossessed of the land; but one of them, a venerable man, refused to abandon his old home. It was found at least necessary to eject him by force; and he was placed gently but firmly without the building. For a little while he stood irresolute before the entrance, trembling with anger, yet loath to depart; and people who stood about the building drew near that they might observe his actions. And he suddenly lifted hand and voice, and cursed the land with a perpetual curse.

"'May no tree, growing upon thee,' he cried: 'ever bear fruit; no seed planted in the bosom ever produce a harvest. May a curse dwell upon the buildings, builded upon thee,—a curse upon the houses and upon the dwellers therein,—a curse upon their undertakings and upon their wealth,—a curse upon their lives and upon their hopes,—a curse upon their slaves and upon their beasts of burthen,—a curse upon the fruits of their labor and works done by the sweat of their brows,—forever and ever until the land shall be restored to the holy keeping of the church.' And the ancient priest, shaking the dust of the place from off his feet, went his way, and left behind him naught save the memory of his curse.

"Generations have passed away since then; yet no prosperity has ever been known by those who own property lying within the enchanted circle of the curse. Within that circle mortgages have fallen thick as a shower of snow flakes; but the new owners fail in their undertakings like the old. And the trees that grow there bear no fruit, nothing but leaves only.

"This was the story that the old French gentleman told me. After he had told it to me, I did not find time to visit him for months. A continued rush of business caused me to forget my old friend. At last came a lull, and I hurried to see him, hoping that I might be able to obtain from him full particulars of the legend, and make a note of many things which I had forgotten. But the quaint house was shut up; the green shutters were closed; and the handle of the door bell muffled with black streamers of the crape. I saw thereto attached a little white paper,—it bore the usual French death notice, headed with the sad word—*Decede*.

"The good old Creole gentleman had been filed away like some old legal document in a marble pigeon hole of the St. Louis Cemetery, and his memories sealed up with him forever. The tradition remains incomplete."

Home

We have all heard curious things said about the peculiarities of New Orleans; we have heard that it was a city where the sun rose in the west and water ran uphill; we have heard it spoken of as built upon a dunghill, and there is a Spanish proverbial expression about it still more uncomplimentary, often uttered by West India captains, which we dare not cite, even in the original. But yesterday we received a visit from an old resident of thirty years' standing, who in the course of a conversation summed up his opinion of New Orleans with the phrase: "New Orleans is a city where it is impossible to make a home for one's self without marrying. I have tried for thirty years to make a home here, and failed." And this observation set us to meditating whether this were, indeed, owing to any peculiarity of the city, or to that vague longing for the quiet comforts of a household which all bachelors feel as life creeps by and each succeeding winter adds its frost to their beards. To the latter, we trust; for we wish to think well of New Orleans.

There is one thing certain: a rich man who understands what the comforts of life are may make a home for himself anywhere without marrying. But rich men form exceptions to the general rule governing human lives, and we are constrained to consider the matter from the standpoint of those who are not rich, and who must expect for the greater part of their lives to work for others, however independent their capacity as artisans or talent as professional men may render them. The more sensitive their disposition and the more artistic their ideas, the more difficult, of course, must it be for them to obtain a home conformable to their desires whether married or unmarried. If unmarried, they may expect to have a hard time of it in any city, if compelled to live there for a number of years. Luckily for themselves, many such men are of wandering dispositions. They soon tire of a city; pack up and go elsewhere, after refusing good offers or neglecting first-class chances of becoming wholly independent by remaining. Being rolling stones, they gather no golden moss; and change of scenery and climate, new places and new faces, new friends and strange experiences become for them almost a necessity of life. These are the world's Bohemians. They are a class apart. They enjoy life, too, in a peculiar fashion which the generality of quiet people of regular habits do not understand. But there are many who, desiring to continue single, and obliged to live where fortune has cast their lot or run the risk of losing all and beginning the struggle with the world over again, do forever pursue after the chimera of a home, and cannot understand, until they have tried all possible expedients and suffered all varieties of disappointments, why they cannot make a home for themselves. To such as these, of course, the idea of a home is coupled with memories of the home of one's youth—cozy rooms, quiet, good fare, kindly attention, liberty to act and think, something to regret leaving, and to delight returning to of evenings;—a pleasant greeting, a dog barking with joy, a cozy chair by the fire, and a cat purring on the rug. And yet how one can obtain these things without a woman's ministry nobody has ever pretended to explain. A woman is the soul of home; and without her there is little more than furniture and brick walls there. She transforms and beautifies everything. You may pooh-pooh and hum-hum!—but you cannot explain how the comforts of a home—a home such as the term was explained to us in childhood—can possibly be obtained without the presence of woman. Without her one may be said to live at such and such a place; but to say that "he has his home there" is sheer humbug. He has no home!

Consequently, many really marry just to obtain a home—which is foolish enough, although the natural consequence of social conditions. We remember one case in this city—a young Frenchman who was continually changing his quarters for years, never being able to find rest or comfort in any one house. At first he had quite a number of effects; but these he gradually disposed of, because they proved serious impediments to his nomadic life, until at last his baggage consisted of a newspaper bundle and a box of matches. His marriage proved unhappy enough in the end. He drew an unlucky number in this great life lottery of ours. But to return to the point under considerataion: what home is there for men circumstanced like those we spoke of? Boarding houses do not offer any. Boarding-houses are good and necessary institutions—but there is no home life about them. No man who longs for home comforts can live in any one boarding-house beyond a certain length of time, or in a hotel. There is no privacy, no seclusion; one is always being brought into contact with persons whom one does not care to know, and obliged to endure things which one does not like to stomach. Life in a private family is better; but, of course, the private-family boarder is always made to feel that he is not one of the family, and the manner of making him feel it is not the most agreeable thing in the world. Renting furnished rooms and boarding in restaurants, of "boarding around" as they call it, is vanity and vexation of spirit, and costs about as much as hotel fare without rendering one any more independent. Furnished rooms!—Furnished rooms! It is an aawful, awful subject—too awful to dilate upon! Neither is there any stability about such a method of living. If one does find just what suits him, he can never tell how long it will last; but of one thing he must always be sure—that the better it seems the sooner something dreadful and unexpected is going to happen. And then?

Well, when you have become tired of boarding-houses and restaurants and furnished rooms, you may try renting or buying a house of your own and furnishing it. But a man must have something round the house, if it is only a dog, to keep him company. And he must also have somebody to take care of his rooms. If he gets a housekeeper, to avoid scandal he must get the oldest and ugliest woman he can find. And servants and others victimize the bachelors terribly. Moreover, everybody living near such a man will regard him as a lunatic or an original, and treat him accordingly. The hand of society is raised against the man who tries to live alone in a house of his own—unless he be very rich. Sometimes five or six bachelors get together, furnish a house, hire a housekeeper, and live a sort of club-life by themselves. But if they should fall out, the whole arrangement would prove more disagreeable than all the combined afflictions common to furnished rooms and boarding houses.

There is no consolation. To get a home, one must get rich or marry, and even then he may not be lucky enough to get it.

A Visitor

"Juan Guerrero y Márquez, su servidor de V."

There are voices which surprise by their sonority. The voice of the speaker, as he introduced himself, made us lift our eyes in surprise to his face;—it was a soft roll of thunder, the richest and deepest bass that had ever vibrated in the writer's ears. To have heard it without seeing the speaker would have compelled the idea that it came from a chest of prodigious depth, from the torso of a giant. Not so, however. The speaker was a young and rather slender man, firmly knit, but with more grace than apparent strength in his frame; not over tall, but with a bearing as proud as his Spanish name. He spoke with the refined accent of Madrid, and the words came from his lips with such a musical depth as when the longest strings of a great harp are touched by strong and skillful fingers. The face was characteristic—a true Latin face, with the strong keenness of the Roman eagle in its profile; eyes large and brilliant as a falcon's; eyebrows thick as mustaches, rising toward the temples, with a slightly sinister elevation; mustaches curling up toward the cheek-bones; and such a short black pointed beard as we see in the portraits of Velásquez. This handsome and daring face belonged to a beautifully formed head, covered with the blackest curls possible to conceive—the head of an antique Roman soldier set upon a columnar neck. With the clear bronze of his skin, no more striking type of the finest of the Latin races could have been asked for by a painter.

Artista español de los primeros, he had been traveling with a Spanish opera company through the West Indies, and enchanting the señoritas of

Havana with the magic of his marvelous voice. Now he wished to visit some distant relatives in one of the far South American republics—members of his own Spanish family and bearing his own name, but born under the Southern cross. He had never seen them; but strangely enough the ancestral family in Spain had maintained relations with its tropical children for a hundred years.

"And there is really a consul of that republic in New Orleans?" we asked in bewilderment; for, alas! we had never heard of him.

"¡Ciertamente, señor!"

So we went to find the consul. It was necessary, first, to find out who he was, and where he lived. The directory refused to yield up the desired information. Then we went successively to see a Spanish tobacconist and a Spanish wine merchant and a Spanish doctor and a Spanish apothecary and a Spanish journalist—who was not at home—and a certain Spanish lady who lives upon a street bearing the name of an ancient Spanish Governor.

It proved easier, however, to find who the consul was than to find where he resided. At one time we began to fancy that he was an illusion or a phantom. Seven different places did we visit in which he had formerly resided, but resided no longer—so that we felt even as wayfarers who vainly pursue after a will-o'-the-wisp.

And a young woman passed by, graceful as a panther, carrying a basket upon her arm. Her eyes were very large and black; her skin the color of gold; and her figure owned those indescribable curves, that cambrure de taille for which there is no expression in the English tongue.

"¡¡Que es bonita!!" exclaimed the singer, with a caressing accent in his deep voice. If the woman did not hear the compliment, she had at least heard the Spanish tongue; for she suddenly turned, and, poised in an attitude of supreme grace like a statue of bronze, addressed the artista in a voice clear as a silver bell:—"¿A quién busca V., señor?" And their black eyes met. It was a tropical look: the man fascinated by the serpent grace of the woman; the woman not seeking to conceal her admiration of the handsome youth before her. Yes: she knew where the consul—Señor Don Alejandro—lived. It was just at the corner. "¡Mil gracias, señorita!" Not a Spanish girl, no—from some strange town with an Aztec name in the heart of Mexico. "¡Yo estaba allá!" cried the artist joyfully: "I remember it well—the plaza, and the old house of Señor—on the corner, where I spent some very pleasant days when I was traveling through Mexico."

And then recalling old memories, they forgot for a moment all about the distant South American republic and the phantom consul. Adiós—a clasp of olive-skinned hands; and with the old-fashioned and tender commendation to God, they departed, never to meet again—as seabirds flying over the sea to opposite coasts look into each other's eyes a moment and pass on.

"I have been to your opera," he said, "I like it. But neither the French nor the Italians know what the Spanish theatre is. It is not merely music and drama. It is a school. It is a medium of national instruction. It teaches feeling, expression, deportment, dress, courtesy, taste, appreciation of the beautiful. And that is why Spanish audiences are so difficult to please."

"I wish I could hear you sing," we said.

"Lo me gustaría mucho," he returned; "but I leave to-night. And you could not judge of what I can do unless you should hear me in the theatre. Do you smoke?" And he presented us with a real "puro."

Suddenly an organ at the corner struck up a fragment of *Faust*—the Gloria chorus of the soldiers. "Ah! I love that," he murmured; and suddenly the martial air rolled from his lips in tones rich and deep, but golden-clear as the voice of a mighty organ. It was only for a moment; but in that moment the children ceased their dances, and people passing through the old-fashioned streets paused and turned and wondered at the witchcraft of that marvelous voice.

"¡Adios, señor!" And we parted forever.

Opening Oysters

"Talk of opening oysters," said old Hurricane, "Why, nothing's easier, if you only knew how." "And how's how?" inquired Starlight. "Scotch snuff," said old Hurricane, very sentitiously. "Scotch snuff. Bring a little of it ever so near their noses, and they'll sneeze their lids off." "I know a genius," observed Meister Karl, who has a better plan. "He spreads the bivalves in a circle, seats himself in the center, and begins spinning a yarn. Sometimes it's an adventure in Mexico—sometimes it's a legend of his loves—sometimes a marvellous stock operation on the Exchange. As he proceeds the 'natives' get interested—one by one they gape with astonishment at the tremendous and direful whoppers which are poured forth; and as they gape my friend whips 'em out, peppers 'em, and swallows 'em." "That'll do," said Starlight, with a long sigh; "I wish we had a bushel of them here now—they'd open easy."

By the Murmuring Waves

Those quiet little resting-places beside the lake could tell such tales had they only tongues. Perhaps it is as well that they have none.

How many little romances have taken place there!

It is so shadowy and quiet. Only the stars are looking; the frogs pay no attention to what does not concern them; the sobbing of the wavelets never interrupts a love story; and the distant music of the band, the cries of waiters, the clinking of glasses and the murmurs of the crowd are too far distant to destroy the delightful sensation of being all alone together by the lake shore.

But they talk in whispers nevertheless.

Doubtless there are many loves of which the fate has been decided by these quiet rendezvous by the lake shore.

Doubtless there are many who will remember to their dying day the story of these evening chats, the whispering of the waves, the chant of frogs and crickets, the winking of the silent stars above, and the distant murmur of the joyous crowd.

Spanish Moss

In goblin looms,
Depending from the many-elbowed arms
Of gnarled oaks, thou weavest Druid charms
    Under weird moons!
    They night-mare hug
Stifles the moaning of the dying pine;
The cedars know that strangler's cord of thine,
    O vegetable Thug.
    Thy robes of rags
The mightiest monarchs of the woods must wear,
And wreathe their crowns with locks of thy grey hair
    Like a Witch-hag's.
    What ghostly foods
Sustain thy spectral sap, thy phantom breath!
Thou Succubus, thou eldritch Life-in-Death,
    Thou Vampire of the Woods!

The Lord Sends Trials and Tribulations to Strengthen and Pacify Our Hearts

It is bad enough to have hot days, but when the heat runs into the night and prevents man from enjoying his slumber, it makes his heart groan in anguish. But who can describe the feelings of the man who has a musically-inclined neighbor by him, who insists in playing on a piano in the late hours of the night.

If the piano was a good one, and the voice of the songster sweet, it might be a lullaby to him; but, in the case in view, the piano is old and out of tune; and the voice of the maiden who warbles the melody, has not improved with age; and is described rather sacrilegiously by the sufferer "cracked." And when the discord echoes on the hot air of the night, the neighboring dogs join in the chorus with their melancholy howlings. Sleeping is banished in the neighborhood, and the sufferers pray, pray devoutly, that lightning will strike that piano at an early day.

Ye Pilot

Bravely the Pilot at his post
Stands, and the guiding wheel
Resolves, responsive to the touch
Of his strong arms of steel.

Fierce winds may blow, fierce storms assail,
Fierce fires may rage around,
But fires, nor lightnings, nor the gale
Can this brave heart confound.

A thousand lives on him depend,
And, careless of his own,
He firmly tries; he does or dies;
And, with his latest moan,

He thinks of those he could not save—
Should fate against him rise—
And sinking in a watery grave,
Still holds the Pilot's prize!

PART III

Of Vices and Virtues

EDITORIALS

At both the *Daily City Item* and the *Times-Democrat*
Hearn served as reporter, critic, essayist, and editorial writer. In spite of his live-and-let-live attitude, he
had a strong judgmental streak, to which he gave
vent in pungent editorials. As an editorialist, he employed humor, irony, sarcasm, and verbal savagery. At his best when on
the attack, Hearn also celebrated the unsung saints and noble
victims of urban life.

Whether attacking or defending, Hearn spoke to the strong
moralizing undercurrent that has always coexisted with the
laissez faire attitudes that prevail on the surface of New Orleans
life. His catalogue of both villains and heroes still resonates in
today's editorials and op-ed pieces.

Latin and Anglo-Saxon

The French papers in Canada have latterly warned their readers that
the Canadian French are being slowly but surely absorbed by the Anglo-
Saxon element, and have been advising them to push forward into the
valley of the Ottawa and there found settlements. This may possibly be
done; but the end will, no doubt, be the same. The Canadian French have,
nevertheless, been among the most thrifty, energetic, and enterprising
pioneers in the world; certainly no other men with Latin blood in their
veins ever showed more endurance and daring than the famous coureurs
des bois and chasseurs de loutre. If the French Canadian is to be absorbed

by the Anglo-Saxon element, we cannot avoid asking ourselves what chance the French element of Louisiana can have to resist absorption when the flood of emigration begins to pour southward with the advancing lines of railway?

The chances, in our opinion, are rather in favor of the Canadian French resisting longer than our own Creoles—unless the French element should be kept up by a continuous immigration. Old manners and customs and dialects and families endure longer in a severe Northern climate than in a semi-tropical land like our own. As we near the tropics decay becomes more rapid—not only material decay of substance, but decay of social conditions and institutions as well. Our French element is not composed, however, of such stern stuff as the French people of Canada. They have become semi-tropicalized here;—they have felt the enchantment of a climate of perennial mildness, and have lived for generations under very different conditions to those which have hardened and invigorated the French people of Canada. It must be remembered also that the French Canadians have had to resist the strongest absorbing influences possible—those of the English, Scotch, and Irish elements in all their purity and force. The geographical position of Louisiana, her climate, and her comparative isolation only recently broken by new railroad lines, have aided the Louisiana Creoles in maintaining their individuality and their pleasant old-fashioned manner of existence.

We have often attempted to analyze the cause of the undoubted predominance of the Anglo-Saxon race wherever it plants itself. Many causes have been adduced, but none seems to us satisfactory. The Latin races are not less hardy and enduring, though inferior in physical strength. They are not less intelligent, though less self-denying. They are not less patriotic, though more cosmopolitan. They possess a number of sterling qualities which are wholly foreign to Anglo-Saxon, Teutonic, or Scandinavian character. In our opinion the real secret of the predominance of Northern races lies in the same causes which may partly account for the conquest of the Western Empire by the Goths, after the Roman armies had been fairly worn out in repelling barbaric invasion. The Northern races are far more prolific than the Latin. The Germans of to-day, for example, are filling up America with emigrants. What Latin race can send out such armies of emigrants? Probably not all the Latin races together could do so! The fact is not perhaps flattering to the Northern races of Europe; for

it is said that the lower organizations propagate most rapidly in all the orders of nature. But history confirms the fact that the real strength of a
people lies not in valor and endurance alone, but in its capacity of self-
multiplication. Nor is this comforting to think of when we gaze toward
China. Idea is stronger than force for a time only; force at length will
carry all before it.

French in Louisiana

The encouragement given by our Legislature to the French language
in Louisiana has been ridiculed a great deal by persons apparently incapable of reflection and clad in the impenetrable mail of prejudice. It has
been said that New Orleans is not a French city, but an American city;
and that the use of the English language alone should be permitted in
public affairs and public schools. It has also been said that the law was
passed through Creole influence and to satisfy the selfish ends of a small
clique. Finally it has been said that this maintenance of a foreign tongue
by legislative complaisance is an ill-advised and ill-timed encouragement
of old fashions, old manners, and old prejudices which should be abolished as soon as possible for the sake of public prosperity.

It is needless to say that these statements are wholly untrue. Even sup-
posing that the law had been passed for the benefit of a few newspaper
publishers, school teachers, and notaries, its actual importance would
not be lessened one jot or tittle thereby. As far as the old-fashioned French
manners and customs go, we must say that we admire and commend
most of them, and are sorry to find that many are falling into disuse. The
good old customs need encouragement; they ought to be maintained;
and they make life in New Orleans more agreeable for strangers—especially Europeans—than may readily be described. It is really the old French
population here which knows most of the philosophy of comfort and hy-
giene, and which lives most naturally and healthily. As to the remarks
about old prejudices, no sensible man can pretend for a moment that
the use of any one language can keep the smouldering fire of old prejudices alive more than the use of any other language could do. In fact, we
believed that the Legislature saw further than the prejudiced myopes

who criticize them, and perceived that the encouragement of the French language in Louisiana was highly important from a purely commercial standpoint.

Let us explain ourselves more fully upon this subject. For years and years we have been conceiving and practicing and abandoning in despair all kinds of schemes for the encouragement of emigration. It would be a waste of time to record our failures. The old conditions are still extant; and the greater number of our real immigrants are from France and Italy. We believe that whatever may be said regarding other immigration, the French has been increasing of late years; and it is exceedingly important that we should do all in our power to encourage it. The French emigrant has almost always a good trade and is a first-class workman; he is remarkably industrious; he understands economy quite as well as the most thrifty German; and he always works with a fixed object in view. There are hundreds of thriving little businesses in this city which have been created out of nothing—one might almost say—by poor French emigrants who are now well-to-do citizens. It is true that the proportion of French immigration is not as large as we could wish, because the French—unlike the Germans—prefer to stay at home as long as any hope of comfort remains rather than go abroad to seek fortune. But there are regular periods in the life of every nation, however prosperous, which develop conditions that force emigration; and France cannot always remain exempt. We believe there will be a considerable increase in French immigration before many years; and we know that such immigrants will be only too glad to seek a French-speaking community in the United States. New Orleans, by proper management, might obtain at least four-fifths of this foreign element, with immense advantage to herself, and might become the central point for America-seeking French emigrants. It is of great moment that the French language be encouraged in Louisiana in view of this fact, and the good effect of the new laws will be felt before many years.

Jewish Emigrants for Louisiana

The lesson civilization received through the result of the persecution of Jews in mediæval Germany and mediæval Spain, and their banishment from both countries, seems to have been forgotten even by modern rulers, especially by the incapable parties who hold in their hands the reins of Russian government. Already the result of persecutions in Russia have had dismal financial effects. Rotten previously to the core the thin skin which held the mouldering fruit of Moscovite finance together is now fissuring and snapping. The brutality and fanaticism of the orthodox peasantry have also recoiled upon themselves. In all parts of the Russian country districts the peasantry, oppressed as they have always been since the time of emancipation by heavy taxes, have been dependent upon the Jews for aid. When crops were short, when seasons of drought or inundation or epidemic or war rendered the payment of taxes almost impossible, it was to the Jews that the peasant made his appeal. With their wonderful economy and thrift, their natural aptitude for finance, their Oriental keenness of foresight, the Jews monopolized without difficulty the role of money lenders in the country districts. When the severe strain of financial disorder,—consequent upon misgovernment, upon tremendous debts incurred in the transportation of troops for thousands of leagues without railroads, upon wars with Turkey, wars in Turkestan, wars on the Chinese frontier, and expensive mischief-making in the East,—fell most heavily upon the country, there was an outcry against the Jews. They were accused of cruel usury, of robbery, of all sorts of crimes which ignorant superstition could imagine; and rascally Russian contractors who had spent all their lives in cheating the government, laid all manner of snares to entrap the authorities into the belief that the Jews were the authors of these frauds. The Jews were robbed, outraged, and murdered; some had their houses burned; some were torn to pieces in the public streets. The number of those who met their deaths by violence is probably not less than a thousand. A vast exodus began—a going forth out of this new land of Egypt. But after the Jews were gone, those who succeeded them soon taught the peasantry what real usury was. Where a Jew would have demanded twenty-five percent, a Russian demanded one hundred; when a Jew might have demanded fifty, a German adventurer asked one hundred and fifty. But this is not all. The great Jewish banking houses in Russia began to tremble; and vast firms on whose prosperity thousands depended for a living were shaken as by an earthquake. A business panic commenced; and the government repented, when too late, of its wicked folly in neglecting to protect the people who created property and gave vitality to commercial enterprise throughout all the Russias.

The immense bodies of Jews now leaving Russia will no doubt for the most part settle in the United States. Their new promised land is here; and their appeals for aid to come here have been answered all the world over by their kindred people. The Jews of France made the greatest efforts in their behalf; exerting as they do the greatest financial influence in Europe; and the Alliance Israelite Universelle has appointed committees to help the Russian Hebrews to emigrate. Subcommittees with the same object are being or have already been organized in all the principal cities of Europe and America. Here in New Orleans a committee was organized the day before yesterday at the Harmony Club rooms. The following report of the proceedings will interest those who have not already seen it:

"Mr. Frank was in the chair, Mr. E. I. Kursheedt acted as secretary and Judge Morris Marks, Messrs. A. Lehman, Sol Marx, Revs. Jas. K. Gutheim, and I. L. Leucht, and Dr. Marx Urwitz, Messrs. Julius Ries, Isaac Bloom, S. Gumbel, and S. Cahn, representing the different lodges of the I.O.B.S. in this city; Mr. Geo. Stern, of the Young Men's Hebrew Association; Mr. G. Kahn, of the Free Sons of Israel, and Mr. Polestrek, of the Keher Shel Barzel, were present. It was decided that those in attendance and Messrs. Max Dinkelspiel and Ferdinand Marks, the other members of the committee, solicit subscriptions, the proceeds to be forwarded to the Alliance for the purpose of defraying the expenses of those who wish to come to the South and establish themselves here."

Louisiana needs all the Jewish emigrants she can obtain,—especially those sturdy Russian Hebrews, who are not afraid to do any work, and many of whom are farmers and mechanics. Once established here they will certainly create capital rapidly, and aid the quick growth of our new prosperity.

Quack! Quack!

Quack! Quack! I am on the rack,
You promised to end my pain;
For a little wealth you'd restore my health
You said; yet here I've lain
For weary weeks and for mournful months,
With pangs that are only known

To the tortured victim of the Quack,
When his faith to the winds has flown.

The Opium Dens

We regret to observe that the City Council are not supporting all the excellent measures recommended by the present excellent Board of Health. We have now the best health board we have had for many years; and yet less attention is paid to some of the recommendations than were paid to the infamous ones of the worst Board of Health we ever had.

We refer especially to the measure taken by the board against the prevalence of the opium vice. The board passed a resolution calling upon the City Council to pass an ordinance closing the opium dens and severely punishing their proprietors. The *Item* at that time improved the opportunity to advocate also that all who frequent those places be liable to punishment. In San Francisco it was found absolutely necessary to pass such laws; and it is better that we should pass the laws at an early date before the evil shall have spread its roots deeply in this community.

The resolution, however, never even came up before the City Council. We should like to ask why? It is true that it might take some time and trouble to enforce the ordinance advocated with our present unfortunate lack of a good police organization; but with the watchful energy of the health board we could hope that great good would result therefrom.

Since we first called attention to the subject, the opium dens have increased in number. There are, we believe, no less than five in the Second district, alone. Daily, early at sunrise, men and women may be seen staggering out of them into the street, drunk with the venomous fumes of the narcotic, and hideous with the pallor of the hideous debauch. The dens are patronized by hundreds and hundreds. It is bad enough that we should have morphine-eaters and opium-eaters; the spread of opium-smoking is a far more alarming evil.

Some may well say that it is only the most vicious classes who practice the vice, and that the sooner these are killed off the better! Even allow this strange argument to be true, it must be remembered that nothing is so contagious as vice; and especially strange vices brought from other lands. If the evil be not checked it will bring other evils in its train,—exotic and terrible evils which we need not specify. In another ten years we might be cursed with the curse of San Francisco. The Chinese like our climate. Those who come to this city settle here instead of working only a few months or years and then seeking other places, as they do North. Wherever they settled they send for their countrymen. They have even got emigrating agencies here, which hold correspondence with Mexico and the Antilles. It is true, they have good qualities as citizens; they are industrious and economical and untiring. But while it is right that they should be allowed to make themselves useful, it is folly to permit them to poison any portion of our community with the vices of the Orient.

Scénes de la Vie des Hoodlums

I.

It was mid-night. And silence breeded over the entire community.

The aforesaid silence was suddenly scared into flight by violent screams of "Watch!"

Two policemen heard the screams. They advanced to the neighborhood of the screams cautiously, being greatly afraid they might have something difficult to do, and inwardly hoping they might arrive too late to do it.

To their agreeable surprise their screams were found to proceed from the throat of a very aged and feeble Negro, who was being stamped upon by the enormous hoofs of two very robust and powerful young hoodlums.

When the police saw these things they stood still and said "Hello!" "Hello! Pete, how's your corporosity?" answered the hoodlums.

"First rate, boys," replied the peelers—"what's up?"

"Why, this ——— nigger's been trying to rob us! We want you to arrest him."

"They done robbed me of three dollars and seventy cents," groaned the old negro, "and kicked me all to pieces."

"None of yer gab!" said one of the policemen, giving him a kick. "That'll be all right, boys, we'll fix him," they said to the hoodlums. Then they carried the old man to the station house and locked him up. And in order to account for his used-up condition they put a charge of "resisting officers" against him, in addition to a charge of "disorderly conduct." He went up for sixty days.

II.

It was nearly mid-night—not quite. And the moon shed her luster upon the city. A large hoodlum entered a house, with green shutters on the door, where a certain girl lived. She was a woman of the town. He wanted her to give him some money. She said she was tired of supporting him. Then he knocked her down and stamped on her, and smashed up her furniture, and broke the looking-glass and overturned things generally until the police came.

"What's the matter, Jim?" asked the policeman, timidly looking in, while the hoodlum was stamping upon the woman's face.

"Why, this ——— has robbed me of twenty dollars," said the hoodlum; "and by ———, I want to make a charge against her!"

"Come along, you ———," said one of the policemen, giving the girl a slap across her bleeding face. Then they took her to jail, and charged her with larceny and assault and battery and disorderly conduct. She was sent to the Parish Prison for six months.

(She had not been able to pay her police blackmail regularly.)

III.

It was mid-night and the song of the mocking bird was heard. And also yells of murder.

When the police heard the yells, they hurried away from the direction of the yells as much as possible. Half an hour later, they returned and made their appearance after the victim had been removed to the hospital, and quiet had been restored.

Suddenly six hoodlums came out of the dark, and surrounded them in a friendly manner.

"Say, Tom," began the biggest of the hoodlums,—"there's been ructions round here to-night; and we knocked seventeen different kinds of stuffing out of one fellow,—that long-legged Dutchman round the corner. "Now he's going to make charges against us when he's able to, and you've got to fix that straight." "All right," answered the policeman.

And when the case came up the policeman swore that those particular hoodlums could not have attacked the prosecutor, because the said hoodlums were eight squares away at the time the prosecutor was attacked. And the hoodlums were discharged; and as they left the court room one of them growled out, "I'll get even with you again, you ——— Dutch blankety blank.

IV.

It was mid-night. And the stars were shining; and cries of "watch" were heard. Hoodlums were assaulting a servant girl.

Seven policemen appeared miraculously upon the scene.

They were not afraid, because there were so many of them together.

They fired "ineffectual shots" at the main body of the hoodlums, but only captured two.

These two were being escorted to the station house by four policemen.

"All right," said one of the hoodlums, "we'll get even with you some of these nights. I know how to get even with you, Dick—and you, Jack—and you, Bill—and you—you ———, infernal, miserable blankety-blank!"

"See here," returned the aforesaid ——— miserable infernal blankety-blank, "we've let you off more'n twenty times and you have never acted the gentleman, —never as much as said 'thank you,' or offered us a drink. Now we'll see what the judge will make you pay for this."

"I'll give you a ten."

"A ten won't go round. Make it twenty."

"I ain't got it," answered the hoodlum, "but my pard here, if he'll pony up, we'll make it all right."

They ponied up; and it was right. Next day the Chief of Police ordered "an investigation," in order to find out who the perpetrators of the assault were. The investigating officers reported that they could not find out anything, and that they believed the girl must have been lying!

V.

It was mid-night. And the hoodlums were breaking the street lamps.

"You really oughten't to do that, Jake," observed a policeman who was timidly looking up.

(The doctor pronounced the policeman's wounds "dangerous" but not necessarily fatal!)

Blackmailing

We are daily in receipt of reports regarding the manner in which the police collect money from the houses of ill-fame; and the brutal abuse which they make of their power. Our testimony is accumulating.

We would suggest to Judge Miltenberger, for example, that certain women arrested and brought before him, be allowed to testify occasionally in their own behalf.

If the city authorities made a fair investigation of the existing evils, and would assure the witnesses protection, a mass of disgusting testimony could be obtained ample enough to fill a thousand newspaper columns.

The police know, however, that their victims are at their mercy; and under present circumstances dare not testify.

Names of officers have been given to us which we have filed away intending to use as soon as we receive such testimony as will not leave the witnesses without protection.

This sort of abuse of authority is something which did not exist as it does now even under the Radical regime.

It must not be supposed that in speaking of these things we do not desire that social evils be properly restrained by law.

On the contrary, we speak of them because we desire that they shall not increase; and also because it is a disgrace to any city that her police should draw money from the practice of crime.

It is said that if a humane policeman be assigned to certain patrols, where their practices are carried on, and that he is unwilling to disgrace his manhood, he is quietly shunted off to the outlying districts.

A good patrolman—we happen to have met one or two very recently—said to a person connected with this paper: "Why do you give it to us poor peelers; it is not we who make the money; it is the men with the double row of buttons."

Another said: "That article in *The Item* the other day, entitled the "Statement of a Victim," is true. I have been on the police twelve years; and I can tell you that these things happen almost every day."

And will the citizen-voters of New Orleans allow this state of things to continue forever?

The Indignant Dead

If they are not indignant as a certain worthy Administrator declared they were, they ought to be.

During the last ten years three hundred and three persons have been murdered in New Orleans or vicinity.

And yet only FIVE of the murderers have been hung.

Only five—although eleven were actually sentenced to death.

Consequently the chance of being hung for committing a murder in this community is as five to three hundred and three.

Almost as little danger of being hung for having committed murder as of being run over by a railroad train or cut in two by a buzz saw or brained by a brick falling from a chimney.

It is really horrible to read the report made to Governor Wiltz. Of perhaps more than three hundred murderers—for many of these murders were committed by several persons—only three escaped from justice. What became of the rest? Where are the three hundred?

One hundred and sixteen were declared NOT GUILTY.

A nolle prosequi was entered in fifty-nine cases.

In nine cases it was "not a true bill."

There were three mistrials.

Twelve cases were transferred to the dead docket.

Without going much further into particulars we need only remark that the rest mostly escaped with light sentences, or were pardoned out of the Penitentiary.

Only five murderers were punished by death.

And that was only because they were strangers,—

Because they had no money to pay lawyers,—

Because they had no political influence.

Two Italians, two negroes and a Malay—probably less guilty than some who are now walking the streets!

There are nearly three hundred unavenged dead,—the blood of nearly three hundred victims crying vainly to heaven for vengeance!

If the dead are not indignant, in the immortal words of our Administrator, they ought to be.

Improved Police Ideas

The happy idea of one of our patrolmen in turning in a fire alarm the other day, and thus dispersing a mob, ought to be universally adopted.

We should recommend that the present police be simply employed to stand at street corners and turn in fire alarms when arrests ought to be made.

We'll bet on the fire department every time.

We don't think the fire department would ever back down when there is good hard work to do.

In other cities firemen hold commissions as guardians of the peace; and if policemen are not around when there is trouble the firemen usually turn up. And when they lay their hands on a disturber of the peace he always goes where they want him to go.

Firemen never stand any nonsense. When they go in to work they mean business.

We recommend an occasional application of the cold-water cure to hoodlumism, as above represented.

Coming Events Cast Their Shadow Before

It will come sooner or later; but the parties who should be most interested in such matters do not pay any attention to the shadows of coming

events. The Widow with Wooden Legs, as the Spaniards call the Gibbet, is waiting to celebrate her nuptials with some of our hoodlums; and yet the latter do not seem to know it. A long time has elapsed since the Widow was last married here, although the number of fellows who ought to have been married to her by force is legion. She is becoming tired of widowhood; and this is leap year. She is going to propose pretty soon; and when she proposes it will be no use to try backing out.

A Visit to New Orleans

The Devil arrived at New Orleans early yesterday morning, having left his winter residence in Chicago at midnight. There was little need, he thought, to bother himself further about Chicago during the present summer, as he holds a mortgage upon that city, which has at present no prospect of being able to prevent him from foreclosing.

Sensitive to the beauties of Nature,—a trait for which he has ever been famous since that primeval morning when, hiding in the leafy shadows of Paradise, he beheld fair Eve admiring the reflection of her snowy limbs in the crystal waters of Gehon,—the Devil could not suppress a sigh of regret as he gazed with far-reaching eyes along the old-fashioned streets of the city, whose gables were bronzed by the first yellow glow of sunrise. "Ah!" he exclaimed, "is this, indeed, the great City of Pleasure, the Sybaris of America, the fair capital which once seemed to slumber in enchanted sunlight, and to exhale a perfume of luxury even as the palaces of the old Cæsars? Her streets are surely green with grass; her palaces are gray with mould; and her glory is departed from her. And perhaps her good old sins have also departed with her glory; for riches are a snare, and gold is a temptation." And the Devil frowned anxiously, and his deep eyes glowed under his brows even as smouldering charcoal glows in the shadows of night.

The Devil had not been in New Orleans since the period of Reconstruction—a period at which, our readers may remember, it was proverbially said that New Orleans was "going to the Devil." Such also appears to have been the Devil's own personal opinion. He found things in such a condition about that time that he had not been able to find room in his voluminous breast-pockets for all the mortgages which he had obtained upon men's souls; and believing, from the mad career of Radicalism, that the whole city must be made over to him in the course of a few years, he had departed elsewhere in search of employment. "They have no need of me," said the Devil, "in the State of Louisiana."

The history of the overthrow of Radicalism, however, which the Devil read in the *Chicago Times,* filled him with consternation. He had a gigantic job on his hands in Chicago, and could not just then afford to leave Illinois, for reasons which we have at the present writing no need to specify. But the rumor of a reform in politics in Louisiana, and a just government, pleased him not at all; and he felt exceedingly anxious to visit the Crescent City. It happened, however, that he could not get away until the midnight between the death of Thursday and the birth of Friday. And, moreover, the Devil has private reasons for objecting to travel on Friday.

The odor of the gutters displeased him as he walked down Saint Charles Street, and he stopped his nose with a handkerchief bearing a pattern of green skeletons and red cupids intertwined upon a saffron ground. "Poverty and dirt are sometimes virtuous," said the Devil, as he proceeded on his way. At the next corner he bought all the papers of the previous day. He put the *Picayune* in his pistol-pocket; cursed the *New Orleans Bee* and the *City Item,* and, flinging them back upon the dealer's stand after a brief examination of their contents, he folded up the other papers in a bundle for future reference. "There is too much virtue in the press, I am afraid," said the Devil; "the *Picayune* is the only paper which suits me."

The police stations were next visited; and the Devil smiled a ghastly smile. "I have no fault to find with the police," he said; "and that reminds me that my own police force below is getting disorganized. I'll have to recruit in New Orleans."

An examination of the records in the Auditor's office tickled him, until he exploded in an abysmal laugh—a series of bass notes singularly like the famous laugh of Mephistopheles in *Faust*. "Why, this system is almost as good as Radicalism," he said. "Forty-five thousand dollars for running an Auditor's office!"

He next read the order of the Mayor to the colored churches, and nodded his head approvingly. "Good enough in its way," he said. By twelve o'clock he had visited all the public institutions;—the Sanitary Association highly displeased him; but the Board of Health put him into an uproarious good humor. "I was a fool to come down here at all," he said; "this Board of Health can do my work better than I can do it myself, and the people seem to be just fools enough to let them do it. Instead of honest poverty, I find vicious poverty; instead of reform, demoralization; instead of law, I find lawyers; instead of justice, oppression. What Carnival King ever found a city so well prepared for him? I guess I shall leave at once; for I have no work to do as yet in Louisiana."

But before leaving, the Devil took a notion to alight upon the top of the State House to watch the Convention. He listened for several hours to the proceedings, much to his own surprise; and it was nearly three o'clock before he knew it.

"Half-past two o'clock on Friday," muttered the Devil; "and I have to be in Pandemonium by a quarter to three. I don't quite like the state of affairs in that old hotel; but I doubt if the situation really demands my presence; I think I shall send a subaltern up to the Convention; for the Devil's interests are not sufficiently represented. But I shall not come back here for twenty years. What is the use of staying in a city that is going just where I am going? Besides, if anything serious happens, my representative can inform me. They have an embargo on reform here, it seems to me—just as they have on commerce. After all, New Orleans in 1879 is not very much holier than New Orleans in 1866. I guess I'll adjourn."

And he adjourned, after having copied the word "Choppinism" into his new *Dictionnaire Infernale*.

Whited Sepulchres

It is rather ghastly to have death in the midst of life as we have it in New Orleans; but ghastlier when it is presented without even the ordinary masks. The skeleton of our public closet is exposed to broad day-light. Are we becoming like the Orientals who never repair?—do we accept all

things with the fatalistic *Kismet?* Our bat-haunted prisons and our ruined cemeteries seem to answer in the affirmative.

They are hideous Golgothas, these old intramural cemeteries of ours. In other cities the cemeteries are beautiful with all that the art of the gardener and the sculptor can give. They are often beautiful parks, in which shafts of rosy granite or pale marble rise in pleasant relief against a background of ornamental shrubbery;—birds are singing in the trees;—flowers are growing upon the gently swelling eminences which mark the sleep of the dead. There horror is masked and hidden. Here it glares at us with empty sockets.

The tombs are fissured, or have caved in, or have crumbled down into shapeless masses of brick and mortar;—the plaster, falling away, betrays the hollow mockery of the frail monuments;—the vases are full of green water and foulness;—the flowers are dying in their coffins of glass;—the crawfish undermine the walls to fatten upon what is hidden within;—and instead of birds, the tombs are haunted by lizards.

If we must have intramural cemeteries, at least let them be worthy of a civilized people. As they are, they are nightmares.

Old-Fashioned Houses

Probably there are as fine residences in New Orleans as in any other city of equal population in the United States; and the almost tropical beauty of the grounds and gardens which surround them lends them a charm that cannot be found in many other cities of North America. Most of these fine residences are built upon designs entirely different from the prevailing architecture of New Orleans houses; and it is pleasant to observe that a new style of building even small houses is coming into fashion in different parts of the city. Few of us can afford to live in palaces; and excepting residences that are absolutely palatial, there are very few comfortable dwellings, comparatively speaking, in the Crescent City. There is much picturesqueness; but picturesqueness is not comfort; there is much of outward charm in old-fashioned places, in quaint rooms, in audacious balconies, in mediæval-looking dormers, in peaked roofs, in maisonettes tinted lemon-yellow, pale rose, or faint green; but all this does not give the coziness of a home. The New Orleans of half a century ago is not suited to the wants of the New Orleans of today. The population has increased; there are infinitely fewer rich people here than formerly; there are many more inhabitants to the square mile, and the great houses which formerly constituted the winter residences of wealthy planters and others must now be portioned out among many families or transformed into boarding-houses in order to be made profitable to their owners. A change in the old style of building dwellings is becoming more and more imperative every succeeding year.

The causes of the old style of building are attributable to a wholly different social condition which still existed a generation ago; and there is really no reason why it should survive at present. Nevertheless, we frequently see new houses in process of erection, being constructed upon precisely the same uncomfortable and antiquated plans which should be abolished forever. We have nothing to say against the outward appearance of New Orleans houses. The general effect is very pleasing;—no one with an artistic eye can avoid loving the zigzag outline of peaked roofs with the pretty dormers; the iron arabesques of graceful balconies, the solid doors and burglar-proof shutters, so brightly green. The old-fashioned houses are by no means ugly. But their interior arrangement is altogether condemnable and renders them almost unfit for modern homes. Take, for example, the ordinary double cottages of which there are thousands upon thousands in New Orleans. Not only do all the rooms open into each other, either with large folding or sliding or the ordinary doors; but each room of each house often opens into each room of its twin on the other side. Thus there are from two to three doors to each room, besides windows; rendering it difficult to warm any apartment in a damp New Orleans winter. Privacy is impossible; seclusion a mockery. Even the attics of two houses open into one another. Suppose one is looking for a house, and expresses his dissatisfaction with this plan, the proprietor will exclaim with astonishment: "Why! there is a door; and the door is closed!" A thin door does not ensure seclusion or even quiet. Every sound can be heard distinctly in both houses—the crying of children in the night; family quarrels; noises of household work; and many other things which should not be heard at all. And the doors are not even double. In nine cases out of ten daylight shows through them. The same thing renders it very difficult to obtain comfortable furnished rooms in the city. Every room opens into another; and every movement of one's neighbor or neighboress is distinctly audible. All this might be avoided by the construction of hallways; and certainly it is not for want or value of space that we have so few hallways in the city. Immense rooms, high and airy!—but cold and comfortless—opening into other immense rooms—all opening into other houses: of such there is no end.

Now if there is one thing more essential than any other to the comfort of a house, it is seclusion! The English understand this fact even better than the Americans, and their cottages are model homes. When a man enters his house he wishes to be able when he pleases to shut himself up from the rest of the world, to be alone with his family or with his thoughts, to rest himself after the day's anxieties without further turmoil or annoyance. But how is he to do this when he finds only a partition thin as the cover of a novel between himself and others who are not of his family, and who live practically on the same floor and almost in the same room? If he wishes to enjoy an hour in his private study, it is not pleasant to be obliged all the time to listen to noises in the next room, even if made by his own servants or his own children. For members of a family themselves require at times to seclude themselves from other members of the family;—there are business matters to be talked of; there are projects which children or servants should not hear; there are numberless things which the heads of a household wish to discuss by themselves. And to warm such houses in winter there must be a fire in every room upon the same floor; otherwise one will find that folding doors are a mockery and sliding doors a vexation of spirit. The double cottage is an abomination; and even the single cottage without a hallway is an affliction. Is it agreeable to be unable to go to bed either without passing through somebody else's room or having somebody else passing through your room? It is not even a civilized way of living; and certainly a vast majority of New Orleans houses would appear to a stranger to have been constructed with little regard to common decency. The truth is simply that twenty-five years ago people here lived very differently from what they can afford to do now;—everything was on a larger and more generous scale; and perhaps the dwellings were excellently adapted at that time to the wants of their tenants. To-day all is changed. Picturesque and uncomfortable New Orleans must disappear to give place to one perhaps less outwardly attractive but less illusive and more substantial. The result will certainly be less consumption and less rheumatism.

La Douane

That vast gray building on Canal Street, which seemeth ancient as Karnac, and upon which princely sums have vainly been expended in the foolish hope of completing it, has long troubled us with a strange impression difficult to analyze. A sense of weight and antiquity oppresses the beholder when he gazes upon it. Kinglake's nightmare of "solid immensity" may be realized by a careful study of it; and its loftiest portion affords an artistic effect of ruin—not the picturesque ruin of feudal remains, but ruin as of Egypt, vast and shadowy and dusty. It has been to the United States Treasury what the sieve was to the daughters of Danaüs. Rivers of gold have been poured into it; yet it remaineth as before. Its marble hall seems like the Pharaonic burial-chamber in the heart of the granite monument of Cheops; and its doors exhale in the most arid and burning weather a breath of damp chilliness, such as smites a mourner in the face when he opens the iron gates of a family vault. So weirdly does it seem to hint of Death and the Past that one cannot help wondering why its corridors are not hypogea and its offices filled with mummies. Without, in sooth, its very shape is ominous. It is, despite its windows and entrances, its pilasters and niches, a huge sarcophagus of granite. Its form is funeral; and against the dismal immensity of its exterior, the openings in its awful walls seem but as carvings upon some ancient stone coffin.

It is in very truth a sarcophagus, wherein repose the mummified remains of that which was once mighty, but not magnanimous; of that which was once rich, yet not honest; of that which once believed itself eternal and invulnerable, yet which expired like Herod of self-engendered corruption. Its corridors are indeed hypogea, filled with the mummies of Radical Pharaohs; and its marble hall a burial-chamber, empty, indeed, like that in the stony heart of the Great Pyramid, yet haunted by the ghost of that régime for which none are left to mourn.

But those empty niches in the great waste surfaces of the quadruple façade! Ah, those niches!—those niches! Why are they accursed with emptiness; why made hideous with vacuity? The statues of stone created to fill them were chiseled out a quarter of a century ago; and yet never have beheld the light of day. Their stone eyes have never gazed upon the glory of Canal Street; their marble ears have never hearkened to the gossip of politicians; their rigid forms have never left the enclosure of the wooden coffins into which they were first packed for importation. They sleep in the awful silence and darkness of the most dismal chamber in the whole gray building. They sleep, and the dust thickens upon their faces; and sometimes in the dead waste and middle of the night they do converse dismally together. They represent Faiths not worshiped under the old régime, Hopes that had failed, and Charities that would have been scorned; Virtues that had fled, or had hidden themselves in lonesome places; Saintly Personages who could not in those days have received respect; and Great Statesmen, perhaps, whose marble faces would have blushed into Egyptian granite, could they have seen that which was, but will never be again. And Radicalism, therefore, hid them away—not, indeed, out of consideration for their feelings, but out of consideration for its own. For it could not have endured the silent reproach of those eyes of marble, or dare to concoct plots within the reach of those ears of marble; and therefore the Faiths and the Virtues were cunningly hidden away where their presence could offend nobody. And now they ask, "When shall we be delivered from darkness and silence and oblivion? When shall the trumpet sound for our resurrection day? When shall we behold the great glory of the Southern sun and the splendor of Canal Street? Better even with broken noses to stand on our pedestals, better even to lose several of our Carrara limbs than this." But the silence and the darkness and the dampness remain; and echo answereth nothing.

The Haunted and the Haunters

In ancient times criminals were delivered to wild beasts, who tortured and devoured them. In modern Louisiana criminals are delivered not to lions, tigers, or panthers, to be devoured; but to certain fiendish winged things, which were anciently termed flitter-mice, and which possess, like certain monsters described by Rabelais, the power of stinking people to death.

The building chosen for the infliction of this dreadful punishment is an antiquated structure, modelled after the Spanish prisons of Colonial time, crowned with turrets from which vigilant sentries, armed with rifles, may slay those who strive vainly to escape from the silent fury of the odoriferous monsters.

Any wayfarer who lingers in the neighbourhood of Congo Square about sundown may behold the weird prison, and a vast flock of winged demons hovering above it, preparing to hold their ghastly revels under a gibbous moon.

He may also smell the ghoulish odour outshaken from the wings of the innumerable host of imps. The odour is never to be forgotten. It contains suggestions of many odours—decaying shoe-leather, miscarried eggs, and dead cats—and yet is unlike any of these. It is an original and astonishing odour which inspires fantastic visions of death and dissolution.

There are many people who hold that criminals should not be tortured. Humanitarians declare that the object of capital punishment is not punishment in reality, but only a necessary means of protecting society against crime. In order to save ourselves from being bitten by snakes we must kill the snakes; but we cannot blame the reptile for using its fangs according to the dictates of its ophidian proclivities.

We feel inclined to this belief ourselves. We do not consider that the cause of morality is aided in the least by delivering unhappy criminals to the bats. Better, we think, that the wicked be favoured with a speedy death than that they be slowly driven out of the world by the most indescribable of stinks.

But even granting, for the sake of argument, that it is right and proper that evil doers be delivered up to the bats;—granting even that they ought to be smeared all over with bat guano seven times a day—let us ask why should the innocent be made to suffer with the guilty?

Why should property be depreciated in the immediate neighbourhood of the prison and beyond it by the wild and savage violence of the stink?—why should unoffending and law-abiding citizens be compelled to bear the punishment of convicts?—why should no efforts be made to prevent the stench from extending over a square mile of peaceable neighbourhood?—why in short should not the bat-torture be inflicted only without the corporate limits of the city?

Why? Oh! why?

Is there no sulphur, no carbolic acid, no gunpowder, no vitriol, no dynamite in Louisiana? Is there no balm in Gilead?

The Unspeakable Velocipede

A mad dog, a runaway horse, a drove of Texas steers on a stampede, a locomotive off the track, a hundred thousand firemen rushing to a fire, a drunken man reeling down the street with a fifty-pound can of nitroglycerine nicely balanced on his oscillating shoulder and liable to fall off without notice,—are things which may all be avoided by pedestrians possessing presence of mind and steady nerves. Because the bull, the locomotive, the mad dog, the nitroglycerine have all certain invariable and eternal rules of action, unchangeable as the laws of the Medes and Persians.

Given such and such conditions, we know how the terrible things above referred to will conduct themselves.

But no man ever lived—not even Moses or Solomon—who could discover any principle of action, any law governing movement, in the gyra-

tions of the wild, treacherous, diabolical and unspeakable velocipede. You might suppose on seeing a velocipede steering straight toward you that its furious charge might be escaped by a flank movement to right or left. But you are sadly mistaken.

You might escape an African lion or a Bengal tiger by a flank movement, but never a velocipede, which unites all the vices of ferocious beasts with none of their virtues.

The velocipede is like a vicious dog, because it always attacks any one who runs away from it; but it is also like a lion which attacks any one who dares to face it boldly. It is like a fox in treachery, like a panther in agility, like a tiger in cruelty, like a gorilla in ferocity, like a greyhound in speed, like a badger in taking a good hold of the calf of your leg, and like the Devil for impudence.

You cannot turn a corner so quickly that a velocipede cannot turn after you still quicker. There is but one possible means of escaping a velocipede. Velocipedes are like grizzly bears; they cannot climb trees.

You must, therefore, climb a tree when you see a velocipede; but if you are near-sighted it will do you no good; for in order to climb a tree quick enough to escape a velocipede, you must be able to see the velocipede coming at the distance of at least a mile. Greased lightning does not travel so quick as the most vicious and terrible species of velocipede, known as the Bicycle.

Happily the Bicycle is so vicious that few, even among the wickedest of New Orleans boys, dare to ride it.

A velocipede seems very light; but its weight increases according to the speed with which it is propelled. Sometimes it weighs several tons.

If you do not believe this, you have never been bitten in the calf of the leg by a furious velocipede.

The only way to attack the velocipede successfully is to attack their riders,—as the Romans learned to do in fighting against trained elephants. Trained elephants sometimes turned and trampled down their own supporters. So with velocipedes. If you stand your ground well and direct your just rage and wholly excusable indignation against the rider, you will find the velocipede treacherously abandon its owner and fling him in the dust and trample wildly upon him.

But we have nothing more to say on this subject. We can only hope that all who disagree with us may be made muddy victims of velocipede wrath, and have their legs smitten by bicycles running at the rate of one thousand miles per hour.

The Organ Grinder

Where is the man with soul so dead as not to be moved by the music of the organ grinder well ground out?

Echoes of Verdi, of Gounod, of Lecocq, of Donizetti, of Meyerbeer;— memories of gorgeous gas-lit opera nights, of splendid scenery, and the white-limbed witches of the ballet;—fragments of mountain airs which recall blue peaks of the Tyrol or braes bathed in Scotch mists, or fair outlines of Irish hills,—all these and many other delightful things, are they not evoked from the magical heart of the organ?

Have not men thousands of leagues from their native land, wandering among the streets of a strange city where their own tongue was not spoken, often started and paused and listened with tears in their eyes to tunes which brought back visions of their native land again?

Are not these organ grinders, who voyage through all the cities of the civilized world, the Apostles of music,—preaching in all lands the universal religion of music, and the holy magic of expressing human passion in harmony?

For these and all other things must we not honor and bless the olivaceous complexioned organ grinder?

Yea, verily, but there are likewise Certain Things the Organ Grinder doth, which at times make men to wax wroth, and to pour out their souls in fierce malediction.

O reader, thou who lovest the music of the hand organ, has thou never in the solemn hours of the night been lying upon a sleepless bed,—

While the starry heaven flamed above thee, and the perfumed breath of the luke-warm night was about thee, and a most romantic and operatic-looking moon was gazing in upon thee through the window, with flitting mosquitoes sharply defined against its white face?

And while thus lying bathed in the moonlight and filled with a sense of contentment, thou wert suddenly startled by hearing an organ at the corner of the street.

A rich organ which began to play the very tune thou didst most desire to hear, not having heard it before for lo! these many years.

And having ground out several tantalizing notes suggestive of the exceeding beauty of the air in question, the organ grinder suddenly ceased to grind, and when thou didst seek to call him back, he had passed away and was not.

But upon retiring to thy couch in disappointment thou didst again hear the same cursed organ grinder grinding afar off—and suddenly ceasing to grind as before. Has it not often been so?—even so?

Ought there not to be a law to prohibit organ grinders from thus torturing expectation and enervating hope?

Forasmuch as they do these things we do abhor organ grinders.

Also we do abhor the organ grinder who for vile lucre doth consent to grind out everlastingly but one tune—and that a dancing tune—instead of the variety of tunes with which good organs are blessed. Surely this is a prostitution of the barrel organ.

Give the poor organ a show, oh lucre accumulating organ grinder!

The Puller of Noses

Thou, O barber, pullest the noses of the oldest and best.

Also dost thou tickle the most dignified under the chin.

Thou tellest the vainest that their heads need washing badly.

Thou stickest the teeth of the comb in the rims of the ears of judges.

Also thy patience is great and thy good nature large.

Otherwise thou couldst not be a barber at all.

Nevertheless thou hast thy faults.

After having smoked cigarettes thou shouldst carefully wash thy fingers, and yet thou dost not.

And the odor of burnt paper and tobacco is not soothing to the olfactory nerves.

Wherefore, one wisheth that women were barbers,—nice young women who do not smoke.

Old women smoke sometimes, you know.

This is why we should like young girls to shave us.

Don't you believe that is the only reason?

Then you mean to say we are not telling the truth;

That we are prevaricators and equivocators!

Then we have nothing more to say upon the subject.

The Glamour of New Orleans

The season has come at last when strangers may visit us without fear, and experience with unalloyed pleasure the first delicious impression of the most beautiful and picturesque old city in North America. For in this season is the glamour of New Orleans strongest upon those whom she attracts to her from less hospitable climates, and fascinates by her nights of magical moonlight, and her days of dreamy languors and perfumes. There are few who can visit her for the first time without delight; and few who can ever leave her without regret; and none who can forget her strange charm when they have once felt its influence. To a native of the bleaker Northern clime—if he have any poetical sense of the beautiful in nature, any love of bright verdure and luxuriance of landscape—the approach to the city by river must be in itself something indescribably pleasant. The white steamer gliding through an unfamiliar world of blue and green—blue above and blue below, with a long strip of low green land alone to break the ethereal azure; the waving cane; the evergreen fringe of groves weird with moss; the tepid breezes and golden sunlight—all deepening in their charm as the city is neared, making the voyage seem beautiful as though one were sailing to some far-off glimmering Eden, into the garden of Paradise itself. And then, the first impression of the old Creole city slumbering under the glorious sun; of its quaint houses; its shaded streets; its suggestions of a hundred years ago; its contrasts of agreeable color; its streets re-echoing the tongues of many nations; its general look of somnolent contentment; its verdant antiquity; its venerable memorials and monuments; its eccentricities of architecture; its tropical gardens; its picturesque surprises; its warm atmosphere, drowsy perhaps with the perfume of orange flowers, and thrilled with the fantastic music of mockingbirds—cannot ever be wholly forgotten. For a hundred years and more has New Orleans been drawing hither wandering souls from all the ends of the earth. The natives of India and of Japan have walked upon her pavements; Chinese and swarthy natives of Manila; children of the Antilles and of South America; subjects of the Sultan and sailors of the Ionian Sea have sought homes here. All civilized nations have sent wandering children hither. All cities of the North, East, and West have yielded up some restless souls to the far-off Southern city, whose spell is so mystic, so sweet, so universal. And to these wondering and wandering ones, this sleepy, beautiful, quaint old city murmurs: "Rest with me. I am old; but thou hast never met with a younger more beautiful than I. I dwell in eternal summer; I dream in perennial sunshine; I sleep in magical moonlight. My streets are flecked with strange sharp shadows; and sometimes also the Shadow of Death falleth upon them; but if thou wilt not fear, thou are safe. My charms are not the charms of much gold and great riches; but thou mayest feel with me such hope and content as thou hast never felt before. I offer thee eternal summer, and a sky divinely blue; sweet breezes and sweet perfumes, bright fruits, and flowers fairer than the rainbow. Rest with me. For if thou leavest me, thou must forever remember me with regret." And assuredly those who wander from her may never cease to behold her in their dreams—quaint, beautiful, and sunny as of old— and to feel at long intervals the return of the first charm—the first delicious fascination of the fairest city of the South.

The Dawn of the Carnival

The Night cometh in which we take no note of time, and forget that we are living in a practical age which mostly relegates romance to printed pages and merriment to the stage. Yet what is more romantic than the Night of the Masked Ball—the too brief hours of light, music, and fantastic merriment which seem to belong to no century and yet to all? Somehow or other, in spite of all the noisy frolic of such nights, the spectacle of a Mardi Gras Ball impresses one at moments as a ghostly and unreal scene. The apparitions of figures which belong to other ages; the Venetian mysteries of the domino; the witchery of beauty half-veiled; the tantalizing salutes from enigmatic figures you cannot recognize; the pretty mockeries whispered into your ear by some ruddy lips whose syllabling seems so strangely familiar and yet defies recognition; the King himself seated above the shifting rout impenetrable as a Sphinx; and the kaleidescopic changing and flashing of colors as the merry crowd whirls and sways under the musical breath of the orchestra—seem hardly real, hardly possible to belong in any manner to the prosaic life of the century. Even the few unimpassional spectators who remain maskless and motionless form so strange a contrast that they seem like watchers in a haunted palace silently gazing upon a shadowy festival which occurs only once a year in the great hall exactly between the hours of twelve and three. While the most beautiful class of costumes seem ghostly only in that they really do belong to past ages, the more grotesque and outlandish sort seem strangely suggestive of a goblin festival. And above all the charms of the domino! Does it not seem magical that a woman can, by a little bright velvet and shimmering silk, thus make herself a fairy? And the glorious Night is approaching—this quaint old-time night, star-jeweled, fantastically robed; and the blue river is bearing us fleets of white boats thronged with strangers who doubtless are dreaming of lights and music, the tepid, perfumed air of Rex's Palace, and the motley rout of merry ghosts, droll goblins, and sweet fairies, who will dance the dance of the Carnival until blue day puts out at once the trembling tapers of the stars and lights of the great ball.

The Pelican's Ghost

There used to be a Pelican in the neighborhood of Jackson Square.

We used to attach considerable interest to that bird. It seemed to us like one of the sacred geese at the Capitol must have seemed to the old Romans. The destiny of the city seemed somehow connected with it. It enjoyed universal respect. Even the wicked little Creole boys refrained from tormenting it. Yet one day it mysteriously disappeared.

We never knew whom it belonged to, and never discovered exactly what had become of it. A friend hinted that it was really a sort of guardian genius, and had left the State in disgust, owing to the corruption of politics.

But it would seem that it simply went the way of all flesh; for an aged man who haunts the Passage de Saint-Antoine declares that he sees its ghost sometimes of clear nights, perched upon the head of Gen. Jackson. He knows it is a ghost, because the stars shine through it.

And the bird says—according to the ancient—something to the following effect, shortly before the midnight hour:—

"I was a Symbol. I am still a Symbol in my ghostliness. I betoken the old-fashioned life of the Pelican State that is passing away. I represent the quaintness that is dying out, and the antiquated thing that shall soon become as ghostly as myself. The old city is becoming Americanized; and I am glad that I am dead."

PART IV

Reports from the Field

LONGER STUDIES

Hearn was a writer and journalist but he lived in an era when scientists were busy collecting and classifying information on all nature and humankind. His papers are full of notes probably intended for future volumes on Louisiana's ethnic groups, its music, and even its wildlife (see the passages on hunting and fishing in part 1).

Hearn was a born collector and classifier, but he actually completed only two such projects: compilations on Creole cuisine and on the Creole dialect. The following selections from these studies suggest why they have produced so many literary offspring down to our own day.

La Cuisine Créole

Introduction

"La Cuisine Créole" (Creole cookery) partakes of the natures of its birthplace—New Orleans—which is cosmopolitan in its nature, blending the characteristics of the American, French, Spanish, Italian, West Indian and Mexican. In this compilation will be found many original recipes and other valuable ones heretofore unpublished, notably those of Gombo filé, Bouill abaisse, Courtbouillon, Jambolaya, Salade a la Russe, Bisque of Cray-fish à la Créole, Pusse Café, Café Brulé, Brulot, together with many confections and delicacies for the sick, including a number of mixed drinks. Much domestic contentment deepens upon the successful preparation of the meal; and as food rendered indigestible through ignorance in cooking often creates discord and unhappiness, it behooves the young housekeeper to learn the art of cooking.

It is the author's endeavor to present to her a number of recipes all thoroughly tested by experience, and embracing the entire field of the "Cuisine," set forth in such clear, concise terms, as to be readily understood and easily made practicable, thereby unveiling the mysteries which surround her, upon the *entrée* into the kitchen. Economy and simplicity govern "La Cuisine Créole"; and its many savory dishes are rendered palatable more as the result of care in their preparation, than any great skill or expensive outlay in the selection of materials. The Creole housewife often makes delicious *morceaux* from the things usually thrown away by the extravagant servant. She is proud of her art, and deservedly receives the compliments of her friends. This volume will be found quite different from the average cook-book in its treatment of recipes, and is the only one in print containing dishes peculiar to "la Cuisine Créole."

Soup

Soup being the first course served at all ordinary dinners, we make it the basis for preliminary remarks. Nothing more palatable than good, well-made soup, and nothing less appetising [sic] than poor soup. Now to attain perfection in any line, care and attention are requisite, careful study a necessity, and application the moving force. Hence, cooking in all its branches should be studied as a science, and not be looked upon as a haphazard mode of getting through life. Cooking is in a great measure a chemical process, and the ingredients of certain dishes should be as carefully weighed and tested as though emanating from the laboratory. Few female cooks think of this, but men with their superior instinctive reasoning power are more governed by law and abide more closely to rule; therefore, are better cooks, and command higher prices for services.

Now, with regard to soup making, the first care is to have the fire brisk, the vessel in which it is cooked thoroughly cleaned and free from odor. To insure this, keep one vessel sacred to soup as nearly as possible; and after serving wash the pot with potash water, or take a piece of washing soda the size of a nutmeg, dissolve in hot water and then cleanse the vessel. A good workman is known by his tools, so also a good cook will look well to the utensils before commencing operations. Good results follow carefulness.

Soup must have time to cook, and should always boil gently, that the meat may become tender, and give out its juices. Allow a quart of water and a teaspoonful of salt for each pound of meat. Soup meat must always be put down in cold water. Skim well before it comes to the boiling point, and again skim off superfluous fat before putting in the vegetables. The vegetables most used in soups are carrots, leeks, parsley, turnip, celery, tomatoes, okras, cabbage, cauliflower, peas and potatoes.

One large leek, two carrots, one bunch of parsley, two turnips and a potato, will be enough for one pot of soup. One head of celery, two leeks, two turnips, and five or six small potatoes will be enough another time. Six tomatoes skinned, the juice strained from the seeds, a leek, a bunch of parsley, and six potatoes will answer for another style; a carrot, some cabbage, tomatoes, and potatoes will do another time. Okra alone is vegetable enough for a gombo, unless onion is liked with it. Green peas, lettuce, and new potatoes are enough for spring lamb soup. Vermicelli and macaroni are for chicken, lamb or veal soup, with the addition of onion if liked.

It is well to prepare the vegetables when the meat is put over the fire to boil; allow a quart of water to a pound of meat. Trim and scrape carrots, then cut or grate them. Wash parsley and cut it small. Pare turnips and cut them in slices a quarter of an inch thick. Cut leeks in thick slices. Cut celery in half lengths; the delicate green leaves give a fine flavor to the soup.

Pour boiling water on tomatoes, which will cause the skins to peel off easily; when cool, squeeze out the seeds, and reserve the juice for use in soup.

Shave a cabbage in thin slices. Slice okra for gombo or ochra soup. Pare the potatoes, shell the peas, and cut off green corn from the cob, for all these add fine flavor to soup.

To color soup brown, use browned flour or a little burnt sugar. Spinach leaves give a fine green color. Pound the leaves, tie them in a cloth, and squeeze out all the juice, which, add to the soup five minutes before serving. This is also used to give color to mock-turtle soup.

You may color soup red by putting in the strained juice of tomatoes, or the whole tomato, if it is run through a sieve; grated carrot gives a fine amber color; okra gives a pale green.

For white soups, which are made of veal, lamb, and chicken, white vegetables are best, such as rice, pearl barley, vermicelli, and macaroni; the thickening should then be made of unbrowned flour.

Oyster Soup. Delicate.

Take the oysters from their liquor. To every quart of the liquor add a pint of water or milk (milk is preferable); season with salt, pepper, butter, and toasted bread-crumbs that have been toasted and pounded. When this has boiled put in a quart of oysters to two quarts of liquor. Let all boil a few minutes, and serve.

Turtle Soup for a Large Company, No. 1.

Cut the head off the turtle the day before you dress it, and drain the blood thoroughly from the body. Then cut it up in the following manner: Divide the back, belly, head and fins from the intestines and lean parts. Be careful not to cut the gall bag. Scald in boiling water to remove the skin and shell. Cut up in neat pieces and throw into cold water. Boil the back and belly in a little water long enough to extract the bones easily. If for a large company a leg of veal will also be required, and a slice of ham, which must be stewed with the lean parts till well browned; then add boiling water, and the liquor and bones of the boiled turtle. Season with sliced lemon, whole pepper, a bunch of parsley, two leaks sliced, and salt to taste. Let this all boil slowly for four hours then strain. Add the pieces of back, belly, head and fins (take the bones from the fins), pour in half a pint of Madeira wine and quarter of a pound of good sweet butter, with a tablespoonful of flour worked in it; also, a lemon sliced thin. Let it boil gently for two hours, then serve.

In cutting up the turtle great care should be taken of the fat, which should be separated, cut up neatly, and stewed til tender in a little of the liquor, and put into the tureen when ready to serve. Garnish with the eggs, if any; if not, use hard-boiled eggs of fowls.

Crayfish Bisque à la Créole

Wash the cray-fishes, boil and drain them. Separate the heads from the tails. Clean out some of the heads, allowing two or three heads to each person. Peel the tails. Chop up a part of them, add to them some bread, onions, salt, black pepper and an egg or two. With this dressing, stuff the heads that you have cleaned out. Chop the claws and the parts adhering to them. Fry a little garlic, onions, ham, one turnip, one carrot, and a little flour; add some water, the chopped claws, a few tomatoes, thyme, sweet bay, parsley and a little rice stirring often to avoid scorching. When well boiled, strain through a colander. After straining, put back to the fire and season to taste. Put the stuffed heads into the oven until brown. When ready to serve, put them and the tails in a soup dish and pour the soup over them. Before serving, add a little butter and nutmeg, stirring until the butter is melted.

Maigre Shrimp Gombo for Lent

Boil a pint of shrimps in a quart of water; give them only one boil up; then set them to drain and cool, reserving the water they were boiled in. Chop up three dozen okra pods; two onions, a pod of pepper, and a little parsley, and fry them brown in a little lard or butter; add to the okra the shrimps and the strained water in which they were boiled. Let all boil for an hour, and season with salt and pepper to taste. When shrimp and crabs can not be procured, half a pound of dry codfish, soaked an hour or two, and chopped fine, will do very well. All gombo should be thickened with a little flour—browned if preferred—and stirred in just before adding the water; then boil an hour.

Chefs D'oeuvre.

The Service Of Wines.

Cosmopolite Louisiana is undoubtedly the wine-drinking section of the Union, and a word as to the manner of serving the wines which play no small part in the discussion of "La Cuisine Creole," will not be out of place.

The inherited French taste of the greater portion of the population, and the education by contact of the American element, makes claret the universal table wine. The climate, too, renders this wine particularly palatable, and during the long heated term it is seldom absent from the table of even the most economical. At the restaurant it is the exception to see a person dining without a bottle of *vin ordinaire,* while for breakfast, during hot weather, white wines of the lighter kinds are much used.

As to the manner of serving wines at dinner the following menu will convey the most adequate idea:

With Soup,	...	Sherry.
" Fish,	...	White Wine.
" Entrees,	}	Claret, vin Ordinaire.
" Entremets,		

With Roast,	}	Claret, vin Ordinaire.
" Salad,		
" Dessert		Fine Claret or Café Noir, Cognac.

At large dinners in New Orleans a great deal of wine is served, and you will be expected to drink with your raw oysters, a light white wine; with soup and hors d'euvre, sherry or Madeira; with fish and entrées, a heavy white wine; with releves and entremets, a good claret followed by a *Ponche Romaine*, which is the turning point of the feast, or rest; after which will be served with the roast, champagne; game and salad, fine claret or burgundy, and with dessert café noir and liqueurs.

The most acceptable distribution of wines at a plain dinner—which we think should never be over five, or six courses at most—is given below. It is one which has the endorsement of the best authorities:

With Oysters,	...	White Wine.
" Soup,	...	Sherry or Madeira.
" Fish,	...	Heavy White Wine.*
" Entrees,	...	Champagne.
" Salad,	}	Fine Claret.
" Roast or Game,		

*not absolutely necessary.

with the usual after-dinner wines as preferred.

Grand Brule a la Boulanger   (From a Gourmet.)

The crowning of a grand dinner is a brule. It is the *piece de resistance,* the grandest *pousse café* of all. After the coffee has been served, the lights are turned down or extinguished, brule is brought in and placed in the centre of the table upon a pedestal surrounded by flowers. A match is lighted, and after allowing the sulphur to burn entirely off is applied to the brandy, and as it burns it sheds its weird light upon the faces of the company, making them appear like ghouls in striking contrast to the gay surroundings. The stillness that follows gives an opportunity for thoughts that break out in ripples of laughter which pave the way for the exhilaration that ensues.

Pour into a large silver bowl two wineglasses of best French brandy, one half wineglass of kirsch, the same of maraschino, and a small quantity of cinnamon and allspice. Put in about ten cubes of white sugar; do not crush them, but let them become saturated with the liquor. Remove the lumps of sugar, place in a ladle and cover with brandy. Ignite it as before directed, then lift it with the contents from the bowl, but do not mix. After it has burned about fifteen minutes serve in wine glasses. The above is for five persons, and should the company be larger add in proportion. Green tea and champagne are sometimes added.

Petit Brulé.

Take an ordinary-sized, thick-skinned orange; cut through the peel entirely around the orange like the line of the equator, then force off the peel by passing the handle of a spoon between it and the pulp. Into the cup thus formed put two lumps of sugar and some cinnamon, and fill with fine French brandy (cognac), and ignite it the same as the above and pour into glasses. The brule will be found to have a pleasant flavor given to it by the orange.

Hints On Cooking.

When salt hams or tongues are cooked they should be instantly thrown into cold water, as the change from the boiling water they were cooked in, to the cold water, instantly loosens the skin from the flesh, and it peels off without trouble.

Fresh vinegar should be added to chapped capers, because it brings out their flavor, and makes the sauces more appetizing.

Butter sauce should never be boiled, as it becomes oily if boiled in making. The whites and yolks of eggs should be beaten separately, because the tissues of both can be better separated; and a tablespoonful of water beaten with each is an improvement, and should never be omitted.

Onions, turnips and carrots should be cut across the fibre, as it makes them more tender when cooked.

Plenty of fast-boiling water should be used in cooking vegetables, as the greater the volume of water the greater the heat. If only a little water is used the whole affair soon cools, the vegetables become tough, and no length of time will render them tender.

Hints On Housecleaning: Soap Boiling, Etc.

House cleaning should commence at the top of the house and work downwards. In this case it may be undertaken by spells, with intervening rests.

After the floors are cleaned, the walls and ceilings claim attention.

A very beautiful whitening for walls and ceilings may be made by shaking the best lime in hot water, covering up to keep in the steam, and straining the milk of lime through a fine sieve; add to a pailful half a pound of common alum, two pounds of sugar, three pints of rice-flour made into a thin, well-boiled paste, and one pound of white glue dissolved slowly over the fire. It should be applied with a paint-brush when warm.

Paint should be cleaned by using only a little water at a time and changing often; a soft flannel cloth or sponge is better than cotton or a brush; a piece of pine wood with a sharp point should be used for the corners. Where the paint is stained with smoke, some ashes or potash lye may be used. A soft linen towel should be used for wiping dry. Glass should not be cleaned with soap; a little paste of whiting and water should be rubbed over, and with another cloth it should be rinsed off, and the glass polished with a soft linen or old silk handkerchief. Alcohol or benzine is a good thing to clean glass, and clean paper is probably better than any cloth, sponge or towel; dry paper leaves an excellent polish. Marble may be cleaned with a mixture of two parts of common soda, one part of pumice stone, and one of chalk, finely powdered and tied up in a fine muslin rag; the marble is wetted with water, the powder shaken over it, and it is rubbed with a soft cloth until clean, then washed in clean water and dried with a soft linen or silk handkerchief. No soap or potash should be allowed on marble. A good furniture polish is made by melting two ounces of beeswax, one ounce of turpentine, and one dram of powdered rosin together, with a gentle heat, and rubbing on when cold, with a soft flannel cloth, and polishing with a soft linen or silk cloth. If for mahogany, a little Indian red may be used. Cracks in furniture may be filled with putty, mixed with Indian-red or burnt umber, to get the desired shade. When dry it will take an equal polish with the wood.

Gombo Zhèbes: Little Dictionary of Creole Proverbs, Selected from Six Creole Dialects

Introduction

Any one who has ever paid a flying visit to New Orleans probably knows something about those various culinary preparations whose generic name is "Gombo" compounded of many odds and ends, with the okra-plant, or true gombo for a basis, but also comprising occasionally *"losé, zepinard, laitie,"* and the other vegetables sold in bunches in the French market. At all events any person who has remained in the city for a season must have become familiar with the nature of *"gombo filé," "gombo févi,"* and *"gombo aux herbes,"* or as our colored cook calls it, "gombo zhèbes"—for she belongs to the older generation of *creole cuisinières,* and speaks the patois in its primitive purity, without using a single "r." Her daughter, who has been to school, would pronounce it *gombo zhairbes:*—the modern patois is becoming more and more Frenchified, and will soon be altogether forgotten, not only throughout Louisiana, but even in the Antilles. It still, however, retains originality enough to be understood with difficulty by persons thoroughly familiar with French; and even those who know nothing of any language but English, readily recognize it by the peculiarly rapid syllabification and musical intonation. Such English-speaking residents of New Orleans seldom speak of it as "Creole": they call it *gombo,* for some mysterious reason which I have never been able to explain satisfactorily. The colored Creoles of the city have themselves begun to use the term to characterize the patois spoken by the survivors of slavery days. Turiault tells us that in the towns of Martinique, where the Creole is gradually changing into French, the *Bitacos,* or country negroes who still speak the patois nearly pure, are much ridiculed by their municipal brethren: *"Ça ou ka palé là, chè, c'est nèg:— Ça pas Créole!"* (*"What you talk is 'nigger,' my dear: that isn't Creole!"*) In like manner a young Creole negro or negress of New Orleans might tell an aged member of his race: *Ça qui to parlé pas Créole: ça c'est gombo!* I have sometimes heard the pure and primitive Creole also called "Congo" by colored folks of the new generation.

The literature of "gombo" has perhaps even more varieties than there are preparations of the esculents above referred to;—the patois has certainly its gombo févi, its gombo filé, its "gombo zhèbes"—both written and unwritten. A work like Marbot's "Bambous" would deserve to be classed with the pure "févi";—the treatises of Turiault, Baissac, St. Quentin, Thomas, rather resemble that fully prepared dish, in which crabs seem to struggle with fragments of many well-stewed meats, all strongly seasoned with pepper. The present essay at Creole folklore can only be classed as "gombo zhèbes"—(*Zhèbes çe feuil-chou, cresson, laitie, betts-av, losé, zépinard*);— the true okra is not the basis of our preparation;—it is a Creole dish, if you please, but a salmagundi of inferior quality.

* * *

For the collection of Louisiana proverbs in this work I am almost wholly indebted to my friend Professor William Henry, Principal of the Jefferson Academy in New Orleans; not a few of the notes, Creole quotations, and examples of the local patois were also contributed by him. The sources of the other proverbs will be found under the head of Creole Bibliography. The translations of the proverbs into French will greatly aid in exhibiting the curious process of transformation to which the negro slave subjected the language of his masters, and will also serve to show the peculiar simplicity of Creole grammar. My French is not always elegant, or even strictly correct;—for with the above object in view it has been necessary to make the translation as literal as is possible without adopting the interlinear system. Out of nearly five hundred proverbs I selected about three hundred and fifty only for publication—some being rejected because of their naïve indecency, others because they offered mere variations of one and the same maxim. Even after the sifting process, I was partly disappointed with the results; the proportions of true Creole proverbs—proverbs of indubitably negro invention—proved to be much smaller than I had expected. Nevertheless all which I have utilized exhibit the peculiarities of the vernacular sufficiently to justify their presence.

* * *

While some of these proverbs are witty enough to call a smile to the most serious lips, many others must, no doubt, seem vapid, enigmatic, or even meaningless. But a large majority of negro sayings depend altogether upon application for their color or their effectiveness; they possess a chameleon power of changing hue according to the manner in which they are placed. (See for examples: Prov. 161, 251, or 308.) Every saying of this kind is susceptible of numerous applications; and the art of applying one proverb to many different situations is one in which the negro has no rival—not

even among the Arabs themselves, whose use of such folklore has been
so admirably illustrated by Carlo Landberg.

* * *

No two authors spell the Creole in the same way; and three writers whom
I have borrowed largely from—Thomas, Baissac, and Turiault—actually
vary the orthography of the same word in quite an arbitrary manner. At
first I thought of remodeling all my proverbs according to the phonetic
system of spelling; but I soon found that this would not only disguise the
Creole etymology almost beyond recognition, but would further interfere
with my plan of arrangement. Finally I concluded to publish the Creole
text almost precisely as I had found it, with the various spellings and peculiarities of accentuation. The reader will find *cabrit,* for example, written
in four or five ways. Where the final t—never pronounced in our own patois—is fully sounded, the several authorities upon Creole grammar have
indicated the fact in various fashions: one spelling it *calbritt;* another
cabrite, etc.

* * *

The grammatical peculiarities and the pronounciation of the several
Creole dialects are matters which could not be satisfactorily treated within
the compass of a small pamphlet. Some few general rules might, indeed,
be mentioned as applying to most Creole dialects. It is tolerably safe to say
that in no one of the West Indian dialects was the French "*r*" pronounced
in former days; it was either totally suppressed, as in the word "*fòcé*" (force)
or exchanged for a vowel sound, as in *bouanche* (for *branche*). The delicate
and difficult French sound of *u* was changed into *ou;* the sound *en* was
simplified into *é;* the clear European *o* became a nasal *au;* and into many
French words containing the sound of *am,* such as *amour,* the negro wedged
the true African *n,* making the singular Creole pronounciation *lanmou,*
canmarade, janmain. But the black slaves from the Ivory and Gold Coasts,
from Congo or Angola, pronounced differently. The Eboes and Mandin-
goes spoke the patois with varying accentuations;—it were therefore very
difficult to define rules of pronounciation applicable to the patois spoken
in all parts of one island like Guadaloupe, or one colonial province like
Guyana. Not so in regard to grammar. In all forms of the patois (whether
the musical and peculiarly picturesque Creole of Martinique, or the more
fantastic Creole of Mauritius, adulterated with Malgache and Chinese
words)—the true article is either suppressed or transformed into a prefix

or affix of the noun, as in *femme-la,* "the woman," or *yon lagrimace,* a grimace;—there is no true gender, no true singular and plural; verbs have rarely more than six tenses—sometimes less—and the tense is not indicated by the termination of the verb; there is a remarkable paucity of auxiliaries, and in some dialects none whatever; participles are unknown, and prepositions few. A very fair knowledge of comparative Creole grammar and pronunciation may be acquired, by any one familiar with French, from the authors cited at the beginning of this volume. I would also recommend those interested in such folklore to peruse the Creole novel of Dr. Alfred Mercier—*Les Saint-Ybars,* which contains excellent examples of the Louisiana dialect; and Baissac's beautiful little stories, *Recits Créoles,* rich in pictures of the old French colonial life. The foreign philological reviews and periodicals, especially those of Paris, have published quite a variety of animal fables, proverbs, stories in various Creole dialects; and among the recent contributions of French ethnologists to science will be also discovered some remarkable observations upon the actual formation of various patois—strongly resembling our own Creole—in the French African colonies.

* * *

Needless to say this collection is far from perfect;—the most I can hope for is that it may constitute the nucleus of a more exhaustive publication to appear in course of time. No one person could hope to make a really complete collection of Creole proverbs—even with all the advantages of linguistic knowledge, leisure, wealth, and travel. Only a society of folklorists might bring such an undertaking to a successful issue; but as no systematic effort is being made in this direction, I have no hesitation in attempting—not indeed to fill a want—but to set an example. *Gouïe passé, difil sivré:* let the needle but pass, the thread will follow.

Creole Bibliography.

The selection of Haytian proverbs in this collection was made by kindly permission of Messrs. Harper Bros., from the four articles contributed by Hon. John Bigelow, to *Harper's Magazine,* 1875. The following list includes only those works consulted or quoted from in the preparation of this dictionary, and comprises but a small portion of all the curious books, essays, poems, etc., written upon, or in the Creole patois of the Antilles and of Louisiana.

Bruyère (Loys) — "Proverbes Créoles de la Guane Fançaise." (In *l'Almanach des Traditions Populaires*, 1883. Paris: Maisonneuve et Cie.)

Baissac (M. C.) — "Étude sur le Patois Créole Mauricien." Nancy: Imprimerie Berger-Levrault & Cie., 1880.

Marbot — "Les Bambous." *Fables de La Fontaine travesties en Patois Créole par un Vieux Commandeur*. Fort-de-France, Martinique: Librarie de Frederic Thomas, 1869. (Second Edition. Both editions of this admirable work are now unfortunately out of print.

Thomas (J. J.) — "The Theory and Practice of Creole Grammar." Port of Spain, Trinidad: The Chronicle Publishing Office, 1869.

Turiault (J.) — "Étude sur le Langage Créole de la Martinique." (Extrait du *Bulletin de la Société Academique*.) Brest: Lefournier, 1869.

De St.-Quentin (Auguste) — *Introduction à l'Histoire de Cayenne, suivie d'un Recueil dContes, Fables, et Chansons en Créole*. Notes et Comentaires par Auguste de St. Quentin. Étude sur la Grammaire Créole par Auguste de St. Quentin. Antibes: J. Marchand, 1872.

Bigelow (Hon. John) — "The Wit and Wisdom of the Haytians." Being four articles upon the Creole Proverbs of Hayti, respectively published in the June, July, August, and September numbers of *Harper's Magazine*, 1875.

Little Dictionary of Creole Proverbs

[*Most of the proverbs quoted in Martinique are current also in Guadaloupe, only 90 miles distant. All proverbs recognized in Louisiana are marked by an asterisk(*). The indications, Mauritius, Guyana, Martinique, Hayti, etc, do not necessarily imply origin; they refer only to the dialects in which the proverbs are written,[1] and to the works from which they are selected.*]

21. Bef pas jamain ka dîe savane, "Meçi!" (Le bœuf ne dit jamais à la savane, "Merci!")

"Ox never says 'Thank you,' to the pasture." — [*Trinidad.*]

A proverb current in Martinique, Louisiana, etc., with slight variations. Favors or services done through selfish policy, or compelled by necessity, do not merit acknowledgment.

23. Bel tignon pas fait bel négresse. (Le beau tignon ne fait pas la belle negresse.)

---

[1] The Louisiana dialect is that of New Orleans.

"It isn't the fine head-dress that makes the fine negress." [*Louisiana*.]

The Louisiana *tiyon* or *tignon* [*tiyon* is the true Creole word] is the famously picturesque handkerchief which in old days all slave women twisted about their heads. It is yet worn by the older colored folk: and there are several styles of arranging it—*tiyon chinoise, tiyon Créole*, etc. An old New Orleans ditty is still sung, of which the refrain is:—

> Madame Caba!
> Tiyon vous tombé!
> Madame Caba,
> Tiyon vous tiombé!
> ["Madame Caba, your tiyon's falling off!"]

26. Bon blanc mouri; mauvais rêté. (Le bon blanc meurt; le mauvais [méchant] reste.)
"The good white man dies; the bad remains."—[*Hayti*.]

*28. Bon chien pas janmain trappé bon zo. (Jamais un bon chien n'obtient un bon os.)
"A good dog never gets a good bone."—Creole adaptation of an old French proverb.—[*Martinique*.]

31. Bon-Guè ka baille ti zouèseau dans bois mangé, jigé sì li pas ké baille chritien mangé. (Le Bon Dieu donne à manger aux petits oiseaux qui sont dans les bois; jugez s'il ne donnera pas à manger à un chrétien.)
"God gives the little birds in the wood something to eat; judge for yourself, then, whether he will not give a Christian something to eat."—[*Martinique*.]

Such a conversation as the following may not unfrequently be heard among the old colored folk in New Orleans:—

—"Eh! Marie! to papé travaï jordi?"

—"Moin?—non!"

—"Eh, ben! comment to fé pou vive alors?"

—"*Ah!... ti zozo li ka boi, li ka mangé, li pas travaï toujou!*"

["Hey, Marie!—Ain't you going to work to-day?" "I?—no!" "Well then, how do you manage to live?" "Ah.... *little bird drinks, little bird eats, little bird does'nt work all the same!*"]

*34. Bon-temps fait crapaud manqué bounda. (Le bon temps fait manquer de derrière au crapaud.)
"Idleness leaves the frogs without buttocks."—[*Louisiana*.]

*35. -Bon-temps pas bosco. (Le bon temps n'est pas bossu.)
"Good fortune is never hunch-backed."—[*Trinidad.*]
  Same proverb in Martinique dialect, and in that of Louisiana.
  In Creole *bon temps* most generally signifies "idleness," and is not always used in a pleasant sense. Proverb 35 is susceptible of several different applications.

36. Bon valett ni lakhé coupé. (Le bon valet a la queue coupée.)
"The good servant's tail is cut off."—[*Martinique.*]
  Reference to the condition of a dog whose tail is cut off: he can't wag his tail, because he has no tail to wag.
  The good servant does not fawn, does not flatter, does not affect to be pleased with everything his master does—he may emulate the dog in constant faithfulness, not in fawning.

*37. Bouche li pas ni dimanche. (Sa bouche n'a pas de dimanche.)
"His mouth never keeps Sunday"—lit: "has no Sunday"—no day of rest.—
[*Martinque.*]

*40. Bouki fait gombo, lapin mangé li. (Le bouc fait le gombo, le lapin le mange.)
"He-goat makes the gombo; but Rabbit eats it."—[*Louisiana.*]
  This proverb is founded upon one of the many amusing Creole animal-fables, all bearing the title: *Compè Bouki épis Compè Lapin* ("Daddy Goat and Daddy Rabbit"). The rabbit always comes out victorious, as in the stories of Uncle Remus.

*43. Ça qui bon pou zoie, bon pou canard. (Ce qui est bon pour l'oie, est bon pour le canard.)
"What is good for the goose is good for the duck."—[*Martinique.*]

44. Ça qui boudé manze boudin. (Celui qui boude mange du boudin.)
"He who sulks eats his own belly." That is to say, spites himself. The pun is untranslatable.—[*Mauritius.*]
  Boudin in French signifies a pudding, in Creole it also signifies the belly. Thus there is a double pun in the patois.

45. Ça qui dourmi napas pensé manzé. (Qui dort ne pense pas à manger.)
"When one sleeps, one doesn't think about eating."—[*Mauritius.*]
  "*Qui dort, dine,*" is an old French proverb.

*57. Ça va rivé dans semaine quatte zheudis. (Cela va arriver dans la semaine de quatre jondis.)
"That will happen in the week of four Thursdays."—[*Louisiana.*]
Ironically said to those who make promises which there is no reason to believe will ever be fulfilled.

60. Cabritt li ka monté roche, li descende. (Chèvre qui a monté un rocher doit en descendre.)
"The goat that climbs up the rocks must climb down again."—[*Guyana.*]

64. Canari vié rîe chôdier. (Le canari [le pot] veut rire de la chaudière [la marmite].)
"The clay-pot wishes to laugh at the iron pot."—[*Trinidad.*]
"Pot calls the kettle black." The clay pot (*canari*) has almost disappeared from Creole kitchens in Louisiana; but the term survives in a song of which the burthen is: "*Canari cassé dans difé.*"

*67. Capon vive longtemps. (Le capon vit longtemps.)
"The coward lives a long time."—[*Louisiana.*]
The word *capon* is variously applied by Creoles as a term of reproach. It may refer rather to stinginess, hypocrisy, or untruthfulness, than to cowardice. We have in New Orleans an ancient Creole ballad of which the refrain is:

> Alcée Leblanc
> Mo di toi, chère,
> *To trop capon*
> *Pou payé manage!*
> C'est qui di ça,—
> Ça que di toi chère,
> Alcée Leblanc!

In this case the word evidently refers to the niggardliness of *Alcée,* who did not relish the idea of settling $500 or perhaps $1,000 of furniture upon his favorite quadroon girl. The song itself commemorates customs of slavery days. Those who took to themselves colored mistresses frequently settled much property upon them—the arrangement being usually made by the mother of the girl. Housekeeping outfits of this character, constituting a sort of dowry, ranged in value from $500 to even $2,500; and such dowries formed the foundation of many celebrated private lodging houses in New Orleans kept by colored women. The quadroon house-keepers have now almost all disappeared.

*68. Çaquéne senti so doulére. (Chacun sent sa douleur.)
"Everybody has his own troubles."—[*Mauritius.*]

*76. *C'est couteau qui cannaite ça qui dans cœur geomon. (C'est le couteau qui sait ce qu'il y a dans le cœur du giromon.)*
"It's the knife that knows what's in the heart of the pumpkin."—[*Martinique.*]

This proverb exists in five Creole dialects. In the Guyana patois it is slightly different: Couteau ounso connain quior iniam (le couteau seul connait le cœur de l'igname.) "It's only the knife knows what's in the heart of the yam."

78. C'est douvant tambou nion cannaitt Zamba. (C'est devant le tambour qu'on reconnait Zamba.)
"It's before the drum one learns to know Zamba."—[*Hayti.*]

79. C'est langue crapaud qui ka trahî crapaud. (C'est la langue du crapaud qui le trahit.)
"It's the frog's own tongue that betrays him."—[*Trinidad.*]

In some of the West Indies the French word *crapaud* seems to have been adopted by the Creoles to signify either a toad or a frog, as it is much more easily pronounced by Creole lips than *grenouille,* which they make sound like "gwoonouïlle." But in Louisiana there is a word used for frog, a delightful and absolutely perfect onomatopœia: OUAOUARON (wahwahron).

I think the prettiest collection of Creole onomatopœia made by any folklorist is that in Baissac's *Étude sur le patois créole Mauricien,* pp. 92–95. The delightful little Creole nursery-narrative, in which the cries of all kinds of domestic animals are imitated by patois phrases, deserves special attention.

*86. Chatte brilé pair di feu. (Le chat brulé a peur du feu.)
"A burnt cat dreads the fire."—[*Louisiana.*]

*89. Chien jappé li pas mordé. (Le chien qui jappe ne mord pas.)
"The dog that yelps doesn't bite."—[*Louisiana.*]

90. Chien pas mangé chien. (Les chiens ne mangent pas les chiens.)
"Dogs do not eat dogs."—[*Louisiana.*]

***95.** Cila qui rit vendredi va pleuré dimanche. (Celui qui rit le vandredi va pleurer le dimanche.)
"He who laughs on Friday will cry on Sunday." There is an English proverb, "Sing at your breakfast and you'll cry at your dinner."—[*Louisiana.*]

96. Ciramon pas donne calabasse. (Le giraumon ne donne pas la calebasse.)
"The pumpkin doesn't yield the calabash."—[*Hayti.*]
I give the spelling *Ciramon* as I find it in Mr. Bigelow's contributions to *Harper's Magazine*, 1875. (See Bibliography.) Nevertheless I suspect the spelling is wrong. In Louisiana Creole we say *Giromon*. The French word is *Giraumon*.

***97.** Cochon conné sir qui bois l'apé frotté. (Le cochon sait bien sur quel arbre [bois] il va se frotter.)
"The hog knows well what sort of tree to rub himself against."—[*Louisiana.*]
In most of the Creole dialects several different versions of a popular proverb are current. A friend gives me this one of proverb 97: *Cochon-marron conné enhaut gui bois li frotté.* ("The wild hog knows what tree to rub himself upon.") *Marron* is applied in all forms of the Creole patois to *wild* things; *zhèbes marrons* signifies "wild plants." The term, *couri-marron,* or *nègue-marron* formerly designated a runaway slave in Louisiana as it did in the Antilles. There is an old New Orleans saying:

> "*Après yé tiré cannon*
> *Nègue sans passe c'est nègue-marron.*"

This referred to the old custom in New Orleans of firing a cannon at eight P.M. in winter, and nine P.M. in summer, as a warning to all slaves to retire. It was a species of modern curfew-signal. Any slave found abroad after those hours, without a pass, was liable to arrest and a whipping of twenty-five lashes. *Marron,* from which the English word "Maroon" is derived, has a Spanish origin. "It is," says Skeats, "a clipt form of the Spanish *cimarrón,* wild, unruly; literally, 'living in the mountain-tops.' *Cimarrón,* from Spanish *cima,* a mountain-summit. The original term for 'Maroon' was *negro-cimarrón,* as it still is in some parts of Cuba."

99. Compé Torti va doucement; mais li rívé coté bîte pendant Compé Chivreil apé dormi. (Compère Tortue va doucement; mais il arrive au bût pendant que Compère Chevreuil dort.)
"Daddy Tortoise goes slow; but he gets to the goal while Daddy Deer is asleep."—[*Louisiana.*]

Based upon the Creole fable of *Compère Tortue* and *Comperè Chevreuil,* rather different from the primitive story of the Hare and the Tortoise.

100. Complot plis fort passé ouanga. (Le complot est plus fort que l'ouanga.)
"Conspiracy is stronger than witchcraft."—[*Hayti.*]

> Di moin si to gagnin nhomme!
> Mo va fé ouanga pou li;
> Mo fé li tourné fantôme
> Si to vié mo to mari. . . .

"Tell me if thou has a man [a lover]: I will make a *ouanga* for him—I will change him into a ghost if thou wilt have me for thy husband.". . . This word, of African origin, is applied to all things connected with the voudouism of the negroes. In the song, "*Dipi mo vouè, touè Adèle,*" from which the above lines are taken, the wooer threatens to get rid of a rival by *ouanga*—to "turn him into a ghost." The victims of voudouism are said to have gradually withered away, probably through the influence of secret poison. The word *grigri,* also of African origin, simply refers to a charm, which may be used for an innocent or innocuous purpose. Thus, in a Louisiana Creole song, we find a quadroon mother promising her daughter a charm to prevent the white lover from forsaking her; *Pou tchombé li na fé grigri*—"We shall make a grigri to keep him."

107. Coupé zoré milet fait pas choual. (Couper le oreilles au mulet, n'en fait pas un cheval.)
"Cutting off a mule's ears won't make him a horse."—[*Louisiana.*]

This seems to me much wittier than our old proverb: "You can't make a silk purse out of a sow's ear."

112. Craché nen laire, li va tombé enhaut vou nez. (Crachez dans l'air, il vous en tombera sur le nez).
"If you spit in the air, it will fall back on your own nose.—[*Louisiana.*]

Like our proverb about chickens coming home to roost. If you talk scandal at random, the mischief done will sooner or later recoil upon yourself. I find the same proverb in the Mauritian dialect.

120. Dent mordé langue. (Les dents mordent la langue.)
"The teeth bite the tongue."—[*Hayti.*]

*123. Di moin qui vous laimein, ma di vous qui vous yé. (Dites moi qui vous aimez, et je vous dirai qui vous êtes.)
"Tell me whom you love, and I'll tell you who you are."—[*Louisiana.*]

124. Dileau dourmi touyé dimounde. (L'eau qui dort tue les gens.)
"The water that sleeps kills people."—[*Mauritius.*]
"Still waters run deep." The proverb is susceptible of various applications. Everyone who has sojourned in tropical, or even semi-tropical, latitudes knows the deadly nature of stagnant water in the feverish summer season.

*130. Dolo toujou couri larivière. (L'eau va toujours à la rivière.)
"Water always runs to the river."—[*Louisiana.*]

133. Faut janmain mett racounn dans loge poule. (Il ne faut jamais mettre un raton dans la loge des poules.)
"One must never put a 'coon into a henhouse."—[*Martinique.*]
A Creole friend assures me that in Louisiana patois, the word for coon, is *chaoui.* This bears so singular a resemblance in sound to a French word of very different meaning—*chat-huant* (screech-owl) that it seems possible the negroes have in this, as in other cases, given the name of one creature to another.

134. Faut jamais porté déil avant défint dans cerkeil. (Il ne faut jamais porter le deuil avant que le défunt soit dans le cercueil.)
"Never wear mourning before the dead man's in his coffin."—[*Louisiana.*]
Don't anticipate trouble: "Never bid the devil good morrow till you meet him." "Don't cross a bridge until you come to it."

*137. Faut pas marré tayau avec saucisse. (Il ne faut pas attacher le chien-courant (taïant) avec des saucisses.)
"Musn't tie up the hound with a string of sausages."—[*Louisiana.*]
Adopted from old French "*taïaut*" (tally-ho!), the cry of the huntsman to his hounds. The Creoles have thus curiously, but forcibly, named the hound itself.

138. Fére éne tourou pour boucé laute. (Il fait un trou pour en boucher un autre.)
"Make one hole to stop another." "Borrow money to pay a debt."— [*Mauritius.*]

*****141.** Gens fégnants ka mandé travâï épîs bouche; main khèrs yeaux ka pouier Bondié pou yeaux pas touver. (Les gens fainéants demandent avec leurs bouches pour du travail mais leurs cœurs prient le Bon Dieu [pour] qu'ils n'en trouvent point.)
"Lazy folks ask for work with their lips: but their hearts pray God that they may not find it."—[*Trinidad.*]

*****147.** Jadin loin, gombo gaté. (Jardin loin, gombo gâté.)
"When the garden is far, the gombo is spoiled."—[*Martinique.*]
This appears to be a universal Creole proverb. If you want anything to be well done, you must look after it yourself: to absent oneself from one's business is unwise, etc.

*****148.** Jamais di: Fontaine, mo va jamais boi to dolo. (Ne dis jamais— Fontaine, je ne boirai jamais de ton eau.)
"Never say—'Spring, I will never drink your water.'"—[*Louisiana.*]
The loftiest pride is liable to fall; and we know not how soon we may be glad to seek the aid of the most humble.

*****152.** Joué épis chien ou trappé pice. (Jouez avec les chiens, vous aurez des puces.)
"Play with the dogs, and you will get fleas."—[*Martinique.*]
This seems to be a universal proverb. In Louisiana we say: *Jouè evec 'ti chien,* etc.

*****153.** Joudui pou ous, demain pou moin. (Au jourd'hui pour vous, demain pour moi.)
"To-day for you; to-morrow for me."—[*Hayti.*]
Current also in Louisiana: *Jordi pou vou,* etc.: "Your turn to-day; perhaps it may be mine to-morrow."

*****157.** Lagniappe c'est bitin qui bon. (Lagniappe c'est du bon butin.)
"Lagniappe is lawful booty."—[*Louisiana.*]
Lagniappe, a word familiar to every child in New Orleans, signifies the little present given to purchasers of groceries, provisions, fruit, or other goods sold at retail stores. Groceries, especially, seek to rival each other

in the attractive qualities of their *lagniappe:* consisting of candles, fruits, biscuits, little fancy cakes, etc. The chief purpose is to attract children. The little one sent for a pound of butter, or "a dime's worth" of sugar, never fails to ask for its *lagniappe.*

*159. Laguerre vertie pas tchué beaucoup soldats. (La guerre avertie ne tue pas beaucoup de soldats.)
"Threatened war doesn't kill many soldiers."—[*Louisiana.*]

161. Lalangue napas lézos. (La langue n'a pas d'os.)
"The tongue has no bones." This proverb has various applications. One of the best alludes to promises or engagements made with the secret determination not to keep them.—[*Mauritius.*]

*162. Lamisère à deux, Misère et Compagnie. (La misère à deux, c'est Misère et Compagnie.)
"Misery for two, is Misery & Co."—[*Louisiana.*]
Refers especially to a man who marries without having made proper provision for the future. The Creole does not believe in our reckless proverb: "What will keep one, will keep two." *Non, non, chèr, lamisère à deux, Misère & Cie!*

*166. Laplie tombé, ouaouaron chanté. (Quand la pluie va tomber, les grenouilles chantent.)
"When the rain is coming, the bull-frogs sing."—[*Louisiana.*]

*171. La-tché chatte poussé avec temps. (La queue du chat pousse avec le temps.)
"The cat's tail takes time to grow."—[*Louisiana.*]

172. Lepé di aimé ous pendant li rouge doighte ous. (La lépre dit qu'elle vous aime pendant qu'elle vous rouge les doigts.)
"The leprosy says it loves you, while it is eating your fingers."—[*Hayti.*]

178. Li manque lagale pour gratté. (Il [ne] manque [que] de gale pour se gratter. [*Lit. In good French:* Il ne lui manque que la gale, etc.]
"He only wants the itch so that he may scratch himself." Said of a man who has all that his heart can wish for.—[*Mauritius.*]
We have a singular expression in Louisiana: "*Li metté mantec dans so faillots.*" ("He puts lard in his beans.") That is to say, "He is well off." *Mantec* is a Creolised form of the Spanish *manteca* used in Spanish-America to signify lard.

*185. Macaque dan calebasse. (Le macaque dans la calebasse.)
"Monkey in the calabash."—[*Louisiana.*]

Allusion to the old fable about the monkey, who after putting his hand easily into the orifice of a gourd could not withdraw it without letting go what he sought to steal from within, and so got caught. In the figurative Creole speech one who allows his passions to ruin or disgrace him, is a *macaque dans calebasse.*

*186. Macaque dit si so croupion plimé ças pas gàdé lezautt. (Le macaque dit que si son croupion est plumé, ça ne régarde pas les autres.)
"Monkey says if his rump is bare, it's nobody's business."—[*Louisiana.*]

Allusion to the callosities of the monkey. *Plimé* literally means "plucked," but the Creole negroes use it to signify "bare" from any cause. A negro in rags might use the above proverb as a hint to those who wish to joke him about his personal appearance.

*187. Macaque pas jamain ka dîe ìche li laide. (Le macaque ne dit jamais que son petit est laid.)
"Monkey never says its young is ugly."—[*Trinidad.*]

A widely-spread proverb. In Louisiana we say *piti li* or *so piti* instead of "*yche*" or "*iche li.*" In Martinique Creole: *Macaque pas janmain trouve yche li laide.*

*198. Maringouin perdi so temps quand li piqué caïman. (Le maringoin perd son temps quand il pique le caïman.)
"The mosquito loses his time when he tries to sting the alligator."—[*Louisiana.*]

Ripost to a threat—as we would say: "All that has as little effect on me as water on a duck's back!"

*203. Merci pas couté arien. ("Merci" ne coûte rien.)
"Thanks cost nothing."—[*Louisiana.*]

*204. Metté milâte enhaut choual, li va dî négresses pas so maman. (Mettez un mulâtre [en haut] sur un cheval—il [va dire] dira qu'une négresse n'est pas sa maman.)
"Just put a mulatto on horseback, and he'll tell you his mother was'nt a negress."—[*Louisiana.*]

I usually give but one example of a proverb when it occurs in several dialects; but the Martinique form of this proverb is too amusing to omit. See Prov. 267.

206. Milatt ka batt, cabritt ka mò. (Les mulâtres se battent, ce sont les cabrits qui meurent.)

"When the mulattoes get to fighting, the goats get killed."—[*Martinique.*]

The feeling of the black to the mulatto is likewise revealed in the following dicton:

—Nègue pòté maïs dans so lapoche pou volé poule;—milatt pòté cordon dans so lapoche pou volé chonal;—nhomme blanc pòté larzan dans so lapoche pou trompé fille. (Le négre porte du maïs dans sa poche pour voler des poules;—le mulâtre porte un cordon dans sa poche pour voler des chevaux;—l'homme blanc porte de l'argent dans sa poche pour tromper les filles.)

"The negro carries corn in his pocket to [help him to] steal chickens; the mulatto carries a rope in his pocket to steal horses; the white man carries money in his pocket to deceive girls."—[*Louisiana.*]

*207. Misè fè macaque mangé piment. (La misère force le macaque à manger du piment.)

"Misery makes the monkey eat red pepper."—[*Martinique.*]

*208. "Mo bien comm mo yé," parole rare. ("Jo me trouve bien comme je suis"—ces sont des paroles rares.)

"'I'm well enough as I am,' are words one doesn't often hear."—[*Louisiana.*]

*209. Mo va pas prê é vous bâton pou cassé mo latête. (Je ne vais vous prêter un bâton pour me casser la tête.)

"I'm not going to lend you a stick to break my head with."—[*Louisiana.*]

*219. Napas zoué av difé; wou a boulé vous çimise. (Ne jouez pas avec le feu; vous vous brûlerez la chemise.)

"Play with the fire and you'll burn your shirt."—[*Maritius.*]

This proverb appears to be current wherever any form of the patois prevails.

*223. Oîmso soulié savé si bas tini trou. (Le soulier seul sait si le bas a un trou.)

"The shoe only knows whether the stockings have holes."—[*Guyana.*]

In the Martinique dialect it is: *C'est soulié qui save si bas tini trou.* In the Trinidad patois: *Cé soulier tout-sél qui save si bas tini trou* (Thomas). In Louisiana Creole: *C'est soulier nek-connin si bas gagnin trou. "Nek,"* compound from French *ne . . . que*—"only."

*228. Où y'en a charogne, y'en a carencro. (Où il a charogne, il y a des busards.)
"Wherever there's carrion, there are buzzards."—[*Louisiana.*]
This is one of several instances of the Creole adoption of English words. The name "carrion-crow" has been applied to the buzzard in Louisiana from an early period of its American history.

*235. Parole trop fort, machoir gonflé. (Par la parole trop forte, la machoir est gonflée.)
"By talking too loud the jaw becomes swelled."—[*Louisiana.*]
Literally: "Word too strong, jaw swelled up." Seems to imply the *indirect* rather than the direct consequence of using violent language—*viz.*, a severe beating from the person abused.

*240. Pis faibe toujou tini tò. (Le plus faible a toujours tort.)
"The weakest is always in the wrong."—[*Martinique.*]

*241. Piti à piti, zozo fait son nid. (Petit à petit, l'oiseau fait son nid.)
"Little by little the bird builds its nest."—[*Louisiana.*]

244. Pou manje, tou bon; pouâlé pas tou parole. (Pou manger, tout est bon; pou parler, pas toute parole).
"Anything is good enough to eat; but every word is not good enough to be spoken."—[*Guyana.*]
In the Martinique dialect: *Toutt mangé, toutt paaule pas bon pou di.*—[*Turiault.*]

*248. Pranne garde vaut miè passé mandé pardon. (Prendre garde vaut mieux que demandre pardon.)
"It is better to take care beforehand than to ask pardon afterward."—[*Louisiana.*]

250. Pitit mie tombe, ramassé li; Chrétien tombe, pas reamasé li. (Quand une petite mie tombe, on la ramasse; quand un Chrétien tombe, on ne le ramasse pas [i.e., on ne l'aide pas à se relever].)
"If a little crumb falls, it is picked up; if a Christian falls, he is not picked up."—[*Hayti.*]

*251. Quand bois tombé, cabri monté. (Quand l'arbre tombe, le cabri monte.)
"When the tree falls, the kid can climb it."—[*Louisiana.*]

This saying has quite a variety of curious applications. The last time I heard it, a Creole negress was informing me that the master of the house in which she worked was lying at the point of death: *"pauve diabe!"* I asked after the health of her mistress. *"Ah! Madame se porte bien; mais... quand bois tombé cabri monté,"* she replied, half in French, half in her own patois; signifying that after the husband's death, wife and children would find themselves reduced to destitution.

*253. Quand boyaux grogné bel'evite pas fait yé pé. (Quand les boyaux grognent, un bel habit ne leur fait pas se taire; lit., ne leur fait pas paix.) "When the bowels growl a fine coat won't make them hold their peace."— [*Louisiana.*]

The words *pè*, pé, in Creole are distinguishable only by their accentuation. *Peur* (fear); *peu* (a little); *paix* (peace, or "hush"); *peut* (can), all take the form *pè* or *pé* in various Creole dialects. *Ipas ni pè sépent:* "he is not afraid of snakes." Sometimes one can guess the meaning only by the context, as in the Martinique saying: *Pè bef pè caca bef.*— "Few oxen, little ox-dung"; i.e., "little money, little trouble." The use of *"pè"* for *père* (father), reminds us of a curious note in the Creole studies of the brothers Saint-Quentin (See Bibliography). In the forests of Guyana there is a bird whose song much resembles that of our Louisiana mocking-bird, but which is far more sonorous and solemn. The Creole negroes call it *ZOZO MONPÉ* (*l'oiseau mon-père*), lit., "The my-father bird." Now *monpè* is the Creole name for a priest; as if we should say "a my-father" instead of "a priest." The bird's song, powerful, solemn, far-echoing through the great aisles of the woods by night, suggested the chant of a *monpè*, a "ghostly father"; and its name might be freely translated by "the priest-bird."

254. Quand cannari pas bouï pou ou, ou donè janmain découvri li. *(Quand le pôt ne bout pas pour vous, vous ne devez jamais le découvrir.)* "When the pot won't boil for you, you must never take the lid off."— [*Martinique.*]

"Watched pot never boils." The *canari* was a clay pot as the following Creole refrain testifies:

> Ya pas bouillon pou vous, macommère;
> Canari cassé dans difé (bis),
> Bouillon renvèrsé dans difé

Ya pas bouillon pou vous, macommère
Canari cassé dans difé

["There's no soup for you, my gossipping friend; the pot's broken in the fire; the soup is spilled in the fire," etc.]

*264. Quand li gagnin kichose dans so latête, cé pas dans so lapiè. (Quand il a quelque chose dans sa tête, ce n'est pas dans son pied.)
"When he gets something into his head, it isn't in his foot."—[*Louisiana.*]
   Refers to obstinacy. A man may be compelled to move his feet, but not to change his resolve.

266. Quand maite chanté, nègue dansé; quand 'conome sifflé, nègue sauté. (Quand le maître chante, le nègre danse; quand l'économe siffle, le nègre saute.)
"When the master sings the negro dances; but when the overseer only whistles, the negro jumps."—A relic of the old slave-day Creole folklore.—[*Louisiana.*]

267. Quand milatt tini yon vié chouvral yo dit nègress pas manman yo. (Quand les mulâtres ont un vieux cheval ils disent que les négresses ne sont pas leurs mères.)
"As soon as a mulatto is able to own an old horse, he will tell you that his mother wasn't a nigger."—[*Martinique.*]

*268. Quand napas maman, tété grand-maman. (Quand n'a pas sa mère, on tete sa grand-mère.)
"When one has no mother, one must be suckled by one's grandmother."—[*Louisiana.*]

*271. Quand patate tchuite, faut mangé li. (Quand la patate est cuite, il faut la manger.)
"When the sweet potato is cooked, it must be eaten."—[*Louisiana.*]
   This differs a little from the spelling adopted by Gottschalk in his *Bamboula*—"*Quand potate-la couite ma va mangé li.*" The proverb is used in the sense of our saying: "Strike the iron while it's hot."

277. Quand yo baille ou tête bef pou mangé, n'a pas peur zieux li. (Quand on vous donne une tête de bœuf à manger n'ayez pas peur de ses yeux.)

"When you are given an ox's head to eat, don't be afraid of his eyes."—
[*Hayti.*]

*282. Ratte mangé canne, zanzoli mouri innocent. (Le rat mange la canne-
[à-sucre], le lézard en meurt.)
"'Tis the rat eats the cane; but the lizard dies for it."—[*Louisiana.*]
   This proverb is certainly of West Indian origin, though I first obtained
it from a Louisianian. In consequence of the depredations committed by
rats in the West-Indian cane-fields, it is customary after the crop has been
taken off, to fire the dry cane tops and leaves. The blaze, spreading over
the fields, destroys many rats, but also a variety of harmless lizards and
other creatures.

*284. Ravette pas jamain tini raison douvant poule. (Le ravet n'a jamais
raison devant la poule.)
"Cockroach is never in the right where the fowl is concerned."—(lit.: *before
the fowl.*)—[*Trinidad.*]
   I find this proverb in every dialect I have been able to study. In Martinique
Creole the words vary slightly: "*Douvant poule ravett pas ni raison.*"

*286. Rendé service, baille chagrin. (Rendre service donne du chagrin.)
"Doing favors brings sorrow."—[*Louisiana.*]

291. Si coulev oûlé viv, li pas prouminée grand-chimin. (Si la couleuvre
veut vivre, elle ne se promène pas dans le grand chemin).
"If the snake cares to live, it doesn't journey upon the high-road."—
[*Guyana.*]

*295. Si lamèr té bouilli, poissons sré tchuite. (Si la mer bouillait, les
poissons seraient cuits.)
"If the sea were to boil, the fishes would be cooked."—[*Louisiana.*]

*298. "Si-moin-tè-connaitt" pas janmain douvant; li toujou deïè. (Si-je-
l'avais-su n'est jamais devant; il vient toujours derrière.)
"'*If-I-had-only-known*'" is never before one; he always comes behind."—
[*Martinique.*]

*303. Soleil levé là; li couché là. (Le soleil se lève là; il se couche là.)
"Sun rises there [pointing to the east]; he sets there [pointing to the
west]."—[*Louisiana.*]

A proverb common to all the dialects. In uttering it, with emphatic gesture, the negro signifies that there is no pride which will not be at last brought down, no grandeur which will not have an end.

*305. Tafia toujou dîe la vérité. (Le tafia dit toujours la vérité.)
"Tafia always tells the truth."—[*Louisiana.*]
   Tafia is the rum extracted from sugar-cane. "*In vino veritas.*"

306. Tambou tini grand train pace endidans li vide. (Le tambour va [lit: tient] grand train parcequ'il est vide en dedans.)
"The drum makes a great fuss because it is empty inside."—[*Trinidad.*]
   In Louisiana Creole, *faire di-train* is commonly used in the sense of making a great noise, a big fuss. An old negro-servant might often be heard reproving the children of the house in some such fashion as this:—
"*Ga! — pouki tapé fait tou di-train la? — Toulé pé? — pas fait tou di-train mo di toi!*" ("Here, what are you making all that noise for?—are you going to keep quiet?—musn't make so much noise, I tell you!")

*308. "Tant-pis" n'a pas cabane. ("Tant-pis" n'a pas de cabane.)
"'So-much-the-worse' has no cabin."—[*Louisiana.*]
   This proverb is the retort for the phrase: "So much the worse for you." Sometimes one might hear a colored servant, for example, warning the children of the house to keep out of the kitchen, which in Creole residences usually opens into the great court-yard where the little ones play: *Eh, pitis! Faut pas resler là: vous ka casser tout!* ("Hey! Little ones, musn't stay there: you'll break everything!") If the father or mother should then exclaim "*Tant pis pour eux!*"—so much the worse for them if they do break everything, you would hear the old woman reply: "*Tant-pis n'a pas cabane!*"— "So-much-the-worse has no cabin"—*i.e.*, nothing to lose. She believes in an ounce of prevention rather than a pound of cure.

*310. Temps present gagnin assez comme ça avec so quenne. (Le temps present en a assez comme ça avec le sien.)
"The present has enough to do to mind its own affairs."—[*Louisiana.*]
   Literally the proverb is almost untranslateable. It is cited to those who express needless apprehension of future misfortune. "Mo va gagnin malhé"— (I am going to have trouble.) "*Aïe, aïe! Chère! — temps present gagnin assez comme ça avec so quenne.*" (Ah, my dear! The present has enough trouble of its own.)

*311. Ti chien, ti còdon. (Petit chien, petit lien.)
"A little string for a little dog."—[*Martinique.*]

*317. Tout ça c'est commerce Man Lison. (Tout ça c'est affaire de Maman Lison.)
"All that's like Mammy Lison's doings."—[*Louisiana.*]

Whenever a thing is badly done, this saying is used:—*commerce* in the Creole signifying almost the reverse of what it does in French. Who that traditional *Man Lison* was, I have never been able to find out.

*320. Toutt joué c'est joué; mais cassé bois dans bonda macaque—ça pas joué. (Tout [façon de] jouer c'est jouer; mais ce ne'est pas jouer que de casser du bois dans le derrière du macaque.)........—[*Martinique.*]

This ridiculous observation is unsuitable for translation. Nevertheless we have an English, or perhaps an American, proverb equally vulgar, which may have inspired, or been derived from, the Creole one. In the English saying, the words "joking" and "provoking" are used as rhymes. The moral is precisely similar to that of No. 322.

In old days the Creole story-teller would always announce his intention of beginning a tale by the exclamation "*Tim-tim!*" whereupon the audience would shout in reply, "*Bois sec*"; and the story-teller would cry again, "*Cassez-li,*" to which the chorus would add ".... *dans tchu (bonda) macaque.*" Thus the story-teller intimated that he had no intention of merely "*joking,*" but intended to tell the whole truth and nothing else—"a real good story"—*tois fois bonne conte!*

*321. Toutt jour c'est pas dimanche. (Tous les jours ne sont pas le dimanche.)
"Every day isn't Sunday."—[*Louisiana.*]

322. Tou jwé sa jwé; me bwa là zòrè sa pa jwé. (Tout [façon de] jouer c'est jouer; mais enfoncer du bois dans l'oreille n'est pas jouer.)
"All play is play; but poking a piece of wood into one's ear isn't play."—[*Guyana.*]

*323. Tout macaque trouvé so piti joli. (Tout macaque trouve son petit joli.)
"Every monkey thinks its young one pretty."—[*Louisiana.*]

*325. Toutt mounn save ça qui ka bouï nens canari yo. (Toute personne sait ce qui bout dans son canari [marmite].)

"Everybody knows what boils in his own pot"—i.e., knows his own business best.—[*Martinique.*]

In Thomas's Trinidad version: "*Tout moune connaite ça qui ka bouï nans canari yeaux.*" In Louisiana Creole: "*Chakin connin ça kapé bouilli dans so chodière.*" *Canari* is sometimes used in our Creole, but rarely. I have only heard it in old songs. The iron pot (*chodière*) or tin untensil has superseded the *canari*.

331. Vide éne boutéye pour rempli laute, qui li? (Vider une bouteille pour en remplir une autre, qu'est-ce?)
"What's the good of emptying one bottle only to fill another?"—[*Mauritius.*]
Same signification as Prov. 138.

***332.** Vie cannari ka fé bon bouillon. (Les vieux pots font les bonnes soupes.)
"It's the old pot that makes the good soup."—[*Martinique.*]

337. Yo ka quimbé chritiens pa langue yo, bef pa cóne yo. (On prend les Chrétiens par la langue, les bœufs par les cornes.)
"Christians are known by their tongues, oxen by their horns." (Literally, are taken by or caught by.)—[*Martinique.*]

Quimbé is a verb of African origin. It survives in Louisiana Creole as *tchombé* or *thombo:*

> *Caroline, zolie femme,*
> *Chombo moin dans collet.*

["Caroline, pretty woman: put your arm about my neck!"—lit.: "take me by the neck."]

There are other African words used by the older colored women, such as *macayé*, meaning to eat at all hours; and *Ouendé*, of which the sense is dubious. But the Congo verb *fifa*, to kiss; and the verbs *souyé*, to flatter; *pougalé*, to abuse violently; and such nouns as *soff* (glutton), *yche* or *iche* (baby), which are preserved in other Creole dialects, are apparently unknown in Louisiana to-day.

In Chas. Jeannest's work, *Quatre Années au Congo* [Paris: Charpentier, 1883], I find a scanty vocabulary of words in the Fiot dialect, the native dialect of many slaves imported into Louisiana and the West Indies. In this vocabulary the word *ouenda* is translated by "*partir pour.*" I fancy it also signifies "to be absent," and that it is synonymous with our Louisiana African-Creole *ouendé*, preserved in the song:

Ouendé, ouendé, macaya;
Mo pas, 'barassé, macaya!
Ouendé, ouendé, macaya;
Mo bois bon divin, macaya!
Ouendé, ouendé, macaya;
Mo mangé bon poulé, macaya!
Ouendé, ouendé, macaya; . . . etc.

This is one of the very few songs with a purely African refrain still sung in New Orleans. The theme seems to be that, the master and mistress of a house being absent, some slave is encouraging a slave-friend to eat excessively, to "stuff himself" with wine, chicken, etc. "They are gone, friend: eat, fill yourself; *I'm* not a bit ashamed; stuff yourself!—I'm drinking good wine; stuff yourself!—I'm eating good chicken; gorge yourself," etc. Here *ouendé* seems to mean "they are out; they are gone away,"—therefore there is no danger.

There is another Creole song with the same kind of double refrain, but the meaning of the African words I have not been able to discover.

Nicolas, Nicolas, Nicolas, ou dindin;
Nicolas, Nicolas, Nicolas marché ouaminon:
Quand li marché
Ouarasi, ouarasa!
Quand li marché
Ouarasi, ouarasa!

["Nicholas, etc., you are a turkey-cock! Nicholas walks *ouaminon:* when he walks, it is *ourasi, ourasa*"] The idea is obvious enough; *viz.:* that Nicholas struts like a turkey-cock; but the precise signification of the three italicised words I have failed to learn.

339. Yon lanmain douè lavé laute. (Une main doit laver l'autre.)
"One hand must wash the other."—You must not depend upon others to get you out of trouble.—[*Martinique.*]

343. Zaffaire ça qui sotte, chien mangé diné yo. (Des choses [qui appart-iennent] aux sots les chiens font leur dîner.)
"Dogs make their dinner upon what belongs to fools."—[*Louisiana.*]

*344. Zaffé cabritt pa zaffé mouton. (L'affaire de la chèvre n'est pas l'affaire du mouton.)
"The goat's business is not the sheep's affair."—[*Martinique.*]

Seems to be the same in all Creole dialects, excepting that the rabbit is sometimes substituted for the sheep.

NOTES ON SOURCES

Periodicals

Cincinnati Commercial. Cincinnati, Ohio.
Daily City Item. New Orleans: City Item Printing.
Harper's Illustrated Weekly Magazine. New York: Harper's Magazine Co.
New Orleans Life. New Orleans: American Printing Co.
New York Tribune. New York, New York.
Southern Bivouac. Louisville Kentucky: Southern Historical Association of Louisville.
Times-Democrat. New Orleans: Times-Democrat Publishing Co.

Collections of Writings by Lafcadio Hearn

(AM) Albert Mordell, ed., *American Miscellany by Lafcadio Hearn, articles and stories now first collected by Albert Mordell,* 2 vols. New York: Dodd, Mead, and Company, 1924.

(BB) Ichiro Nishizaki, ed. *Barbarous Barbers, Lafcadio Hearn's American Articles, now first arranged and edited by Ichiro Nishizaki,* vol. IV. Japan: The Hokuseidi Press, 1939.

(CS) Charles Woodward Hutson, ed., *Creole Sketches by Lafcadio Hearn.* Boston and New York: Houston Mifflin Company, 1924.

(ED) Charles Woodward Hutson, ed., *Editorials by Lafcadio Hearn.* New York: Houghton Mifflin Company, 1926.

(FF) R. Tanabé, ed., *Facts and Fancies by Lafcadio Hearn.* Japan: The Hokuseido Press, 1929.

(FO) Charles Woodward Hutson, ed., *Fantastics and Other Fancies by Lafcadio Hearn.* Boston and New York: Houghton Mifflin Company, 1914.

(HC) Hodding Carter, Jr., ed., *Lafcadio Hearn's Creole Cook Book: A Literary and Culinary Adventure, with the addition of a collection of drawings and writings by Lafcadio Hearn during his sojourn in New Orleans from 1877 to 1887.* Gretna: Pelican Publishing Company, 1967.

(NR) Ichiro Neshizaki, ed., *New Radiance, Lafcadio Hearn's American Articles,* vol. 1. Japan: The Hokuseidi Press, 1939.

(OG) Albert Mordell, ed., *Occidental Gleanings by Lafcadio Hearn, sketches and essays now first collected by Albert Mordell,* 2 vols. New York: Dodd, Mead, and Company, 1925.

Notes on Sources

(SW) Henry Goodman, ed., *The Selected Writings of Lafcadio Hearn, with introduction by Malcolm Cowley*. New York: Citadel Press, 1949, 1977; Carol Publishing Group, 1991.
(WR) *Writings of Lafcadio Hearn in Sixteen Volumes*. Boston & New York: Roberts Brothers, 1887; New York: Houghton Mifflin Company, 1911.

Biography

(ET) Edward Laroque Tinker, *Lafcadio Hearn's American Days*. New York: Dodd, Mead, and Company, 1924.
(JC) Jonathan Cott, *Wandering Ghost: The Odyssey of Lafcadio Hearn*. New York: Alfred A. Knopf, 1991.

Volumes written and/or edited by Lafcadio Hearn

(GZ) Lafcadio Hearn, ed., *Gombo Zhèbes: Little Dictionary of Creole Proverbs Selected from Six Creole Dialects*. New York: Will H. Coleman, 1885.
(HS) *Historical Sketch Book and Guide to New Orleans and Environs*. New York: Will H. Coleman, 1885.
(LC) Lafcadio Hearn, *La Cuisine Créole: A Collection of Culinary Recipes, From Leading Chefs and Noted Creole Housewives, Who Have Made New Orleans Famous for its Cuisine*. New York: Will H. Coleman, 1885; second edition, New Orleans: F. F. Hansell & Bros., Ltd.

Other

(CC) Edward Larocque Tinker, *Creole City: Its Past and Its People*. New York, London, Toronto: Longmans, Green & Co., 1953.
(LM) James Gill, *Lords of Misrule: Mardi Gras and the Politics of Race in New Orleans*. Jackson: University Press of Mississippi, 1997.
(LS) Frank de Caro, ed., *Louisiana Sojourns: Traveler's Tales and Literary Journals, as Recounted by James J. Audubon, et. al*. Baton Rouge: Louisiana State University Press, 1998.

I. The Outsider as Insider: Impressions

The following reports of this section were first published in the *Cincinnati Commercial* on the following dates and were reprinted in *Occidental Gleanings* on the indicated pages: "Memphis to New Orleans," November 23, 1877 (OGI: 156–163); "At the Gate of the Tropics," November 26, 1877 (OGI: 164–178); "The City of the South," December 10, 1877 (OGI: 179–194); "New Orleans in Wet Weather," December 22, 1877 (OGI: 208–222); and "New Orleans Letter," January 7, 1878 (OGI: 235–245). Included in "Los Criollos," which appeared in the *Cincinnati Commercial*,

226

December 3, 1877 (OGI: 195–207) are "Some Little Creole Songs," drawn from "Curious Nomenclature of New Orleans Streets," also from the *Commercial,* February 18, 1878 (OGI: 270–275); and "The Creole Patois," an excerpt from the article of the same title first published in *Harper's Weekly* (AMII: 147–148, 152–153). A different version of "Some Little Creole Songs" appeared in "The Streets" (HS: 278–263).

Drawn from *Historical Sketch Book* are "The Streets" (HS: 278–263, *cf* "Curious Nomenclature of New Orleans Streets"); "The French Market" (HS: 43–45); "Under the Oaks" (HS:181–187); "Executions" (HS: 207–209); "St. John's Eve—Voudouism" (HS: 229–231); and "Rod and Gun" (HS:245–251).

"New Orleans in Carnival Garb" (OGII: 269–273; *excerpt,* JG: 132–133) was first published in *Harper's Weekly,* February 24, 1883 (Vol. XXVII, 133); "The Creole Doctor, Some Curiosities of Medicine in Louisiana" (OGII: 195–208) first appeared in the *New York Tribune,* January 3, 1886.

With the exception of "The Death of Marie Laveau," all remaining essays in this section were reprinted in *American Miscellany.* Of these essays, those originally published in *Harper's Weekly* are "The Last of the Voudoos" (AMII: 201–208), November 7, 1885 (Vol. XXVII, 726–727) and "Saint Maló, A Lacustrine Village in Louisiana" (AMII: 89–102), March 3, 1883 (Vol. XXVII, 198). "The Last of the New Orleans Fencing Masters" (AMII: 185–200) first appeared in the *Southern Bivouac* November, 1886. "The Garden of Paradise" (AMII: 103–106) was first published in the *Times-Democrat,* March 27, 1883, and *Facts and Fancies* (FF: 96–98). "The Last of the Voudoos" (AMII: 201–208) was reprinted in *The Selected Writings* (SW: 268–273). "The Death of Marie Laveau" was originally published in the *City Item,* July 17, 1881 (untitled, in column "Wayside Notes").

The following essays are reprinted here for the first time: "The Streets," "The French Market"[1], "Under the Oaks," "Executions," "The Death of Marie Laveau," "St. John's Eve—Voudouism," and "Rod and Gun."

II. From the Land of Dreams: Sketches

Sketches in this section first appeared in the *City Item* on the indicated dates and were subsequently reprinted in the order as follow: "Voices of

---

[1]A condensed version appeared in *Louisiana Sojourns* (89–93), although its true authorship is unidentified, but attributed nonetheless to the publisher, Will H. Coleman (71, 89).

Dawn," July 22, 1881 (CS: 197–198, WR: 206–208, SW: 266–268); "Char-Coal," August 25, 1880 (CS: 70–71, LC: 254a-b, CC: 253); "The Flower-Sellers," September 11, 1880 (CS: 150–152); "Cakes and Candy," September 18, 1880 (ET: 127; LC: 237b, *woodprint only*); "Washerwomen," August 31, 1880 (CS: 98–101, LC: 256a, *woodprint only*); "Des Perches," August 30, 1880 (CS: 35–87, LC: 260a); "Shine?" July 19, 1880; "The Man with the Small Electric Machine," September 12, 1880; "Under the Electric Light," August 6, 1880; "——! ——!! Mosquitoes!!!" July 28, 1880 (EL: 286); "The Festive," October 13, 1880 (ET: 275); "The Wolfish Dog," July 15, 1880 (EL: 81; JC: 150, *woodprint only*); "The Go-At," July 18, 1880; "The Alligators," September 13, 1880 (CS: 164–166); "Wet Enough For You?" December 2, 1880; "Web-Footed," December 3, 1880; "A Creole Type," May 6, 1879 (CS: 26–33, WRI: 118–122, SW: 260–263); "Complaint of a Creole Boarding-House Keeper," September 27, 1879 (CS: 52–56, WRI: 151–152); "The Boarder's Reply," September 28, 1879 (CS: 52–56, WRI: 131–134); "A Kentucky Colonel Renting Rooms," November 15, 1879 (CS: 88–89, WRI: 151–152); "The Restless Boarder," October 27, 1879 (CS: 63–66, WRI: 138–189); "Furnished Rooms," November 2, 1879 (CS: 67–69, WRI: 140–141); "Ghosteses," August 18, 1880 (CS: 34–37; LC: 227b, *woodprint only*; "A Creole Journal," October 5, 1879 (CS: 67–69, WRI: 136–137); "Ultra-Canal," July 17, 1880 (CS: 22–25; HC: v, *woodprint only*); "An Ultra-Canal Talk," July 13, 1880 (CS: 106–110, WRI: 161–163); "Why Crabs are Boiled Alive," October 5, 1879 (CS: 59, WRI: 135, LC: 23a, SW: 266); "Creole Servant Girls," December 20, 1880 (CS: 160–163, WRI: 188–190, SW: 264–265); "The Creole Character," November 13, 1879 (CS: 82–84, WRI: 149–150); "All Saints!" October 31, 1880; "Does Climate Affect the Character of People?" October 30, 1878; "The City of Dreams," March 9, 1879 (CS: 14–21, WRI: 113–117); "A Dream of Kites," June 18, 1880 (FO: 57–59, WRII: 241–243); "The Tale of a Fan," July 1, 1881 (FO: 166–169, WRII: 327–329); "*Les Coulisses*," December 6, 1879 (FO: 43–50, WR-II: 230–236); "French Opera," November 6, 1880 (LC: 165b, *woodprint only*); "Down Among the Dives: A Midnight Sketch," December 1, 1878; "Fire!" October 29, 1880; "That Piano Organ," November 8, 1880 (LC: 93a, *woodprint only*); "A Creole Courtyard, November 11, 1879 (CS: 78–81, WRI: 147–148); "The Accursed Fig Tree," *date unavailable* (BB: 99–102); "Home," January 8, 1881 (CS: 167–174, WRI: 191–195); "A Visitor," November 26, 1880 (CS:

153–159, WRI: 183–187); "Opening Oysters," September 25, 1878; "By the Murmuring Waves," August 15, 1880; "Spanish Moss," October 28, 1880 (EL: 331, LC: 208a); "The Lord Sends Trials and Tribulations to Strengthen and Pacify our Hearts," June 16, 1881, and "Ye Pilot," September 20, 1880.

With the exception of the woodprints only of "French Opera" and "The Organ Grinder," the following are reprinted here for the first time: "Shine?" "The Man with the Small Electric Machine," "Under the Electric Light," "The Go-At," "Wet Enough For You?" "Web-Footed," "All Saints!" "Does Climate Affect the Character of People?" "French Opera," "Down Among the Dives: A Midnight Sketch," "Fire!" "That Piano Organ," "Opening Oysters," "By the Murmuring Waves," "The Lord Sends Trials and Tribulations to Strengthen and Pacify our Hearts," and "Ye Pilot."

III. Of Vice and Virtue: Editorials

Articles included in this section were first published in the *City Item* on the indicated dates and subsequently reprinted in the order as follow: "Latin and Anglo-Saxon," November 24, 1880 (CS: 145–149, WRI: 180–182); "French in Louisiana," March 2, 1880 (ED: 81–83); "Jewish Emigrants for Louisiana," September 20, 1883 (BB: 153–156); "Quack! Quack!" August 20, 1880 (CS: 45–46); "The Opium Dens," October 5, 1880 (NR: 111–112); "*Scénes de la Vie des* Hoodlums," May 15, 1881 (BB: 94–98); "Blackmailing," October 9, 1880; "The Indignant Dead," September 8, 1880 (CS: 124–127); "Improved Police Ideas," October 8, 1880; "Coming Events Cast Their Shadow Before," August 19, 1880 (CS: 57–58); "A Visit to New Orleans," May 10, 1879 (CS: 38–44, WRI: 123–127); "Whited Sepulchres," September 9, 1880 (CS: 135–137, LS: 535, *woodprint only*); "Old-Fashioned Houses," January 12, 1881 (CS: 175–182, WRI: 196–2000); "*La Douane*," December 2, 1878 (CS: 6–10, WRI: 110–112); "The Haunted and the Haunters," May 22, 1880 (ET: 231); "The Unspeakable Velocipede," June, 1880 (*New Orleans Life,* January 1925; ET: 373–374; JC: 131, *woodprint only*); "The Organ Grinder," June 30, 1880; "The Puller of Noses," September 19, 1880; "The Glamour of New Orleans," November 26, 1878 (CS: 1–5, WRI: 107–109); "The Dawn of the Carnival," February 2, 1880 (CS: 90–92, WRI: 153–154, JG: 131–132); and "The Pelican's Ghost, November 19, 1880.

Reprinted here for the first time are "Blackmailing," "Improved Police Ideas," "The Organ Grinder," "The Puller of Noses," and "The Pelican's Ghost."

IV. Reports from the Field: Longer Studies

Contents of *La Cuisine Créole* are extracted from *La Cuisine Créole: A Collection of Culinary Recipes, From Leading Chefs and Noted Creole Housewives, Who Have Made New Orleans Famous for its Cuisine,* of which a facsimile was issued under the title *Lafcadio Hearn's Creole Cookbook* (HC).

The proverbs under "Gombo Zhèbes" are selected from *Gombo Zhèbes: Little Dictionary of Creole Proverbs Selected from Six Creole Dialects.* Proverbs 35, 40, 76, 137, 157, 271, 321, and 337 were also included in *Lafcadio Hearn's Creole Cookbook* (HC).